Good Housekeeping

Favourite
Family Meals

250 Tried, tested, trusted recipes ★ Delicious results

Good Housekeeping

Favourite
Family Meals

250 Tried, tested, trusted recipes ★ Delicious results

COLLINS & BROWN

First published in the United Kingdom in 2010 by
Collins & Brown
10 Southcombe Street
London
W14 0RA

An imprint of Anova Books Company Ltd

The Good Housekeeping website is
www.allaboutyou.com/goodhousekeeping

10 9 8 7 6 5 4 3 2 1

ISBN 978-1-84340-590-0

A catalogue record for this book is available from the British Library.

Reproduction by Dot Gradations UK Ltd
Printed and bound by Times Offset Malaysia

This book can be ordered direct from the publisher at
www.anovabooks.com

Recipes in this book are taken from the Good Housekeeping recipe library and may have been reproduced in previous publications.

Picture Credits:
Neil Barclay (pages 18, 40, 74, 75, 77, 115, 123, 160, 161, 178, 191, 198 and 256); Martin Brigdale (pages 20, 81, 84, 87, 90, 93, 96, 97, 98, 100, 102, 103, 108, 109, 112, 113, 116, 121, 238, 242 and 277); Nicki Dowey (pages 10, 12, 13, 15, 17, 24, 25, 26, 29, 30, 31, 32, 33, 35, 36, 41, 42, 50, 52, 55, 56, 57, 58, 59, 61, 62, 63, 66, 67, 70, 71, 73, 85, 86, 88, 89, 95, 99, 106, 107, 110, 111, 118, 119, 125, 127, 128, 129, 133, 138, 140, 141, 142, 144, 145, 146, 147, 148, 149, 152, 153, 155, 134, 166, 168, 169, 172, 176, 177, 180, 184, 189, 190, 192, 193, 202, 203, 206, 219, 232, 233, 234, 236, 239, 247, 249, 252, 253, 254, 255, 260, 264, 265, 266, 271, 272, 273, 278, 279, 280, 281, 284 and 285); Will Heap (pages 53, 126, 135, 139, 151, 162 and 283); Craig Robertson (pages 16, 19, 21, 34, 37, 38, 39, 44, 45, 48, 49, 51, 64, 69, 82, 94, 101, 117, 124, 134, 136, 143, 154, 158, 163, 170, 171, 173, 174, 179, 181, 182, 188, 197, 199, 200, 204, 209, 210, 211, 212, 214, 216, 217, 218, 221, 222, 223, 226, 227, 228, 229, 231, 244, 246, 257, 258, 261, 263, 267, 274 and 275); Roger Stowell (page 183); Lucinda Symons (pages 11, 22, 27, 28, 43, 54, 68, 76, 83, 92, 114, 120, 137, 150, 159, 165, 175, 185, 186, 187, 213, 215, 220, 230, 235, 240, 241, 245, 248, 259, 262, 268, 269, 270 and 282)
Home economists: Anna Burges-Lumsden, Joanna Farrow, Emma Jane Frost, Teresa Goldfinch, Alice Hart, Lucy McKelvie, Kim Morphew, Katie Rogers, Bridget Sargeson, Sarah Tidesley, Jennifer White and Mari Mererid Williams
Stylists: Susannah Blake, Wei Tang, Helen Trent, Sarah Tidesley and Fanny Ward

NOTES

★ Both metric and imperial measures are given for the recipes. Follow either set of measures, not a mixture of both, as they are not interchangeable.

★ All spoon measures are level.
1 tsp = 5ml spoon; 1 tbsp = 15ml spoon.

★ Ovens and grills must be preheated to the specified temperature.

★ Medium eggs should be used except where otherwise specified.

DIETARY GUIDELINES

★ Note that certain recipes contain raw or lightly cooked eggs. The young, elderly, pregnant women and anyone with immune-deficiency disease should avoid these because of the slight risk of salmonella.

★ Note that some recipes contain alcohol. Check the ingredients list before serving to children.

Contents

Foreword

It always makes me smile when I witness a family food tradition. Sure, there are traditions that are much more widely practised – like eating turkey on Christmas Day or munching on hot cross buns in the run-up to Easter – but it's the more personal ones that I love. Whether that be baking the same gooey chocolate cake every year for a husband's birthday, or eating fish pie only on a Thursday, these traditions are there for one reason – because someone wants them to be.

On one occasion I thought I would test the staying power of a family habit and dared to ask my youngest brother whether he thought it was entirely necessary to have a repeat of the full Christmas lunch just three days after the main event. His answer was simple and efficient, 'Of course it's necessary, it's our family tradition.' True, and it's a tradition I will now honour for as long as I can.

Foodie traditions are invariably made up of recipes that are family favourites; the recipes that speak of home and childhood, of cosy kitchen dinners and raucous celebratory gatherings. The original recipes (or by now, the tenth photocopy!) are well-thumbed and always deliver.

This wonderful book is full of just-such family favourites and each and every recipe has been developed and rigorously triple-tested right here in the GHI: our guarantee to you that they will work first time round.

I hope this book stays by your side for years to come and that the recipes inside grow into new family traditions.

Enjoy!

Meike.

Meike Beck
Chief Home Economist

Soups, Salads and Snacks

French Onion Soup

Preparation Time 30 minutes • Cooking Time about 1 hour • Serves 4 • Per Serving 438 calories, 21g fat (of which 13g saturates), 45g carbohydrate, 1.3g salt • Vegetarian • Easy

75g (3oz) butter
700g (1½lb) small onions, finely
    chopped
3 garlic cloves, crushed
1 tbsp plain flour
200ml (7fl oz) dry white wine
    (optional)
1.5 litres (2½ pints) vegetable stock
bouquet garni (see Cook's Tip)
salt and ground black pepper

TO SERVE

1 small baguette, cut into slices
    1cm (½in) thick
50g (2oz) Gruyère cheese or
    Cheddar, grated

1 Melt the butter in a large heavy-based pan. Add the onions and cook slowly over a very low heat, stirring frequently, until very soft and golden brown; this should take at least 30 minutes. Add the garlic and flour and cook, stirring, for 1 minute.

2 Pour in the wine, if using, and let bubble until reduced by half. Add the stock, bouquet garni and seasoning. Bring to the boil, then reduce the heat and simmer gently, uncovered, for 20–30 minutes.

3 Discard the bouquet garni and let the soup cool a little. Whiz one-third in a food processor or blender until smooth, then stir this back into the soup in the pan.

4 Preheat the grill. Lightly toast the baguette slices on both sides. Reheat the soup and adjust the seasoning.

5 Divide the soup among four ovenproof soup bowls. Float two or three slices of toast on each portion and sprinkle thickly with the grated cheese. Stand the bowls under the hot grill until the cheese has melted and turned golden brown. Serve at once.

COOK'S TIP
To make a bouquet garni, tie together a sprig each of thyme and parsley with a bay leaf and a piece of celery.

Tomato Salad Soup with Bruschetta

★

Preparation Time 15 minutes, plus marinating and chilling • **Cooking Time** 5 minutes • **Serves 4** • **Per Serving** 490 calories, 25g fat (of which 4g saturates), 52g carbohydrate, 1.5g salt • **Vegetarian** • **Dairy Free** • **Easy**

700g (1½lb) ripe plum tomatoes, thinly sliced
6 spring onions, finely chopped
zest of ½ lemon
2 tbsp freshly chopped basil
125ml (4fl oz) extra virgin olive oil, plus extra to drizzle
2 tbsp balsamic vinegar
2–3 garlic cloves
a pinch of sugar
50ml (2fl oz) chilled vodka
1 tbsp Worcestershire sauce
a few drops of Tabasco
150ml (¼ pint) tomato juice
8 thin slices French bread
salt and ground black pepper
fresh basil leaves to garnish

1 Put the tomatoes into a large shallow dish and scatter the spring onions, lemon zest and chopped basil over them. Blend together the oil, vinegar, 1 garlic clove, the sugar, vodka, Worcestershire sauce and Tabasco. Season to taste with salt and pepper and pour over the tomatoes. Cover the dish and leave to marinate for 2 hours at room temperature.

2 Whiz the tomato salad and tomato juice in a blender until very smooth. Transfer to a bowl and leave to chill in the fridge for 1 hour.

3 Just before serving, preheat the grill. Lightly toast the bread slices on both sides. Rub each one with the remaining crushed garlic and drizzle with oil. Spoon the soup into serving bowls, drizzle with a little oil and grind on some black pepper. Garnish the bruschetta with fresh basil leaves and serve with the soup.

★ COOK'S TIP
Not suitable for children due to the alcohol content.

Autumn Barley Soup

Preparation Time 10 minutes • Cooking Time 1 hour 5 minutes • Serves 4 • Per Serving 83 calories, 1g fat (of which trace saturates), 16g carbohydrate, 0.6g salt • Vegetarian • Dairy Free • Easy

25g (1oz) pot barley, washed and drained
1 litre (1¾ pints) hot vegetable stock
2 large carrots, diced
1 turnip, diced
2 leeks, trimmed and sliced
2 celery sticks, diced
1 small onion, finely chopped
1 bouquet garni (see page 10)
2 tbsp freshly chopped parsley
salt and ground black pepper

1 Put the barley and stock into a pan and bring to the boil. Reduce the heat and simmer for 45 minutes or until the barley is tender.

2 Add the vegetables to the pan with the bouquet garni and season to taste with salt and pepper. Bring to the boil, then reduce the heat and simmer for about 20 minutes or until the vegetables are tender.

3 Discard the bouquet garni. Add the parsley to the soup, stir well and serve immediately.

 TRY SOMETHING DIFFERENT
Replace the barley with 75g (3oz) soup pasta: add for the last 10 minutes of cooking.

Gazpacho with Tortilla Chips

Preparation Time 25–30 minutes, plus chilling • Serves 8 • Per Serving 303 calories, 20g fat (of which 5g saturates), 28g carbohydrate, 1.1g salt • Vegetarian • Easy

900g (2lb) ripe tomatoes
4 garlic cloves
50g (2oz) fresh white breadcrumbs
6 tbsp extra virgin olive oil
juice of 1½ small limes
1 red chilli, seeded and chopped
   (see Cook's Tips)
2 cucumbers, halved lengthways,
   seeded and chopped
2 bunches of spring onions, chopped
1 red pepper, seeded and chopped
600ml (1 pint) tomato juice
6 tbsp freshly chopped coriander
salt and ground black pepper
175g bag tortilla chips to serve

TO GARNISH
1 large avocado
juice of ½ small lime
150ml (¼ pint) soured cream
a few fresh coriander sprigs

⭐ COOK'S TIPS
● *Don't be tempted to make the garnish too far in advance, as the delicate pale green flesh of avocado discolours when exposed to air.*
● *Chillies vary enormously in strength, from quite mild to blisteringly hot, depending on the type of chilli and its ripeness. Taste a small piece first to check it's not too hot for you.*
● *Be extremely careful when handling chillies not to touch or rub your eyes with your fingers, as the oil in the chilli will sting. Wash knives immediately after handling chillies for the same reason. As a precaution, use rubber gloves when preparing them, if you like.*

1 Score a cross in the skin at the base of each tomato, then put into a bowl. Pour enough boiling water over to cover them, leave for 30 seconds, then transfer to a bowl of cold water. Peel, discarding the skins, then cut into quarters. Discard the seeds.

2 Put all the gazpacho ingredients into a large bowl and mix well. Whiz in batches in a food processor until smooth. Transfer to a bowl or jug, season generously with salt and pepper and stir well. Cover and chill for at least 2 hours or overnight.

3 Just before serving, halve, stone and peel the avocado, then roughly dice and toss in lime juice to coat. Serve the soup garnished with soured cream, the avocado, a sprinkling of black pepper and fresh coriander. Serve the tortilla chips separately.

Chicken and Bean Soup

Preparation Time 10 minutes • **Cooking Time** 30 minutes • **Serves 4** • **Per Serving** 351 calories, 6g fat (of which 1g saturates), 48g carbohydrate, 2.7g salt • **Dairy Free** • **Easy**

1 tbsp olive oil

1 onion, finely chopped

4 celery sticks, chopped

1 red chilli, seeded and roughly chopped (see Cook's Tips, page 13)

2 boneless, skinless chicken breasts, about 125g (4oz) each, cut into strips

1 litre (1¾ pints) hot chicken or vegetable stock

100g (3½oz) bulgur wheat

2 × 400g cans cannellini beans, drained and rinsed

400g can chopped tomatoes

25g (1oz) flat-leafed parsley, roughly chopped

wholegrain bread and hummus to serve

1 Heat the oil in a large heavy-based pan. Add the onion, celery and chilli and cook over a low heat for 10 minutes or until softened. Add the chicken and stir-fry for 3–4 minutes until golden.

2 Add the hot stock to the pan and bring to a simmer. Stir in the bulgur wheat and simmer for 15 minutes.

3 Stir in the cannellini beans and tomatoes and bring to a simmer. Ladle into four warmed bowls and sprinkle with chopped parsley. Serve with wholegrain bread and hummus

Fast Fish Soup

Preparation Time 10 minutes • Cooking Time about 15 minutes • Serves 4 • Per Serving 269 calories, 10g fat
(of which 2g saturates), 6g carbohydrate, 0.4g salt • **Gluten Free** • **Dairy Free** • **Easy**

1 leek, trimmed and finely chopped
4 fat garlic cloves, crushed
3 celery sticks, finely chopped
1 small fennel bulb, finely chopped
1 red chilli, seeded and finely
  chopped (see page 13)
3 tbsp olive oil
50ml (2fl oz) dry white wine
about 750g (1lb 11oz) mixed fish
  and shellfish, such as haddock
  and monkfish fillets, peeled and
  deveined raw prawns, and fresh
  mussels, scrubbed and cleaned
  (discard any mussels that don't

close when tapped on a
worksurface or that have
broken shells)
4 medium tomatoes, chopped
1½ tbsp freshly chopped thyme
salt and ground black pepper

1 Put the leek into a large pan and add the garlic, celery, fennel, chilli and oil. Cook over a medium heat for 5 minutes or until the vegetables are soft and beginning to colour.

2 Stir in 1.1 litres (2 pints) boiling water and the wine. Bring to the boil, then reduce the heat, cover and simmer for 5 minutes.

3 Cut the white fish into large chunks. Add to the soup with the tomatoes and thyme. Continue to simmer gently until the fish has just turned opaque. Add the prawns and simmer for 1 minute, then add the mussels.

4 As soon as all the mussels have opened, season the soup and ladle into warmed bowls. Discard any mussels that remain closed, then serve immediately.

★ TRY SOMETHING DIFFERENT
● *To give the soup more of a kick, stir in 2 tbsp Pernod instead of the wine.*
● *Garlic croûtes are traditionally served with fish soup; they can be made while the soup is simmering. Toast small slices of baguette, spread with garlic mayonnaise and sprinkle with grated cheese. Float in the hot soup just before serving.*

Quick Winter Minestrone

Preparation Time 10 minutes • **Cooking Time** 45 minutes • **Serves** 4 • **Per Serving** 334 calories, 11g fat (of which 3g saturates), 47g carbohydrate, 1.5g salt • **Easy**

2 tbsp olive oil
1 small onion, finely chopped
1 carrot, chopped
1 celery stick, chopped
1 garlic clove, crushed
2 tbsp freshly chopped thyme
1 litre (1¾ pints) hot vegetable
  stock
400g can chopped tomatoes
400g can borlotti beans, drained
  and rinsed
125g (4oz) minestrone pasta
175g (6oz) Savoy cabbage,
  shredded
salt and ground black pepper
fresh pesto (see Cook's Tip),
  toasted ciabatta and extra virgin
  olive oil to serve

1 Heat the oil in a large pan and add the onion, carrot and celery. Cook for 8–10 minutes until softened, then add the garlic and thyme and fry for another 2–3 minutes.

2 Add the hot stock, tomatoes and half the borlotti beans to the pan and baring to the boil. Mash the remaining beans and stir into the soup, then reduce the heat and simmer for 30 minutes, adding the minestrone pasta and cabbage for the last 10 minutes of cooking time.

3 Check the seasoning, then ladle the soup into four warmed bowls and serve with a dollop of fresh pesto on top and slices of toasted ciabatta drizzled with extra virgin olive oil on the side.

★ COOK'S TIP
Pesto
Put a 20g pack of roughly chopped basil into a food processor. Add 25g (1oz) finely grated Parmesan, 50g (2oz) pinenuts and 4 tbsp extra virgin olive oil and whiz to a rough paste. Alternatively, grind in a pestle and mortar. Season with salt and plenty of ground black pepper.

Cock-a-Leekie Soup

Preparation Time 30–40 minutes • Cooking Time 1 hour 20 minutes • Serves 8 • Per Serving 280 calories, 4g fat
(of which 1g saturates), 40g carbohydrate, 0.2g salt • Easy

1 oven-ready chicken, about
   1.4kg (3lb)
2 onions, roughly chopped
2 carrots, roughly chopped
2 celery sticks, roughly chopped
1 bay leaf
25g (1oz) butter
900g (2lb) leeks, trimmed and
   sliced
125g (4oz) ready-to-eat dried
   prunes, sliced
salt and ground black pepper
freshly chopped parsley to serve

FOR THE DUMPLINGS
125g (4oz) self-raising flour
a pinch of salt
50g (2oz) shredded suet
2 tbsp freshly chopped parsley
2 tbsp freshly chopped thyme

1 Put the chicken into a pan in which it fits quite snugly, then add the chopped vegetables, bay leaf and chicken giblets (if available). Pour in 1.7 litres (3 pints) water and bring to the boil, then reduce the heat, cover and simmer gently for 1 hour.

2 Meanwhile, melt the butter in a large pan, add the leeks and fry gently for 10 minutes or until softened.

3 Remove the chicken from the pan and leave until cool enough to handle. Strain the stock and put to one side. Strip the chicken from the bones and shred roughly. Add to the stock with the prunes and softened leeks.

4 To make the dumplings, sift the flour and salt into a bowl. Stir in the suet, herbs and about 5 tbsp water to make a fairly firm dough. Lightly shape the dough into 2.5cm (1in) balls. Bring the soup just to the boil and season well. Reduce the heat, add the dumplings and cover the pan with a lid. Simmer for 15–20 minutes until the dumplings are light and fluffy. Serve the soup scattered with chopped parsley.

★ COOK'S TIP
Make the stock a day ahead, if possible, then cool overnight. The following day, remove any fat from the surface.

Scotch Broth

Preparation Time 15 minutes • Cooking Time 2 hours • Serves 8 • Per Serving 173 calories, 2g fat (of which trace saturates), 35g carbohydrate, 2.3g salt • **Dairy Free** • **Easy**

1 piece marrow bone, about 350g (12oz)
1.4kg (3lb) piece beef skirt (ask your butcher for this)
300g (11oz) broth mix (to include pearl barley, red lentils, split peas and green peas), soaked according to the pack instructions
2 carrots, finely chopped
1 parsnip, finely chopped
2 onions, finely chopped
¼ white cabbage, finely chopped
1 leek, trimmed and finely chopped
½ tbsp salt
ground black pepper
2 tbsp freshly chopped parsley to serve

1 Put the marrow bone and beef skirt into a 5.7 litre (10 pint) stock pot and add 2.6 litres (4½ pints) cold water – there should be enough to cover the meat.

2 Bring the water to the boil. Remove any scum from the surface with a spoon and discard. Reduce the heat to low, add the broth mix and simmer, partially covered, for 1½ hours, skimming the surface occasionally.

3 Add the carrots, parsnip, onions, cabbage, leek and another 600ml (1 pint) cold water. Cover to bring to the boil quickly, then reduce the heat and simmer for 30 minutes.

4 Remove the marrow bone and piece of beef from the broth. Add a few shreds of beef to the broth, if you like. Season the broth well with the salt and some pepper and stir in the chopped parsley. Ladle into warmed bowls and serve hot.

 COOK'S TIP
This is really two meals in one, a starter and a main course. The beef flavours the stock and is removed before serving. Later, you divide up the meat and serve it with mashed potatoes, swedes or turnips.

Chicken Noodle Soup

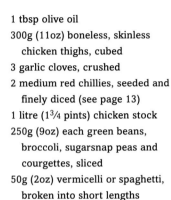

Preparation Time 30 minutes • Cooking Time 15 minutes • Serves 4 • Per Serving 229 calories, 7g fat
(of which 1g saturates), 16g carbohydrate, 1.2g salt • Dairy Free • A Little Effort

1 tbsp olive oil

300g (11oz) boneless, skinless
chicken thighs, cubed

3 garlic cloves, crushed

2 medium red chillies, seeded and
finely diced (see page 13)

1 litre (1¾ pints) chicken stock

250g (9oz) each green beans,
broccoli, sugarsnap peas and
courgettes, sliced

50g (2oz) vermicelli or spaghetti,
broken into short lengths

1 Heat the oil in a large pan, add
the chicken, garlic and chillies and
cook for 5–10 minutes until the
chicken is opaque all over.

2 Add the stock and bring to the
boil, then add the vegetables and
simmer for 5 minutes or until the
chicken is cooked through.

3 Meanwhile, cook the pasta in
a separate pan of lightly salted
boiling water for 5–10 minutes
until al dente, depending on the
type of pasta.

4 Drain the pasta, add to the broth,
and serve immediately.

Leek and Potato Soup

Preparation Time 10 minutes • Cooking Time 45 minutes • Serves 4 • Per Serving 117 calories, 6g fat (of which 4g saturates), 13g carbohydrate, 0.1g salt • **Vegetarian** • **Easy**

25g (1oz) butter
1 onion, finely chopped
1 garlic clove, crushed
550g (1¼lb) leeks, trimmed and
    chopped
200g (7oz) floury potatoes, sliced
1.3 litres (2¼ pints) hot vegetable
    stock
crème fraîche and chopped chives
    to garnish

1 Melt the butter in a pan over a gentle heat, then cook the onion for 10–15 minutes until soft. Add the garlic and cook for a further 1 minute. Add the leeks and cook for 5–10 minutes until softened. Add the potatoes and toss together with the leeks.

2 Pour in the hot stock and bring to the boil, then reduce the heat and simmer the soup for 20 minutes or until the potatoes are tender.

3 Leave the soup to cool a little, then whiz in batches in a blender or food processor until smooth.

4 To serve, reheat the soup gently. Ladle into warmed bowls, drizzle the crème fraîche over it and garnish with chives.

Carrot and Sweet Potato Soup

Preparation Time 15 minutes • **Cooking Time** 45 minutes • **Serves 8** • **Per Serving** 120 calories, 3g fat (of which 1g saturates), 22g carbohydrate, 0.7g salt • **Vegetarian** • **Gluten Free** • **Easy**

1 tbsp olive oil
1 large onion, chopped
1 tbsp coriander seeds
900g (2lb) carrots, roughly chopped
2 medium sweet potatoes, roughly chopped
2 litres (3½ pints) hot vegetable or chicken stock
2 tbsp white wine vinegar
2 tbsp freshly chopped coriander, plus extra coriander leaves to garnish
4 tbsp half-fat crème fraîche
salt and ground black pepper

1 Heat the oil in a large pan, add the onion and coriander seeds and cook over a medium heat for 5 minutes. Add the carrots and sweet potatoes and cook for a further 5 minutes.

2 Add the hot stock and bring to the boil, then reduce the heat and simmer for 25 minutes or until the vegetables are tender.

3 Leave the soup to cool a little, then whiz in batches in a blender or food processor until slightly chunky. Add the wine vinegar and season with salt and pepper.

4 Pour the soup into a clean pan, stir in the chopped coriander and reheat gently.

5 Drizzle the crème fraîche over it and sprinkle with the coriander leaves. Serve in warmed bowls.

★ FREEZING TIP
To freeze *Freeze the soup at step 3 for up to one month.*
To use *Thaw overnight in the fridge. Reheat gently and simmer for 5 minutes.*

Broccoli and Goat's Cheese Soup

Preparation Time 10 minutes • **Cooking Time** 20 minutes • **Serves 6** • **Per Serving** 220 calories, 16g fat (of which 10g saturates), 8g carbohydrate, 0.5g salt • **Easy**

50g (2oz) butter
2 medium onions, chopped
1 litre (1¾ pints) vegetable,
    chicken or turkey stock
700g (1½lb) broccoli, broken into
    florets, stout stalks peeled and
    chopped
1 head of garlic, separated into
    cloves, unpeeled
1 tbsp olive oil
150g (5oz) goat's cheese
salt and ground black pepper

1 Preheat the oven to 200°C (180°C fan oven) mark 6. Melt the butter in a pan over a gentle heat. Add the onions, then cover the pan and cook for 4–5 minutes until translucent. Add half the stock and bring to the boil. Add the broccoli and return to the boil, then cover the pan, reduce the heat and simmer for 15–20 minutes until the broccoli is tender.

2 Toss the cloves of garlic in the oil and tip into a roasting tin. Roast in the oven for 15 minutes or until soft when squeezed.

3 Leave the soup to cool a little, then add the goat's cheese and whiz in batches in a blender or food processor until smooth. Return the soup to the pan and add the remaining stock. Reheat gently on the hob and season to taste with salt and pepper.

4 Ladle the soup into warmed bowls, squeeze the garlic out of their skins and scatter over the soup, add a sprinkling of black pepper and serve.

★ TRY SOMETHING DIFFERENT
● *Double the quantity of goat's cheese if you prefer a stronger taste.*
● *Instead of goat's cheese, substitute a soft garlic cheese for a really garlicky flavour.*

Warm Bacon Salad

Preparation Time 10 minutes • Cooking Time 10–15 minutes • Serves 4 • Per Serving 188 calories, 15g fat (of which 5g saturates), 6g carbohydrate, 0.8g salt • Easy

120g bag soft salad leaves
1 medium red onion, thinly sliced
150g (5oz) diced streaky bacon
2 thick slices white bread, diced
4 medium eggs
40g (1½oz) Parmesan, pared into
   shavings with a vegetable peeler

FOR THE DRESSING
1 tbsp Dijon mustard
2 tbsp red wine vinegar
2 tbsp fruity olive oil
salt and ground black pepper

1 Put the salad leaves and onion into a large bowl. Fry the bacon in a non-stick frying pan until it begins to release some fat. Add the diced bread and continue to fry until the bacon is golden and crisp.

2 Put all the dressing ingredients into a small bowl, season with salt and pepper and whisk together.

3 Half-fill a small pan with cold water and bring to the boil. Turn the heat right down – there should be just a few bubbles on the base of the pan. Break the eggs into a cup, then tip them gently into the pan and cook for 3–4 minutes, using a metal spoon to baste the tops with a little of the hot water. Lift the eggs out of the water with a slotted spoon and drain on kitchen paper.

4 Tip the bacon, bread and any pan juices over the salad leaves. Add the Parmesan, then pour the dressing over the salad. Toss well, then divide between four plates. Top each with an egg, season to taste with salt and pepper and serve.

Spring Chicken Salad with Sweet Chilli Sauce

Preparation Time 15 minutes • Cooking Time 10 minutes • Serves 4 • Per Serving 307 calories, 15g fat (of which 3g saturates), 8g carbohydrate, 0.2g salt • Gluten Free • Dairy Free • Easy

2 tbsp groundnut oil, plus extra to grease
4 boneless, skinless chicken breasts, each cut into four strips
1 tbsp Cajun seasoning (see Cook's Tip)
salt and ground black pepper

FOR THE SALAD
175g (6oz) small young carrots, cut into thin matchsticks
125g (4oz) cucumber, halved lengthways, seeded and cut into matchsticks
6 spring onions, cut into matchsticks

10 radishes, sliced
50g (2oz) bean sprouts, rinsed and dried
50g (2oz) unsalted peanuts, roughly chopped
1 large red chilli, seeded and finely chopped (see page 13)
2 tsp sesame oil
Thai chilli dipping sauce to drizzle

1 Soak eight bamboo skewers in water for 20 minutes. Oil a baking sheet.

2 Preheat the grill. Toss the chicken strips in the Cajun seasoning, then season with salt and pepper and brush with groundnut oil. Thread on to the skewers.

3 Place the skewered chicken strips on the prepared baking sheet and cook under the hot grill for 3–4 minutes on each side until cooked through.

4 Place all the salad vegetables, peanuts and red chilli in a bowl, toss with the sesame oil and season well with salt and pepper.

5 Divide the vegetables among four serving plates, top with the warm chicken skewers and drizzle with the chilli sauce. Serve immediately.

★ COOK'S TIP
Cajun seasoning is a spice and herb mixture, which includes chilli, cumin, cayenne and oregano.

Quick Chicken and Gruyère Salad

Preparation Time 15 minutes, plus chilling • Serves 8 • Per Serving 507 calories, 40g fat (of which 9g saturates), 7g carbohydrate, 0.7g salt • **Gluten Free** • **Easy**

900g–1kg (2–2¼lb) cooked, boned chicken, skinned and cut into bite-size pieces
4 celery sticks, thinly sliced
125g (4oz) Gruyère or Emmenthal cheese, coarsely grated
2 firm red apples, halved, cored and roughly chopped
125g (4oz) seedless black grapes, halved
200ml (7fl oz) olive oil
2 tbsp white wine vinegar
4 tbsp soured cream
4 tbsp mayonnaise
4 tbsp freshly chopped parsley
75g (3oz) toasted pecan nuts or walnuts
mixed green salad to serve

1 Put the chicken, celery, cheese, apples and grapes into a large bowl. Add all the other ingredients and toss well.

2 Adjust the seasoning, cover and leave to chill for at least 10–15 minutes. Serve with a mixed green salad.

★ COOK'S TIPS
● *Any strongly flavoured cheese can be used for this recipe. You could try crumbled Danish blue or blue Stilton.*
● *The whole salad can be completed the day before and kept covered in the fridge until required. Stir well before serving.*

Warm Chicken Liver Salad

Preparation Time 20 minutes • **Cooking Time** 8–10 minutes • **Serves 4** • **Per Serving** 236 calories, 15g fat (of which 3g saturates), 3g carbohydrate, 0.8g salt • **Gluten Free** • **Dairy Free** • **Easy**

450g (1lb) chicken livers
1–2 tbsp balsamic vinegar
1 tsp Dijon mustard
3 tbsp olive oil
50g (2oz) streaky bacon rashers,
   de-rinded and cut into small,
   neat pieces (lardons)
50g (2oz) sun-dried tomatoes or
   roasted red peppers, cut into thin
   strips
½ curly endive, about 175g (6oz)
100g (3½oz) rocket
1 bunch of spring onions, sliced
salt and ground black pepper

1 Drain the chicken livers on kitchen paper, then trim and cut into pieces.

2 To make the dressing, put the vinegar, mustard, 2 tbsp oil, and salt and pepper into a small bowl. Whisk together and put to one side.

3 Fry the lardons in a non-stick frying pan until beginning to brown, stirring from time to time. Add the tomatoes or red peppers and heat through for 1 minute. Add the remaining oil and the chicken livers and stir-fry over a high heat for 2–3 minutes until the livers are just pink in the centre.

4 Meanwhile, toss the endive, rocket and spring onions with the dressing in a large bowl. Divide among four plates, arrange the warm livers and bacon on top and serve at once.

Smoked Mackerel with Potato and Horseradish Salad

Preparation Time 15 minutes • Cooking Time 20 minutes • Serves 4 • Per Serving 320 calories, 23g fat (of which 5g saturates), 22g carbohydrate, 0.7g salt • Gluten Free • Dairy Free • Easy

350g (12oz) new potatoes, scrubbed
2 tbsp horseradish sauce
2 tbsp crème fraîche
1 tbsp lemon juice
4 tbsp olive oil
2 crisp apples, cored
2 smoked mackerel fillets
100g (3½oz) watercress
ground black pepper

1 Cook the potatoes in a pan of lightly salted boiling water for 15–20 minutes until tender. Drain and put to one side.

2 Put the horseradish sauce, crème fraîche, lemon juice and oil into a bowl and mix together, then season with pepper.

3 Roughly chop the apples and the warm potatoes, put into a large bowl and toss in the dressing. Skin and flake the mackerel and add to the bowl with the watercress. Toss together and serve.

★ TRY SOMETHING DIFFERENT
● Try baby leaf spinach instead of watercress.
● Use wholegrain Dijon mustard instead of horseradish.

Tuna, Bean and Red Onion Salad

Preparation Time 5 minutes • Serves 4 • Per Serving 190 calories, 6g fat (of which 1g saturates), 15g carbohydrate, 1.1g salt • Gluten Free • Dairy Free • Easy

400g can cannellini beans, drained
  and rinsed
1 small red onion, very finely sliced
1 tbsp red wine vinegar
225g can tuna steak in oil (see
  Cook's Tip)
2 tbsp freshly chopped parsley
salt and ground black pepper
green salad and warm crusty bread
  to serve

1 Put the cannellini beans, onion and vinegar into a bowl, season with a little salt and mix well. Add the tuna with its oil, breaking the fish into large flakes.

2 Add half the chopped parsley and season generously with pepper. Toss the salad, then scatter the remaining parsley over the top. Serve with a green salad and plenty of warm crusty bread.

★ COOK'S TIP
Buy tuna steak canned in extra virgin olive oil, which flakes easily into large meaty flakes and has a good flavour.

Melon and Prawn Salad

Preparation Time 25 minutes, plus chilling • Serves 4 • Per Serving 571 calories, 39g fat (of which 6g saturates), 44g carbohydrate, 1.1g salt • Gluten Free • Dairy Free • Easy

1 ripe Charentais melon
½ small ripe Galia melon
1 wedge watermelon
1 papaya (optional)
grated zest and juice of 1 lime, plus
    extra lime zest to garnish
200ml (7fl oz) thick mayonnaise
225g (8oz) large cooked and peeled
    prawns
salt and ground black pepper
freshly chopped coriander to
    garnish

1 Thickly slice the melons and remove the skin. Scoop out the seeds and strain them, reserving the juice. Cut the melons into bite-size pieces, then cover and chill. Cut the papaya, if using, into thick slices (removing the seeds, if you like), then chill.

2 Stir the lime zest and 2 tbsp each lime and melon juice into the mayonnaise and season with salt and pepper. Mix the mayonnaise and prawns together.

3 Arrange the chilled melon and papaya on four serving plates. Add the prawns and garnish with extra lime zest and chopped coriander.

★ TRY SOMETHING DIFFERENT
Mango, Crab and Lime Salad
Replace the watermelon and papaya with 2 small ripe mangoes, peeled, stoned and sliced. Use cooked white crabmeat instead of the prawns.

Bacon, Avocado and Pinenut Salad

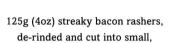

Preparation Time 5 minutes • **Cooking Time** 7 minutes • **Serves 4** • **Per Serving** 352 calories, 34g fat (of which 6g saturates), 3g carbohydrate, 1g salt • **Gluten Free** • **Dairy Free** • **Easy**

125g (4oz) streaky bacon rashers, de-rinded and cut into small, neat pieces (lardons)
1 shallot, finely chopped
120g bag mixed baby salad leaves
1 ripe avocado
50g (2oz) pinenuts
4 tbsp olive oil
4 tbsp red wine vinegar
salt and ground black pepper

1 Put the lardons into a frying pan over a medium heat for 1–2 minutes until the fat starts to run. Add the shallot and fry gently for about 5 minutes or until golden.

2 Meanwhile, divide the salad leaves among four serving plates. Halve, stone and peel the avocado, then slice the flesh. Arrange on the salad leaves.

3 Add the pinenuts, oil and vinegar to the frying pan and let bubble for 1 minute. Season with salt and pepper.

4 Tip the bacon, pinenuts and dressing over the salad and serve at once, while still warm.

★ TRY SOMETHING DIFFERENT
Replace the pinenuts with walnuts.

Antipasto Salad

Preparation Time 15 minutes • **Serves 6** • **Per Serving** 129 calories, 6g fat (of which 3g saturates), 15g carbohydrate, 0.8g salt • Vegetarian • Gluten Free • Easy

juice of 1 lime
4 ripe pears, peaches or nectarines, halved, stoned and sliced
50g (2oz) rocket
4–5 small firm round goat's cheeses, thickly sliced
4 grilled red peppers, sliced, or a 285g jar pimientos, drained
2 small red onions, sliced into petals
a handful of black olives
olive oil to drizzle
ground black pepper

1 Squeeze the lime juice over the fruit and add a sprinkling of black pepper.

2 Arrange all the ingredients on six serving plates.

3 Cover with clingfilm and keep in a cool place. Use within 2 hours. Drizzle with olive oil just before serving.

★ TRY SOMETHING DIFFERENT
Include other ingredients in this Italian-inspired salad, according to what's available: try quartered fresh figs, slices of melon, Parma ham or salami, buffalo mozzarella cheese or marinated grilled artichokes.

Mozzarella Mushrooms

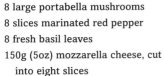

Preparation Time 2–3 minutes • Cooking Time 15–20 minutes • Serves 4 • Per Serving 137 calories, 9g fat (of which 5g saturates), 5g carbohydrate, 0.4g salt • **Vegetarian** • **Easy**

8 large portabella mushrooms
8 slices marinated red pepper
8 fresh basil leaves
150g (5oz) mozzarella cheese, cut into eight slices
4 English muffins, halved
salt and ground black pepper
green salad to serve

1 Preheat the oven to 200°C (180°C fan oven) mark 6. Lay the mushrooms side by side in a roasting tin and season with salt and pepper. Top each mushroom with a slice of red pepper and a basil leaf. Lay a slice of mozzarella on top of each mushroom and season again. Roast in the oven for 15–20 minutes until the mushrooms are tender and the cheese has melted.

2 Meanwhile, toast the muffin halves until golden. Put a mozzarella mushroom on top of each muffin half. Serve immediately with a green salad.

Lemon Hummus with Black Olives

★

Preparation Time 15 minutes • Serves 4 • Per Serving 284 calories, 16g fat (of which 2g saturates), 25g carbohydrate, 1.2g salt • Vegetarian • Gluten Free • Dairy Free • Easy

2 × 400g cans chickpeas, drained and rinsed
1 garlic clove (use fresh garlic when possible, see Cook's Tip), crushed
zest and juice of 1 lemon
4 tbsp olive oil
25g (1oz) pitted black olives, roughly chopped
1 tsp paprika, plus a little extra to sprinkle (optional)
sticks of raw vegetables and breadsticks to serve

1 Put the chickpeas and garlic into a food processor, add the lemon zest and juice and whiz to combine. With the motor running, drizzle in the oil to make a thick paste. If the hummus is too thick, add 1–2 tbsp cold water and whiz again.

2 Spoon into a bowl and stir in the olives and paprika. Sprinkle with a little extra paprika, if you like, and serve with raw vegetables and breadsticks for dipping.

★ COOK'S TIP
Raw garlic is renowned for its curative and protective powers, which include lowering blood pressure and cholesterol levels.
Fresh garlic has juicy mild cloves and is available from May and throughout the summer. It is the classic form of garlic to use for making (for example) pesto, salsa verde, garlic mayonnaise and chilled soups.

Mini Poppadums with Aubergine Purée

Preparation Time 5 minutes, plus cooling • Cooking Time about 1 hour • Serves 8 • Per Serving 161 calories, 11g fat
(of which 3g saturates), 14g carbohydrate, 0.7g salt • Vegetarian • Gluten Free • Dairy Free • Easy

2 large aubergines
1–2 garlic cloves, crushed
1 tbsp tahini (see Cook's Tips)
juice of ½ lemon
3 tbsp freshly chopped coriander,
   plus extra sprigs to garnish
1 pack mini poppadums (40 in
   pack)
salt and ground black pepper
paprika to garnish

1 Preheat the oven to 200°C (180°C fan oven) mark 6. Pierce the aubergines several times with a small sharp knife, put on a baking sheet and cook in the oven for about 1 hour or until very soft. Leave to cool.

2 Peel the aubergines. Wrap the flesh in a clean cloth and squeeze to remove any excess juice. Tip into a bowl. Add the garlic, tahini and lemon juice and mash well with a fork or whiz in a processor. Stir in the chopped coriander and enough water to give a dipping consistency. Season with salt and pepper.

3 Put a little purée on each of the poppadums and garnish with paprika and coriander sprigs.

★ COOK'S TIPS
● *Tahini is a thick creamy paste that is made from ground sesame seeds. Look out for it in good supermarkets and healthfood shops.*
● *For fewer calories, serve the purée with crudités instead.*

Chicken Fajitas

Preparation Time 10 minutes • **Cooking Time** 20 minutes • **Serves 4** • **Per Serving** 651 calories, 23g fat (of which 8g saturates), 63g carbohydrate, 1.6g salt • **Easy**

700g (1½lb) boneless, skinless chicken breasts, cut into chunky strips
2 tbsp fajita seasoning
1 tbsp sunflower oil
1 red pepper, seeded and sliced
360g jar fajita sauce
1 bunch of spring onions, halved
8 large flour tortillas
150g (5oz) tomato salsa
125g (4oz) guacamole dip
150ml (¼ pint) soured cream

1 Put the chicken breasts into a shallow dish and toss together with the fajita seasoning. Heat the oil in a large non-stick frying pan, add the chicken and cook for 5 minutes or until golden brown and tender.

2 Add the red pepper and cook for 2 minutes. Pour in the fajita sauce and bring to the boil, then reduce the heat and simmer for 5 minutes or until thoroughly heated. Add a splash of boiling water if the sauce becomes too thick. Stir in the spring onions and cook for 2 minutes.

3 Meanwhile, warm the tortillas in a microwave on full power for 45 seconds, or wrap in foil and warm in a preheated oven at 180°C (160°C fan oven) mark 4 for 10 minutes.

4 Transfer the chicken to a serving dish and take to the table, along with the tortillas, salsa, guacamole and soured cream. Let everyone help themselves.

Pork Pittas with Salsa

Preparation Time 10 minutes • **Cooking Time** 10 minutes • **Serves 4** • **Per Serving** 518 calories, 17g fat
(of which 5g saturates), 58g carbohydrate, 1.3g salt • **Easy**

1 tbsp olive oil
500g (1lb 2oz) diced pork
4 tbsp spicy seasoning such as
   fajita seasoning
4 large pittas
100g (3½oz) Greek yogurt

FOR THE SALSA
1 ripe avocado
1 red onion, chopped
4 large tomatoes, roughly chopped
a small handful of roughly chopped
   fresh coriander
juice of 1 lime
salt and ground black pepper

1 Heat the oil in a pan over a medium heat and cook the pork, stirring, for 3–4 minutes. Add the spicy seasoning and stir to coat the pork, then cook for a further 4–5 minutes until cooked through.

2 Meanwhile, make the salsa. Halve, stone and peel the avocado, then chop. Put the onion into a bowl and add the avocado, tomatoes, coriander and lime juice. Mix well, season with salt and pepper and put to one side.

3 Toast the pittas until lightly golden, then slit down the side and stuff with the pork, a spoonful of salsa and a dollop of Greek yogurt. Serve immediately.

 COOK'S TIP
Make your own spicy seasoning by mixing 1 crushed garlic clove, 1 tsp ground ginger and ½–1 tsp cayenne pepper. Toss with the pork and complete the recipe.

Tomato Crostini with Feta and Basil

★

Preparation Time 20 minutes • **Cooking Time** 3 minutes • **Serves 4** • **Per Serving** 242 calories, 17g fat (of which 3g saturates), 18g carbohydrate, 1.5g salt • **Vegetarian** • **Easy**

1 small garlic clove, crushed

3 tbsp freshly chopped basil, plus extra basil leaves to garnish

25g (1oz) pinenuts

2 tbsp extra virgin olive oil

grated zest and juice of 1 lime

50g (2oz) vegetarian feta cheese

4 large tomatoes, preferably vine-ripened, thickly sliced

150g tub fresh tomato salsa

50g (2oz) pitted black olives, roughly chopped

4 thick slices country-style bread

salt and ground black pepper

1 Put the garlic, chopped basil, pinenuts, oil, lime zest and juice into a food processor and whiz to form a smooth paste. Add the feta cheese and blend until smooth. Thin with 1 tbsp water if necessary. Season with salt and pepper.

2 Put the tomatoes, salsa and olives into a bowl and gently toss together.

3 Toast the bread. Divide the tomato mixture among the slices of toast and spoon the basil and feta mixture on top. Garnish with basil leaves and serve.

Croque Monsieur

★

Preparation Time 5 minutes • **Cooking Time** 8 minutes • **Serves 2** • **Per Serving** 551 calories, 35g fat (of which 22g saturates), 27g carbohydrate, 3.6g salt • **Easy**

4 slices white bread
butter, softened, to spread, plus extra for frying
Dijon mustard, to taste
125g (4oz) Gruyère cheese
4 slices ham

1 Spread each slice of bread on both sides with the butter. Then spread one side of two slices of bread with a little Dijon mustard.

2 Divide the cheese and ham between the two mustard-spread bread slices. Top each with the remaining bread and press down.

3 Heat a griddle with a little butter until hot and fry the sandwiches for 2–3 minutes on each side until golden and crispy and the cheese starts to melt. Slice in half and serve immediately.

Tuna Melt

Preparation Time 5 minutes • **Cooking Time** 5 minutes • **Serves 2** • **Per Serving** 390 calories, 21g fat (of which 8g saturates), 30g carbohydrate, 1.7g salt • **Easy**

2 slices Granary, sourdough or
    wholemeal bread
2 tomatoes, sliced
75g (3oz) canned tuna in brine,
    drained
2 tbsp mayonnaise
50g (2oz) Cheddar or Red Leicester
    cheese, grated
dash of Worcestershire sauce

1 Preheat the grill. Toast the bread on one side, then turn it over.

2 Divide the sliced tomatoes between the two slices of bread, then add the tuna.

3 Spread the mayonnaise over the tuna, cover with the cheese and sprinkle a dash of Worcestershire sauce on each. Grill until the cheese is golden and bubbling.

★ TRY SOMETHING DIFFERENT
Instead of tuna, use a 120g can of sardines or mackerel.

Low-GI Beans on Toast

Preparation Time 5 minutes • **Cooking Time** 10 minutes • **Serves 4** • **Per Serving** 364 calories, 9g fat
(of which 2g saturates), 55g carbohydrate, 2.1g salt • **Easy**

1 tbsp olive oil
2 garlic cloves, finely sliced
400g can borlotti or cannellini
   beans, drained and rinsed
400g can chickpeas, drained and
   rinsed
400g can chopped tomatoes
leaves from 2 fresh rosemary
   sprigs, finely chopped
4 slices sourdough or Granary
   bread
25g (1oz) Parmesan

1 Heat the oil in a pan over a low heat, add the garlic and cook for 1 minute, stirring gently.

2 Add the beans and chickpeas to the pan with the tomatoes and bring to the boil. Add the chopped rosemary to the pan. Reduce the heat and simmer for 8–10 minutes until thickened.

3 Meanwhile, toast the bread and put on plates. Grate the Parmesan into the bean mixture, stir once, then spoon over the bread. Serve immediately.

Garden Frittata

Preparation Time 10 minutes • Cooking Time 10–15 minutes • Serves 6 • Per Serving 208 calories, 13g fat (of which 7g saturates), 8g carbohydrate, 0.4g salt • Gluten Free • Easy

125g (4oz) small new potatoes
125g (4oz) shelled broad beans
50g (2oz) soft cheese, preferably
   fresh goat's cheese
4 medium eggs
2 tbsp freshly chopped thyme, plus
   extra to serve
2 tbsp olive oil
125g (4oz) onions, roughly chopped
225g (8oz) courgettes, sliced
125g (4oz) cooked and peeled
   prawns
125g (4oz) lightly cooked salmon
salt and ground black pepper

1 Preheat the grill. Cook the potatoes and broad beans separately in lightly salted boiling water until just tender, then drain. Whisk together the cheese, eggs, thyme and seasoning.

2 Heat the oil in a large shallow flameproof pan. Add the onions, courgettes, potatoes and beans and cook, stirring, for 2–3 minutes, then add the prawns and salmon. Pour in the egg mixture.

3 As the eggs cook, push the mixture into the centre of the pan to allow the raw egg to flow down to the edge. When the mixture is lightly set, put the pan under the hot grill for 2–3 minutes until golden. Sprinkle with thyme to serve.

★ TRY SOMETHING DIFFERENT
● *You could substitute fresh sorrel for the thyme.*
● *The broad beans can be skinned for extra colour.*

Quiche Lorraine

Preparation Time 35 minutes, plus chilling • **Cooking Time** 1 hour • **Serves 8** • **Per Serving** 595 calories, 50g fat (of which 29g saturates), 22g carbohydrate, 1.5g salt • **Easy**

Shortcrust Pastry (see page 255) made with 200g (7oz) plain flour, a pinch of salt, 100g (3½oz) chilled butter and 1 large egg

FOR THE FILLING
5 large eggs
225g (8oz) unsmoked streaky bacon, rind removed
40g (1½oz) butter
125g (4oz) shallots, onions or spring onions, finely chopped
400g (14oz) crème fraîche
100g (3½oz) Gruyère cheese, grated
salt and ground black pepper

crispy bacon and fried spring onions to garnish

1 Preheat the oven to 200°C (180°C fan oven) mark 6. Roll out the pastry thinly and use to line a 23cm (9in), 3cm (1¼in) deep, loose-based tart tin. Prick the base all over and cover with foil or greaseproof paper 7.5cm (3in) larger than the tin. Spread baking beans on top and bake blind for 15–20 minutes. Remove the foil or paper and beans and bake for 5–10 minutes until the pastry is light golden.

2 Meanwhile, lightly whisk the eggs for the filling. Use a little to brush the inside of the pastry case and return it to the oven for 5 minutes to seal any cracks. Remove from the oven. Reduce the oven temperature to 190°C (170°C fan oven) mark 5.

3 Cut the bacon into 5mm (¼in) strips. Put the bacon into a pan of cold water and bring to the boil. Drain, refresh under cold water and dry on kitchen paper.

4 Melt the butter in a frying pan, add the shallots or onions and cook for 1 minute. Add the bacon and cook, stirring, until brown.

5 Mix the eggs with the crème fraîche and Gruyère cheese, then season. Put the bacon mixture in the pastry case and spoon the crème fraîche mixture on top (see Cook's Tip). Cook for 30–35 minutes until golden and just set. Cool for 10 minutes before serving. Garnish with bacon and fried spring onions.

 COOK'S TIP
Fill the pastry case as full as possible. You may find you have a little mixture left, as flan tins vary in size.

Sausage Rolls

Preparation Time 25 minutes • **Cooking Time** 30 minutes • **Makes 28** • **Per Sausage Roll** 119 calories, 9g fat (of which 2g saturates), 8g carbohydrate, 0.4g salt • **Easy**

**450g (1lb) puff pastry, thawed
    if frozen
plain flour to dust
450g (1lb) pork sausagemeat
milk to brush
beaten egg to glaze**

1 Preheat the oven to 220°C (200°C fan oven) mark 7. Roll out half the pastry on a lightly floured surface to a 40.5 x 20.5cm (16 x 8in) rectangle, then cut lengthways into two strips.

2 Divide the sausagemeat into four, dust with flour and form two portions into rolls, the length of the pastry. Lay a sausagemeat roll on each strip of pastry. Brush the pastry edges with a little milk, fold one side of the pastry over and press the long edges together to seal. Repeat with the remaining pastry and sausagemeat. Trim the ends.

3 Brush the pastry with egg to glaze and cut each roll into 5cm (2in) lengths. Make two or three slits in the top of each one.

4 Transfer to a baking sheet and bake for 15 minutes. Reduce the oven temperature to 180°C (160°C fan oven) mark 4 and bake for a further 15 minutes. Transfer to a wire rack. Serve hot or cold.

★ TRY SOMETHING DIFFERENT

Add 1 seeded and finely chopped hot red chilli, 1 tbsp freshly grated ginger and a handful of freshly chopped coriander leaves to the pork sausagemeat.

Pizza and Pasta

Pizza Base

225g (8oz) strong white bread flour
7g sachet fast-action (easy-blend)
    dried yeast
½ tsp salt
4 tbsp extra virgin olive oil
cornmeal or flour to sprinkle

1 Sift the flour into a large bowl, stir in the yeast and salt and make a well in the centre. Pour 150ml (¼ pint) water into the well with 1 tbsp oil. Use your fingertips or a large spoon to stir the mixture together.

2 Turn out on to a lightly floured surface and knead for 5 minutes or until the dough is smooth. It should be quite soft. Lightly oil the mixing bowl, put in the dough and turn it over to coat in the remaining oil. Cover with oiled clingfilm or a clean teatowel. Put in a warm draught-free place to rise for 45 minutes or until doubled in size.

3 Preheat the oven to 240°C (220°C fan oven) mark 9. Quickly punch the dough to knock it back, then roll it out into a circle or rectangle about 1cm (½ in) thick.

4 Sprinkle a baking sheet fairly generously with cornmeal or plain flour. Roll the dough over the rolling pin and lift it on to the baking sheet, then unroll and spread with Fresh Tomato Sauce (see opposite).

5 Add your choice of toppings (see below) and bake for 20–25 minutes until the rim is crusty and the topping is bubbling.

★ TOPPINGS
Scatter one or two of the following on top of a basic cheese and tomato pizza:
● *Bacon or pancetta bits, or slices of prosciutto*
● *Rocket leaves*
● *Dried chilli flakes*
● *Capers*
● *Sliced sun-dried tomatoes*
● *Pepperoni slices*
● *Roasted peppers*
● *Artichoke hearts, drained and quartered*
● *Sliced mushrooms*

★ PERFECT PIZZAS
● *A ceramic baking stone (from good kitchen shops) is extremely useful for cooking pizza, to help cook the pizza evenly and give crunchiness to the base. (Put the stone into the oven before preheating.) Alternatively, use a metal baking sheet.*
● *Pizza should not be a heavy dish, so add toppings with a light hand.*
● *If you can't get good mozzarella, use another cheese instead – Taleggio, Fontina, or even just a good Cheddar all work well.*

Fresh Tomato Sauce

900g (2lb) vine-ripened tomatoes,
   roughly chopped
2 tbsp extra virgin olive oil
2 garlic cloves, crushed
grated zest of 1 lemon
1 tsp dried oregano
2 tbsp freshly chopped basil
a pinch of sugar, or to taste
   (optional)
salt and ground black pepper

1 Put the tomatoes into a pan with the oil, garlic, lemon zest and oregano. Bring to the boil, then cover the pan, reduce the heat and simmer gently for 20 minutes.

2 Add the basil, salt and pepper to taste and a little sugar if required. Simmer, uncovered, for a further 10 minutes or until the sauce is slightly thickened. If a smooth sauce is preferred, pass through a sieve and reheat before serving.

3 To use, stir into cooked pasta; use as a sauce to braise white fish or chicken; stir in cheese or herbs and serve as a sauce with fish or chicken; reduce until thick and use to spread on a pizza before adding a topping.

⭐ TO STORE

● *In the fridge*
Store, covered, and use within three days.

● *In the freezer*
Freeze in small portions in freezer bags or boxes for up to a month; thaw before use.

Tuna Melt Pizza

Preparation Time 5 minutes • Cooking Time 10–12 minutes • Serves 4 • Per Serving 688 calories, 26g fat (of which 9g saturates), 72g carbohydrate, 3.5g salt • Easy

2 large pizza bases, ready made, or make your own (see page 48)
4 tbsp sun-dried tomato pesto
2 × 185g cans tuna, drained
50g can anchovies, drained and chopped
125g (4oz) mature Cheddar, grated
rocket to serve

1 Preheat the oven to 220°C (200°C fan oven) mark 7. Spread each pizza base with 2 tbsp sun-dried tomato pesto. Top each with half the tuna, half the anchovies and half the grated cheese.

2 Put on a baking sheet and cook in the oven for 10–12 minutes until the cheese has melted. Sprinkle with rocket to serve.

★ TRY SOMETHING DIFFERENT

Mozzarella and Tomato Pizza
Spread the pizza bases with 4 tbsp pesto and top with 125g (4oz) chopped sunblush tomatoes and 2 x 125g sliced mozzarella balls. Cook, then serve topped with a handful of baby spinach leaves.

Ham and Pineapple Pizza
Spread the pizza bases with 4 tbsp Fresh Tomato Sauce (see page 49). Top with a 225g can drained unsweetened pineapple chunks, 125g (4oz) diced ham and 125g (4oz) grated Gruyère.

Deli Pizza

Preparation Time 5 minutes • Cooking Time 15 minutes • Serves 4 • Per Serving 440 calories, 15g fat (of which 5g saturates), 64g carbohydrate, 2.8g salt • **Vegetarian** • **Easy**

6 tbsp Fresh Tomato Sauce (see page 49)
2 pizzeria-style pizza bases
100g (3½oz) soft goat's cheese
1 red onion, finely sliced
100g (3½oz) sunblush tomatoes
100g (3½oz) pitted black olives
a handful of fresh basil, roughly torn
green salad to serve

1 Preheat the oven to 220°C (200°C fan oven) mark 7. Put a large baking sheet on the top shelf to heat up.

2 Spread a thin layer of the tomato sauce over each of the pizza bases, leaving a 2.5cm (1in) border around the edge. Top with dollops of goat's cheese, then scatter on the onion, tomatoes and olives.

3 Slide one of the pizzas on to the hot baking sheet and bake for 15 minutes or until golden and crisp. Repeat with the second pizza base. Scatter the torn basil over each pizza and serve immediately with a green salad.

★ TRY SOMETHING DIFFERENT
Try marinated peppers, artichokes or chargrilled aubergines instead of the olives and sunblush tomatoes.

Garlic Cheese Pizza

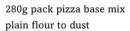

Preparation Time 20 minutes • **Cooking Time** 30 minutes • **Serves 4** • **Per Serving** 536 calories, 30g fat (of which 9g saturates), 54g carbohydrate, 0.6g salt • **Vegetarian** • **Easy**

280g pack pizza base mix
plain flour to dust
2 × 150g packs garlic and herb
  cheese
12 whole sun-dried tomatoes,
  drained of oil and cut into rough
  pieces
40g (1½oz) pinenuts
12 fresh basil leaves
3 tbsp olive oil
green salad to serve

1 Preheat the oven to 220°C (200°C fan oven) mark 7. Put a pizza stone or large baking sheet in the oven to heat up.

2 Mix the pizza base dough according to the pack instructions. Turn out on to a lightly floured worksurface and knead for a few minutes or until smooth. Roll out to a 33cm (13in) round. Transfer the dough to the preheated pizza stone or baking sheet. Pinch a lip around the edge.

3 Crumble the cheese over the dough and flatten with a palette knife, then sprinkle on the sun-dried tomatoes, pinenuts and basil leaves.

4 Drizzle with the oil and bake for 20–30 minutes until pale golden and cooked to the centre. Serve with a green salad.

★ TRY SOMETHING DIFFERENT
Use goat's cheese instead of the garlic and herb cheese.

Egg and Pepper Pizza

Preparation Time 15 minutes • **Cooking Time** 12 minutes • **Serves 4** • **Per Serving** 403 calories, 13g fat (of which 2g saturates), 61g carbohydrate, 1g salt • **Vegetarian** • **Easy**

150g (5oz) red and yellow marinated peppers in oil, drained and oil reserved
8 tbsp passata
4 small wheat-free pizza bases
4 medium eggs
125g (4oz) watercress, washed and stalks removed

1 Preheat the oven to 220°C (200°C fan oven) mark 7. Put two large baking sheets, big enough to hold two pizzas each, into the oven to heat up.

2 Chop the peppers into thin strips. Spoon 2 tbsp passata over each pizza base and scatter the pepper around the edges. Make a dip in the passata in the middle of each pizza and break an egg into it. Carefully slide the pizzas on to the preheated baking sheets. Place in the oven and cook for 12 minutes or until the egg is thoroughly cooked.

3 Top the pizzas with watercress, drizzle with a little of the reserved oil from the peppers and serve.

★ COOK'S TIP
Watercress is the salad superfood par excellence. It is a good source of iron, and vitamins C and E.

Mozzarella, Parma Ham and Rocket Pizza

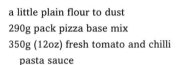

Preparation Time 10 minutes • Cooking Time 15–18 minutes • Serves 4 • Per Serving 508 calories, 19g fat (of which 11g saturates), 64g carbohydrate, 1.9g salt • Easy

a little plain flour to dust
290g pack pizza base mix
350g (12oz) fresh tomato and chilli pasta sauce
250g (9oz) buffalo mozzarella cheese, drained and roughly chopped
6 slices Parma ham, torn into strips
50g (2oz) rocket
a little extra virgin olive oil to drizzle
salt and ground black pepper

1 Preheat the oven to 200°C (180°C fan oven) mark 6 and lightly flour two large baking sheets. Mix the pizza base dough according to the pack instructions. Divide the dough into two and knead each ball on a lightly floured surface for about 5 minutes, then roll them out to make two 23cm (9in) rounds. Put one on each of the prepared baking sheets.

2 Divide the tomato sauce between the pizza bases and spread it over, leaving a small border around each edge. Scatter on the mozzarella pieces, then scatter with ham. Season well with salt and pepper.

3 Cook the pizzas for 15–18 minutes until golden. Slide on to a wooden board, top with rocket leaves and drizzle with oil. Cut in half to serve.

 COOK'S TIP
If you're short of time, buy two ready-made pizza bases.

Funny Face Pizzas

Preparation Time 40 minutes, plus 1 hour rising • Cooking Time 20 minutes • Makes 12 • Per Serving 231 calories, 9g fat (of which 5g saturates), 28g carbohydrate, 1g salt • Easy

400g (14oz) strong white flour, plus extra to dust
1 tsp salt
2 tsp fast-action (easy-blend) dried yeast
2 tbsp olive oil, plus extra to grease
100ml (3½fl oz) pizza sauce or tomato pasta sauce
250g bag grated Cheddar or mozzarella cheese
a few slices ham or salami
a few pitted olives
12 cherry tomatoes, sliced
green, red or yellow peppers, seeded and cut into strips

1 Sift the flour with the salt into a large bowl. Stir in the yeast. Make a well in the centre and pour in about 200ml (7fl oz) warm water and the oil. Mix together with a wooden spoon to form a soft dough.

2 Tip the dough out on to a floured worksurface and knead for 10 minutes or until smooth and elastic. Put into a lightly oiled bowl and cover with a clean teatowel. Leave to rise for 1 hour or until doubled in size. Lightly oil several baking sheets.

3 Preheat the oven to 230°C (210°C fan oven) mark 8. Divide the dough into twelve pieces. Roll out each piece to the size of a saucer – about 14cm (5½ in) – and arrange on the prepared baking sheets.

4 Spread some sauce on each pizza base, then sprinkle with cheese. Use the ham or salami, olives, cherry tomatoes and pepper strips to make faces on the pizzas. Bake for 5 minutes, then reduce the temperature to 200°C (180°C fan oven) mark 6 and bake for another 10–15 minutes. Serve immediately.

Seafood Spaghetti with Pepper and Almond Sauce

Preparation Time 20 minutes • Cooking Time 25 minutes • Serves 4 • Per Serving 426 calories, 9g fat (of which 1g saturates), 62g carbohydrate, 0.9g salt • Dairy Free • Easy

1 small red pepper
1 red chilli (see page 13)
50g (2oz) blanched almonds
2–3 garlic cloves, chopped
2 tbsp red wine vinegar
350ml (12fl oz) tomato juice
a small handful of flat-leafed parsley
300g (11oz) spaghetti
450g (1lb) mixed cooked seafood, such as prawns, mussels and squid
salt and ground black pepper

1 Preheat the grill. Grill the red pepper and chilli, turning occasionally, until the skins char and blacken. Cover and leave to cool slightly, then peel off the skins. Halve, discard the seeds, then put the flesh into a food processor.

2 Toast the almonds under the grill until golden. Add the toasted almonds and garlic to the processor with the vinegar, tomato juice and half the parsley, then season with salt and pepper. Whiz until almost smooth, then transfer the sauce to a large pan.

3 Meanwhile, cook the spaghetti in a pan of lightly salted boiling water according to the pack instructions; keep it al dente.

4 Heat the sauce gently until it simmers, then add the seafood. Simmer for 3–4 minutes until the sauce and seafood have heated through, stirring frequently.

5 Roughly chop the remaining parsley. Drain the pasta and return to the pan, then add the sauce together with the parsley and toss well.

Quick and Easy Carbonara

Preparation Time 5 minutes • Cooking Time 10 minutes • Serves 4 • Per Serving 688 calories, 39g fat (of which 19g saturates), 65g carbohydrate, 1.6g salt • **Easy**

350g (12oz) tagliatelle
150g (5oz) smoked bacon, chopped
1 tbsp olive oil
2 large egg yolks
150ml (¼ pint) double cream
50g (2oz) freshly grated Parmesan
2 tbsp freshly chopped parsley

1 Cook the pasta in a large pan of lightly salted boiling water according to the pack instructions. Drain.

2 Meanwhile, fry the bacon in the oil for 4–5 minutes. Add to the drained pasta and keep hot.

3 Put the egg yolks into a bowl, add the cream and whisk together. Add to the pasta with the Parmesan and parsley, toss well and serve.

Fusilli with Chilli and Tomatoes

Preparation Time 10 minutes • **Cooking Time** 10–15 minutes • **Serves 4** • **Per Serving** 479 calories, 17g fat (of which 4g saturates), 69g carbohydrate, 0.4g salt • **Easy**

350g (12oz) fusilli or other short pasta
4 tbsp olive oil
1 large red chilli, seeded and finely chopped (see page 13)
1 garlic clove, crushed
500g (1lb 2oz) cherry tomatoes
2 tbsp freshly chopped basil
50g (2oz) Parmesan, shaved (see Cook's Tip)
salt and ground black pepper

1 Cook the pasta in a large pan of lightly salted boiling water according to the pack instructions. Drain.

2 Meanwhile, heat the oil in a large frying pan over a high heat. Add the chilli and garlic and cook for 30 seconds. Add the tomatoes, season with salt and pepper and cook over a high heat for 3 minutes or until the tomato skins begin to split.

3 Add the basil and drained pasta and toss together. Transfer to a serving dish, sprinkle the Parmesan shavings over the top and serve immediately.

★ COOK'S TIP
Make Parmesan shavings with a vegetable peeler. Hold the piece of Parmesan in one hand and, using the peeler, pare off wafer-thin strips of cheese.

Chilli Bolognese

Preparation Time 15 minutes • **Cooking Time** 30–40 minutes • **Serves 4** • **Per Serving** 756 calories, 33g fat (of which 13g saturates), 74g carbohydrate, 1.4g salt • **Easy**

1 tbsp olive oil
1 large onion, finely chopped
½ large red chilli, seeded and
    thinly sliced (see page 13)
450g (1lb) minced beef or lamb
125g (4oz) smoked bacon, rind
    removed, cut into strips
3 roasted red peppers, drained and
    finely chopped
400g can chopped tomatoes
125ml (4fl oz) red wine
300g (11oz) spaghetti
25g (1oz) freshly grated Cheddar or
    Gruyère cheese
2 tbsp freshly chopped flat-leafed
    parsley (optional)
salt and ground black pepper

1 Heat the oil in a large pan over a medium heat. Add the onion and chilli and fry for 5–10 minutes until soft and golden. Add the beef or lamb and the bacon and stir over the heat for 5–7 minutes until well browned.

2 Stir in the red peppers, tomatoes and wine. Season with salt and pepper and bring to the boil, then reduce the heat and simmer over a low heat for 15–20 minutes.

3 Meanwhile, cook the pasta in a large pan of lightly salted boiling water according to the pack instructions. Drain.

4 Just before serving, stir the grated cheese, parsley, if using, and the sauce into the spaghetti.

Italian Meatballs

Preparation Time 15 minutes • Cooking Time 50 minutes • Serves 4 • Per Serving 275 calories, 12g fat (of which 4g saturates), 16g carbohydrate, 1.8g salt • **Dairy Free** • **Easy**

50g (2oz) fresh breadcrumbs
450g (1lb) minced lean pork
1 tsp fennel seeds, crushed
¼ tsp chilli flakes, or to taste
3 garlic cloves, crushed
4 tbsp freshly chopped flat-leafed
    parsley
3 tbsp red wine
oil-water spray (see Cook's Tip)
roughly chopped fresh oregano to
    garnish
spaghetti to serve

FOR THE TOMATO SAUCE
oil-water spray
2 large shallots, finely chopped
3 pitted black olives, shredded
2 garlic cloves, crushed
2 pinches of chilli flakes
250ml (9fl oz) vegetable or chicken
    stock
500g carton passata
2 tbsp each freshly chopped flat-
    leafed parsley, basil and oregano
salt and ground black pepper

1 To make the tomato sauce, spray a pan with the oil-water spray and add the shallots. Cook gently for 5 minutes. Add the olives, garlic, chilli flakes and stock and bring to the boil, then reduce the heat, cover and simmer for 3–4 minutes.

2 Uncover and simmer for 10 minutes or until the shallots and garlic are soft and the liquid syrupy. Stir in the passata and season with salt and pepper. Bring to the boil, then reduce the heat and simmer for 10–15 minutes. Stir in the herbs.

3 Meanwhile, put the breadcrumbs, pork, fennel seeds, chilli flakes, garlic, parsley and wine into a large bowl, season and mix together, using your hands, until thoroughly combined. (If you wish to check the seasoning, fry a little mixture, taste and adjust if necessary.)

4 With wet hands, roll the mixture into balls. Line a grill pan with foil, shiny side up, and spray with the oil-water spray. Cook the meatballs under a preheated grill for 3–4 minutes on each side. Serve with the tomato sauce and spaghetti, garnished with oregano.

 COOK'S TIP
Oil-water spray is far lower in calories than oil alone and, as it sprays on thinly and evenly, you'll use less. Fill one-eighth of a travel-sized spray bottle with oil such as sunflower, light olive or vegetable (rapeseed) oil, then top up with water. To use, shake well before spraying. Store in the fridge.

Pasta with Chicken, Cream and Basil

Preparation Time 10 minutes • Cooking Time 25 minutes • Serves 4 • Per Serving 612 calories, 27g fat (of which 12g saturates), 67g carbohydrate, 0.4g salt • **Easy**

1 tbsp olive oil
2 shallots, chopped
400g (14oz) boneless chicken, cubed
125g (4oz) chestnut mushrooms, sliced
50g (2oz) sultanas
a pinch of ground cinnamon
50ml (2fl oz) dry white wine
125ml (4fl oz) hot chicken stock
300g (11oz) farfalle pasta
142ml carton double cream
2 tsp Dijon mustard
2 tsp freshly chopped basil
salt

1 Heat the oil in a pan. Add the shallots and fry for 4–5 minutes. Add the chicken and cook until browned. Add the mushrooms and cook for 2 minutes. Stir in the sultanas and cinnamon.

2 Pour in the wine and hot stock and simmer for 12–15 minutes until the chicken is cooked.

3 Meanwhile, cook the pasta in a large pan of lightly salted boiling water according to the pack instructions.

4 Stir the cream, mustard and basil into the chicken and season with salt. Drain the pasta and return to the pan, then add the sauce, toss and serve.

Ham and Mushroom Pasta

Preparation Time 5 minutes • Cooking Time 15 minutes • Serves 4 • Per Serving 415 calories, 10g fat
(of which 4g saturates), 67g carbohydrate, 1g salt • **Easy**

350g (12oz) penne pasta
1 tbsp olive oil
2 shallots, sliced
200g (7oz) small button mushrooms
3 tbsp crème fraîche
125g (4oz) smoked ham, roughly
   chopped
2 tbsp freshly chopped flat-leafed
   parsley
salt and ground black pepper

1 Cook the pasta in a large pan of lightly salted boiling water until al dente.

2 Meanwhile, heat the oil in a pan. Add the shallots and fry gently for 3 minutes or until starting to soften. Add the mushrooms and fry for 5–6 minutes.

3 Drain the pasta, put back into the pan and add the shallots and mushrooms. Stir in the crème fraîche, ham and parsley. Toss everything together, season with salt and pepper and heat through to serve.

Spicy Salami and Pasta Supper

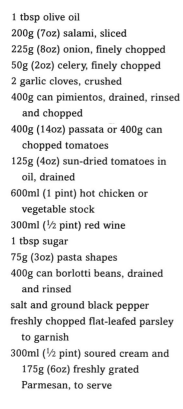

Preparation Time 15 minutes • **Cooking Time** 30 minutes • **Serves 6** • **Per Serving** 629 calories, 39g fat (of which 18g saturates), 36g carbohydrate, 3.1g salt • **Easy**

1 tbsp olive oil
200g (7oz) salami, sliced
225g (8oz) onion, finely chopped
50g (2oz) celery, finely chopped
2 garlic cloves, crushed
400g can pimientos, drained, rinsed
    and chopped
400g (14oz) passata or 400g can
    chopped tomatoes
125g (4oz) sun-dried tomatoes in
    oil, drained
600ml (1 pint) hot chicken or
    vegetable stock
300ml (½ pint) red wine
1 tbsp sugar
75g (3oz) pasta shapes
400g can borlotti beans, drained
    and rinsed
salt and ground black pepper
freshly chopped flat-leafed parsley
    to garnish
300ml (½ pint) soured cream and
    175g (6oz) freshly grated
    Parmesan, to serve

1 Heat the oil in a large pan over a medium heat and fry the salami for 5 minutes or until golden and crisp. Drain on kitchen paper.

2 Fry the onion and celery in the hot oil for 10 minutes or until soft and golden. Add the garlic and fry for 1 minute. Put the salami back in the pan with the pimientos, passata or chopped tomatoes, the sun-dried tomatoes, hot stock, wine and sugar and bring to the boil.

3 Stir in the pasta, bring back to the boil and cook for about 10 minutes, or according to the pack instructions, until the pasta is almost tender.

4 Stir in the beans and simmer for 3–4 minutes. Top up with more stock if the pasta is not tender when the liquid has been absorbed. Season with salt and pepper.

5 Ladle into warmed bowls and serve topped with soured cream and garnished with chopped parsley. Serve the grated Parmesan separately.

★ GET AHEAD

To prepare ahead *Complete the recipe to the end of step 2, cool quickly, cover and chill for up to one day.*
To use *Bring back to the boil, stir in the pasta and complete the recipe.*

Greek Pasta Bake

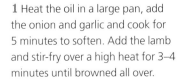

Preparation Time 10 minutes • Cooking Time about 1½ hours • Serves 4 • Per Serving 736 calories, 30g fat (of which 13g saturates), 80g carbohydrate, 0.8g salt • **Easy**

2 tbsp vegetable oil
1 onion, finely chopped
2 garlic cloves, crushed
450g (1lb) extra-lean minced lamb
2 tbsp tomato purée
400g can chopped tomatoes
2 bay leaves
150ml (¼ pint) hot beef stock
350g (12oz) macaroni
50g (2oz) Cheddar, grated
salt and ground black pepper

FOR THE SAUCE
15g (½oz) butter
15g (½oz) plain flour
300ml (½ pint) milk
1 medium egg, beaten

1 Heat the oil in a large pan, add the onion and garlic and cook for 5 minutes to soften. Add the lamb and stir-fry over a high heat for 3–4 minutes until browned all over.

2 Stir in the tomato purée and cook for 1–2 minutes. Stir in the tomatoes, bay leaves and hot stock and season with salt and pepper. Bring to the boil, then reduce the heat and cook for 35–40 minutes.

3 Meanwhile, make the sauce. Melt the butter in a small pan, then stir in the flour and cook over a medium heat for 1–2 minutes. Gradually add the milk, stirring constantly. Reduce the heat to low and cook, stirring, for 4–5 minutes. Remove from the heat and cool slightly. Stir in the beaten egg and season well with salt and pepper. Put to one side.

4 Preheat the oven to 180°C (160°C fan oven) mark 4. Cook the macaroni in a large pan of lightly salted boiling water according to the pack instructions until al dente.

5 Drain the pasta well and spoon half into a 2 litre (3½ pint) ovenproof dish. Spoon the meat mixture over it, then top with the remaining macaroni. Pour the sauce evenly over the top and scatter with the grated cheese. Bake for 25–30 minutes until golden brown.

Pasta with Leeks, Bacon and Mushrooms

Preparation Time 5 minutes • Cooking Time 15–20 minutes • Serves 4 • Per Serving 765 calories, 39g fat (of which 22g saturates), 86g carbohydrate, 1.5g salt • Easy

450g (1lb) conchiglie pasta
50g (2oz) butter
125g (4oz) streaky bacon, diced
2 medium leeks, trimmed and thickly sliced
225g (8oz) chestnut or button mushrooms, sliced
1 garlic clove, crushed
150g pack soft cream cheese with herbs
salt and ground black pepper
basil leaves to garnish

1 Cook the pasta in a large pan of lightly salted boiling water according to the pack instructions until al dente.

2 Meanwhile, melt the butter in a pan and add the bacon, leeks, mushrooms and garlic. Cook over a medium heat for 5–10 minutes until the leeks are tender. Reduce the heat, add the cream cheese and season well with salt and pepper.

3 Drain the pasta, add to the sauce and toss well. Garnish with basil and serve.

Ribbon Pasta with Courgettes and Capers

Preparation Time about 5 minutes • **Cooking Time** 8–10 minutes • **Serves 4** • **Per Serving** 556 calories, 18g fat (of which 2g saturates), 86g carbohydrate, 2.1g salt • **Dairy Free** • **Easy**

450g (1lb) pappardelle pasta

2 large courgettes, coarsely grated

50g can anchovies, drained and
   roughly chopped

1 red chilli, seeded and finely
   chopped (see page 13)

2 tbsp salted capers, rinsed

1 garlic clove, crushed

4 tbsp pitted black Kalamata olives,
   roughly chopped

4 tbsp extra virgin olive oil

2 tbsp freshly chopped flat-leafed
   parsley

salt and ground black pepper

1 Cook the pappardelle in a large pan of boiling water until al dente. About 1 minute before the end of the cooking time, add the courgettes, then simmer until the pasta is just cooked.

2 Meanwhile, put the anchovies into a small pan and add the chilli, capers, garlic, olives and oil. Stir over a low heat for 2–3 minutes.

3 Drain the pasta and put back in the pan. Pour the hot anchovy mixture on top, mix well and toss with the parsley. Season with salt and pepper and serve immediately.

★ COOK'S TIP
If cooking for vegetarians, omit the anchovies and serve with freshly grated vegetarian Parmesan cheese.

Lamb and Pasta Pot

Preparation Time 10 minutes • Cooking Time 50 minutes • Serves 4 • Per Serving 686 calories, 36g fat (of which 16g saturates), 18g carbohydrate, 1.4g salt • **Dairy Free** • **Easy**

1 half leg of lamb roasting joint – about 1.1kg (2½lb) total weight
125g (4oz) smoked streaky bacon, chopped
150ml (¼ pint) red wine
400g can chopped tomatoes with chilli, or 400g (14oz) passata
75g (3oz) pasta shapes
12 sunblush tomatoes
150g (5oz) chargrilled artichokes in oil, drained and halved
a handful of basil leaves to garnish

1 Preheat the oven to 200°C (180°C fan oven) mark 6. Put the lamb and bacon into a small deep roasting tin and fry for 5 minutes or until the lamb is brown all over and the bacon is beginning to crisp.

2 Remove the lamb and put to one side. Pour the wine into the tin with the bacon – it should bubble immediately. Stir well, scraping the base to loosen any crusty bits, then leave to bubble until half the wine has evaporated. Stir in 300ml (½ pint) water and add the chopped tomatoes or passata, the pasta and sunblush tomatoes.

3 Put the lamb on a rack over the roasting tin so that the juices drip into the pasta. Cook, uncovered, in the oven for about 35 minutes.

4 Stir the artichokes into the pasta and put everything back in the oven for 5 minutes or until the lamb is tender and the pasta cooked. Slice the lamb thickly and serve with the pasta, garnished with the basil.

Mixed Mushroom Cannelloni

Preparation Time 15 minutes • **Cooking Time** 50–55 minutes • **Serves** 4 • **Per Serving** 631 calories, 37g fat (of which 18g saturates), 50g carbohydrate, 1.9g salt • **A Little Effort**

6 sheets fresh lasagne

3 tbsp olive oil

1 small onion, finely sliced

3 garlic cloves, sliced

20g pack fresh thyme, finely chopped

225g (8oz) chestnut or brown-cap mushrooms, roughly chopped

125g (4oz) flat-cap mushrooms, roughly chopped

2 × 125g goat's cheese logs, with rind

350g carton cheese sauce

salt and ground black pepper

green salad to serve

1 Preheat the oven to 180°C (160°C fan oven) mark 4. Cook the lasagne in boiling water until just tender. Drain well and run it under cold water to cool. Keep covered with cold water until ready to use.

2 Heat the oil in a large pan and add the onion. Cook over a medium heat for 7–10 minutes until the onion is soft. Add the garlic and fry for 1–2 minutes. Keep a few slices of garlic to one side. Keep a little thyme for sprinkling later, then add the rest to the pan with the mushrooms. Cook for a further 5 minutes or until the mushrooms are golden brown and there is no excess liquid in the pan. Season, remove from the heat and put to one side.

3 Crumble one of the goat's cheese logs into the cooled mushroom mixture and stir together. Drain the lasagne sheets and pat dry with kitchen paper. Spoon 2–3 tbsp of the mushroom mixture along the long edge of each lasagne sheet, leaving a 1cm (½in) border. Roll up the pasta sheets and cut each roll in half. Put the pasta into a shallow ovenproof dish and spoon the cheese sauce over it. Slice the remaining goat's cheese into thick rounds and arrange across the middle of the pasta rolls. Sprinkle the reserved garlic and thyme on top. Cook in the oven for 30–35 minutes until golden and bubbling. Serve with a green salad.

★ COOK'S TIP
Fresh lasagne sheets wrapped around a filling are used here to make cannelloni, but you can also buy cannelloni tubes, which can easily be filled using a teaspoon.

Stuffed Pasta Shells

Preparation Time 15 minutes • **Cooking Time** about 1 hour • **Serves 6** • **Per Serving** 378 calories, 17g fat (of which 5g saturates), 41g carbohydrate, 1.1g salt • **Easy**

2 tbsp olive oil

1 large onion, finely chopped

a few fresh rosemary or oregano sprigs, chopped

125g (4oz) small flat mushrooms, sliced

6 plump coarse sausages, skinned

175ml (6fl oz) red wine

300ml (½ pint) passata

4 tbsp sun-dried tomato paste

sugar to taste, if necessary

250g (9oz) large pasta shells, such as conchiglioni rigati

150ml (¼ pint) half-fat single cream (optional)

freshly grated Parmesan to garnish

green salad to serve

1 Preheat the oven to 180°C (160°C fan oven) mark 4. Heat the oil in a deep frying pan. Stir in the onion and rosemary or oregano and cook over a gentle heat for 10 minutes or until the onion is soft and golden. Add the mushrooms and cook over a medium heat until the vegetables are soft and beginning to brown at the edges. Tip the onion mixture into a bowl.

2 Crumble the sausagemeat into the hot pan and stir over a high heat with a wooden spoon, breaking the meat up as you do so, until browned all over. Reduce the heat slightly and pour in the wine. Leave to bubble and reduce by about half. Return the onion mixture to the pan and add the passata and sun-dried tomato paste. Bubble gently for another 10 minutes. Add a pinch of sugar if the sauce tastes a little sharp.

3 While the sauce is simmering, cook the pasta shells in plenty of boiling water for 10 minutes or until just tender. Drain well and run under the cold tap to cool.

4 Fill the shells with the sauce and put into a shallow ovenproof dish. Drizzle with any extra sauce and the cream, if using, and bake for 30 minutes or until piping hot. Sprinkle with Parmesan and serve with a big bowl of green salad.

★ TRY SOMETHING DIFFERENT

● *Turkey or chicken mince would make a lighter alternative to the sausages: you will need 450g (1lb).*

● *Use a small aubergine, diced, instead of the mushrooms.*

Classic Lasagne

Preparation Time about 1 hour • Cooking Time 45 minutes • Serves 6 • Per Serving 326 calories, 13g fat (of which 6g saturates), 37g carbohydrate, 0.5g salt • **Easy**

butter to grease

350g (12oz) fresh lasagne, or 225g (8oz) 'no need to pre-cook' lasagne (12–15 sheets, see Cook's Tip)

3 tbsp freshly grated Parmesan

FOR THE BOLOGNESE SAUCE

2 tbsp olive oil

1 onion, finely chopped

2 garlic cloves, crushed

450g (1lb) extra-lean minced beef

2 tbsp sun-dried tomato paste

300ml (½ pint) red wine

400g can chopped tomatoes

125g (4oz) chestnut mushrooms, sliced

2 tbsp Worcestershire sauce

salt and ground black pepper

FOR THE BÉCHAMEL SAUCE

300ml (½ pint) semi-skimmed milk

1 onion slice

6 peppercorns

1 mace blade

1 bay leaf

15g (½oz) butter

15g (½oz) plain flour

freshly grated nutmeg

salt and ground black pepper

1 To make the Bolognese sauce, heat the oil in a large pan, add the onion and fry over a medium heat for 10 minutes or until softened and golden. Add the garlic and cook for 1 minute. Add the beef and brown evenly, using a wooden spoon to break up the pieces. Stir in the tomato paste and wine, cover and bring to the boil. Add the tomatoes, mushrooms and Worcestershire sauce and season well with salt and pepper. Bring back to the boil, reduce the heat and simmer for 20 minutes.

2 To make the béchamel sauce, pour the milk into a pan and add the onion, peppercorns, mace and bay leaf. Bring almost to the boil, then remove from the heat, cover and leave to infuse for about 20 minutes. Strain. Melt the butter in a pan, stir in the flour and cook, stirring, for 1 minute or until cooked but not coloured. Remove from the heat and gradually pour in the milk, whisking constantly. Season lightly with nutmeg, salt and pepper. Return to the heat and cook, stirring constantly, until the sauce is thickened and smooth. Simmer gently for 2 minutes.

3 Preheat the oven to 180°C (160°C fan oven) mark 4. Spoon one-third of the Bolognese sauce over the base of a greased 2.3 litre (4 pint) ovenproof dish. Cover with a layer of lasagne sheets, then a layer of béchamel. Repeat these layers twice more, finishing with a layer of béchamel to cover the lasagne.

4 Sprinkle the Parmesan over the top and stand the dish on a baking sheet. Cook in the oven for 45 minutes or until well browned and bubbling.

★ COOK'S TIP

If using 'no need to pre-cook' lasagne, add a little extra stock or water to the sauce.

Tagliatelle Bake

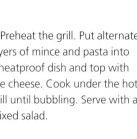

Preparation Time 5 minutes • **Cooking Time** 45 minutes • **Serves** 4 • **Per Serving** 935 calories, 42g fat (of which 19g saturates), 97g carbohydrate, 1.6g salt • **Easy**

1 tbsp olive oil
1 large onion, finely chopped
450g (1lb) minced beef
2 garlic cloves, crushed
290g jar marinated vegetables
2 × 400g cans chopped tomatoes
1 tsp dried marjoram
375g (12oz) fresh garlic and herb
    tagliatelle
330g jar ready-made cheese sauce
4 tbsp milk
75g (3oz) Cheddar, grated
salt
mixed salad to serve

1 Heat the oil in a pan. Add the onion and fry until soft. Add the beef and fry, stirring, until the meat is brown. Add the garlic, vegetables, tomatoes and marjoram. Simmer for 25 minutes or until the meat is tender.

2 Cook the tagliatelle in a pan of lightly salted boiling water according to the pack instructions. Drain, put back into the pan and stir in the cheese sauce and milk. Heat through for 3 minutes.

3 Preheat the grill. Put alternate layers of mince and pasta into a heatproof dish and top with the cheese. Cook under the hot grill until bubbling. Serve with a mixed salad.

★ FREEZING TIP

To freeze Double the quantities and make another meal for four or make two meals for two people and freeze. Complete the recipe to the end of step 2, then layer the mince and pasta in a freezerproof, heatproof container. Cool and freeze for up to three months.
To use Thaw overnight in the fridge. Bake in the oven at 190°C (170°C fan oven) mark 5 for 25 minutes, then place under a hot grill for 2–3 minutes until bubbling.
Alternatively, make double the meat mixture, freeze half and serve with spaghetti or flour tortillas.

Chunky One-pot Bolognese

Preparation Time 15 minutes • **Cooking Time** about 1 hour • **Serves 6** • **Per Serving** 506 calories, 31g fat (of which 11g saturates), 40g carbohydrate, 1.5g salt • **Dairy Free** • **Easy**

3 tbsp olive oil
2 large red onions, finely diced
a few fresh rosemary sprigs
1 large aubergine, finely diced
8 plump coarse sausages
350ml (12fl oz) full-bodied red wine
700g (1½lb) passata
4 tbsp sun-dried tomato paste
300ml (½ pint) hot vegetable stock
175g (6oz) small pasta, such as
    orecchiette
salt and ground black pepper

1 Heat 2 tbsp oil in a large shallow non-stick pan. Add the onions and rosemary and cook over a gentle heat for 10 minutes or until soft and golden.

2 Add the aubergine and remaining oil and cook over a medium heat for 8–10 minutes until soft and golden.

3 Meanwhile, pull the skin off the sausages and divide each into four rough chunks. Tip the aubergine mixture on to a plate and add the sausage chunks to the hot pan. You won't need any extra oil.

4 Stir the sausage pieces over a high heat for 6–8 minutes until golden and beginning to turn crisp at the edges. Pour in the wine and allow to bubble for 6–8 minutes until only a little liquid remains. Put the aubergine mixture back into the pan, along with the passata, tomato paste and hot stock.

5 Stir the pasta into the liquid and cover the pan, then simmer for 20 minutes or until the pasta is cooked. Taste and season with salt and pepper if necessary.

★ FREEZING TIP
To freeze *Complete the recipe to the end of step 4. Add the pasta and cook for 10 minutes – it will continue to cook right through when you reheat the Bolognese. Cool, put into a freezerproof container and freeze for up to three months.*
To use *Thaw overnight at cool room temperature, put into a pan and add 150ml (¼ pint) water. Bring to the boil, then simmer gently for 10 minutes or until the sauce is hot and the pasta is cooked.*

Very Easy Four-cheese Gnocchi

Preparation Time 3 minutes • **Cooking Time** 10 minutes • **Serves 2** • **Per Serving** 630 calories, 28g fat (of which 15g saturates), 77g carbohydrate, 0g salt • **Gluten Free** • **Easy**

350g pack fresh gnocchi
300g tub fresh four-cheese sauce
240g pack sunblush tomatoes
2 tbsp freshly torn basil leaves, plus
   basil sprigs to garnish
1 tbsp freshly grated Parmesan
15g (½oz) butter, chopped
salt and ground black pepper
salad to serve

1 Bring a large pan of water to the boil, then add 1 tsp salt and the gnocchi and cook according to the pack instructions or until all the gnocchi have floated to the surface. Drain well and put the gnocchi back into the pan.

2 Preheat the grill. Add the four-cheese sauce and tomatoes to the gnocchi and heat gently, stirring, for 2 minutes.

3 Season with salt and pepper, then add the basil and stir again. Spoon into individual heatproof bowls, sprinkle a little Parmesan over each one and dot with butter.

4 Cook under the grill for 3–5 minutes until golden and bubbling. Garnish with basil sprigs and serve with salad.

Fast Macaroni Cheese

Preparation Time 5 minutes • Cooking Time 15 minutes • Serves 4 • Per Serving 1137 calories, 69g fat (of which 44g saturates), 96g carbohydrate, 2g salt • Easy

500g (1lb 2oz) macaroni
500ml (17fl oz) crème fraîche
200g (7oz) freshly grated Parmesan
2 tbsp ready-made English or Dijon mustard
5 tbsp freshly chopped flat-leafed parsley
ground black pepper
green salad to serve

1 Bring a large pan of lightly salted water to the boil and cook the macaroni according to the pack instructions. Drain and keep to one side.

2 Preheat the grill to high. Put the crème fraîche into a pan and heat gently. Stir in 175g (6oz) Parmesan, the mustard and parsley and season well with black pepper. Stir the pasta through the sauce, spoon into bowls and sprinkle with the remaining cheese. Grill until golden and serve immediately with salad.

Stir-fries and Noodles

Sweet and Sour Duck

★

Preparation Time 15 minutes, plus marinating • **Cooking Time** about 15 minutes • **Serves 4** • **Per Serving** 278 calories, 13g fat (of which 2g saturates), 29g carbohydrate, 1.9g salt • **Dairy Free** • **Easy**

3 tbsp dark soy sauce
1 tbsp dry sherry
1 tsp sesame oil
225g (8oz) duck breast fillets, thinly
    sliced
1 tbsp sugar
2 tsp cornflour
3 tbsp distilled malt vinegar
1 tbsp tomato ketchup
4 tbsp vegetable oil
125g (4oz) aubergine, sliced
1 red onion, sliced
1 garlic clove, sliced
125g (4oz) carrot, sliced lengthways
    into strips
125g (4oz) sugarsnap peas or
    mangetouts
1 mango, peeled, stoned and thinly
    sliced
noodles to serve

1 Mix 1 tbsp soy sauce with the sherry and sesame oil. Pour the mixture over the duck, cover and leave to marinate for at least 30 minutes.

2 Mix together the sugar, cornflour, vinegar, ketchup and remaining 2 tbsp soy sauce. Put to one side.

3 Heat 2 tbsp vegetable oil in a wok or large non-stick frying pan. Drain the duck from the marinade and reserve the marinade. Fry the duck slices over a high heat for 3–4 minutes until golden and the fat is crisp. Remove from the pan and put to one side.

4 Add 1 tbsp vegetable oil to the pan and fry the aubergine for about 2 minutes on each side or until golden. Add the remaining 1 tbsp oil and fry the onion, garlic and carrot for 2–3 minutes, then add the sugarsnap peas or mangetouts and fry for a further 1–2 minutes.

5 Add the mango to the pan along with the duck, the soy sauce mixture and the reserved marinade. Bring to the boil, stirring gently all the time, and allow to bubble for 2–3 minutes until slightly thickened. Serve immediately, with noodles.

Chicken Stir-fry with Noodles

Preparation Time 20 minutes • **Cooking Time** 20 minutes • **Serves 4** • **Per Serving** 355 calories, 10g fat (of which 2g saturates), 29g carbohydrate, 0.5g salt • **Dairy Free** • **Easy**

2 tbsp vegetable oil
2 garlic cloves, crushed
4 boneless, skinless chicken
    breasts, each sliced into
    10 pieces
3 medium carrots, about 450g (1lb),
    cut into thin strips, about 5cm
    (2in) long
250g pack thick egg noodles
1 bunch of spring onions, sliced
200g (7oz) mangetouts
155g jar sweet chilli and
    lemongrass sauce

1 Cook the noodles in boiling water according to the pack instructions.

2 Meanwhile, heat the oil in a wok or frying pan, then add the garlic and stir-fry for 1–2 minutes. Add the chicken pieces and stir-fry for 5 minutes, then add the carrot strips and stir-fry for a further 5 minutes.

3 Add the spring onions, mangetouts and sauce to the wok and stir-fry for 5 minutes.

4 Drain the cooked noodles well and add to the wok. Toss everything together and serve.

⭐ TRY SOMETHING DIFFERENT
Use turkey or pork escalopes instead of the chicken: you will need 450g (1lb), cut into thin strips.

Chilli-fried Chicken with Coconut Noodles

Preparation Time 15–20 minutes • Cooking Time 15 minutes • Serves 6 • Per Serving 567 calories, 26g fat (of which 5g saturates), 40g carbohydrate, 0.6g salt • Dairy Free • Easy

2 tbsp plain flour
1 tsp mild chilli powder
1 tsp ground ginger
½ tsp salt
1 tsp caster sugar
6 boneless, skinless chicken breasts, about 150g (5oz) each, cut diagonally into three
250g (9oz) thread egg noodles
3 tbsp groundnut oil
1 large bunch of spring onions, sliced
1½ tsp Thai red curry paste or tandoori paste
150g (5oz) salted roasted peanuts, finely chopped
6 tbsp coconut milk

1 Mix the flour, chilli powder, ground ginger, salt and sugar in a bowl. Dip the chicken into the spiced flour and coat well.

2 Cook the noodles in boiling water according to the pack instructions, then drain.

3 Heat the oil in a frying pan. Add the chicken and fry for 5 minutes or until cooked. Put to one side, cover and keep warm. Add the spring onions to the pan and fry for 1 minute. Put to one side and keep warm.

4 Add the curry paste to the pan with 75g (3oz) peanuts and fry for 1 minute. Add the noodles and fry for 1 minute. Stir in the coconut milk and toss the noodles over a high heat for 30 seconds.

5 Put the chicken and spring onions on the coconut noodles. Scatter with the remaining peanuts and serve.

⭐ COOK'S TIP
Coconut milk gives a thick creaminess to stir-fries, soups and curries.

Chicken Chow Mein

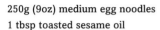

Preparation Time 10 minutes • **Cooking Time** 10 minutes • **Serves 4** • **Per Serving** 451 calories, 11g fat (of which 2g saturates), 59g carbohydrate, 1.3g salt • **Dairy Free** • **Easy**

250g (9oz) medium egg noodles
1 tbsp toasted sesame oil
2 boneless, skinless chicken
   breasts, about 125g (4oz) each,
   cut into thin strips
1 bunch of spring onions, thinly
   sliced diagonally
150g (5oz) mangetouts, thickly
   sliced diagonally
125g (4oz) bean sprouts
100g (3½oz) cooked ham, finely
   shredded
120g sachet chow mein sauce
salt and ground black pepper
light soy sauce to serve

1 Cook the noodles in boiling water for 4 minutes or according to the pack instructions. Drain, rinse thoroughly in cold water, drain again and put to one side.

2 Meanwhile, heat a wok or large frying pan until hot, then add the oil. Add the chicken and stir-fry over a high heat for 3–4 minutes until browned all over. Add the spring onions and mangetouts and stir-fry for 2 minutes. Stir in the bean sprouts and ham and cook for a further 2 minutes.

3 Add the drained noodles, then pour in the chow mein sauce and toss together to coat evenly. Stir-fry for 2 minutes or until piping hot. Season with salt and pepper and serve immediately with light soy sauce to drizzle over the chow mein.

Turkey and Sesame Stir-fry with Noodles

Preparation Time 5 minutes, plus marinating • Cooking Time 10 minutes • Serves 4 • Per Serving 672 calories, 18g fat (of which 4g saturates), 97g carbohydrate, 0.7g salt • **Dairy Free** • **Easy**

300g (11oz) turkey breast fillets, cut into thin strips
3 tbsp teriyaki marinade
3 tbsp clear honey
500g (1lb 2oz) medium egg noodles
about 1 tbsp sesame oil, plus extra for the noodles
300g (11oz) ready-prepared mixed stir-fry vegetables, such as carrots, broccoli, red cabbage, mangetouts, bean sprouts and purple spring onions
2 tbsp sesame seeds, lightly toasted in a dry wok or heavy-based pan

1 Put the turkey strips into a large bowl with the teriyaki marinade and honey and stir to coat. Cover and put to one side for 5 minutes.

2 Cook the noodles in boiling water for about 4 minutes or according to the pack instructions. Drain well, then toss in a little oil.

3 Heat 1 tbsp oil in a wok or large frying pan and add the turkey, reserving the marinade. Stir-fry over a very high heat for 2–3 minutes until cooked through and beginning to brown. Add a drop more oil, if needed, then add the vegetables and reserved marinade. Continue to cook over a high heat, stirring, until the vegetables have started to soften and the sauce is warmed through.

4 Scatter with the sesame seeds and serve immediately with the noodles.

Sweet Chilli Beef Stir-fry

Preparation Time 10 minutes • Cooking Time 10–15 minutes • Serves 4 • Per Serving 273 calories, 13g fat (of which 5g saturates), 8g carbohydrate, 0.2g salt • **Gluten Free** • **Dairy Free** • **Easy**

1 tsp chilli oil

1 tbsp each tamari (wheat-free Japanese soy sauce) and runny honey

1 garlic clove, crushed

1 large red chilli, seeded and chopped (see page 13)

400g (14oz) lean beef, cut into strips

1 tsp sunflower oil

1 broccoli head, thinly sliced

200g (7oz) mangetouts, halved

1 red pepper, halved, seeded and cut into strips

rice to serve

1 Pour the chilli oil into a medium-sized shallow bowl. Add the tamari, honey, garlic and chilli and stir well. Add the strips of beef and toss in the marinade.

2 Heat the sunflower oil in a wok over a high heat until it is very hot. Cook the strips of beef in two batches, for 3–4 minutes until just cooked through, then remove from the wok and put to one side. Wipe the wok with kitchen paper to remove any residue.

3 Add the broccoli, mangetouts, red pepper and 2 tbsp water and stir-fry for 5–6 minutes until starting to soften. Return the beef to the wok to heat through. Serve with rice.

★ TRY SOMETHING DIFFERENT
Use pork fillet instead of beef, trimmed of fat and cut into thin slices.

Beef Chow Mein

Preparation Time 15 minutes, plus marinating • Cooking Time 15 minutes • Serves 4 • Per Serving 408 calories, 20g fat (of which 5g saturates), 38g carbohydrate, 1.2g salt • Dairy Free • Easy

2 tsp dark soy sauce

4 tsp dry sherry

1 tsp cornflour

1 tsp sugar

1 tbsp sesame oil

225g (8oz) rump steak, cut into thin strips about 7.5cm (3in) long

175g (6oz) egg noodles

3 tbsp vegetable oil

1 bunch of spring onions, sliced

3 garlic cloves, crushed

1 large green chilli, seeded and sliced (see page 13)

125g (4oz) Chinese leaves, or cabbage, sliced

50g (2oz) bean sprouts

salt and ground black pepper

1 Put the soy sauce, sherry, cornflour, sugar and 1 tsp sesame oil into a bowl and whisk together. Pour this mixture over the beef, then cover, chill and leave to marinate for at least 1 hour or overnight.

2 Cook the noodles in boiling water for 4 minutes or according to the pack instructions. Rinse in cold water and drain.

3 Drain the beef, reserving the marinade. Heat the vegetable oil in a wok or large non-stick frying pan and fry the beef over a high heat until well browned. Remove with a slotted spoon and put to one side.

4 Add the spring onions, garlic, chilli, Chinese leaves or cabbage and the bean sprouts to the pan and stir-fry for 2–3 minutes. Return the beef to the pan with the noodles and reserved marinade. Bring to the boil, stirring all the time, and bubble for 2–3 minutes. Sprinkle the remaining sesame oil over it, season with salt and pepper and serve immediately.

Sesame Beef

★

Preparation Time 20 minutes • Cooking Time 10 minutes • Serves 4 • Per Serving 207 calories, 10g fat (of which 3g saturates), 4g carbohydrate, 2g salt • **Dairy Free** • **Easy**

2 tbsp soy sauce
2 tbsp Worcestershire sauce
2 tsp tomato purée
juice of ½ lemon
1 tbsp sesame seeds
1 garlic clove, crushed
400g (14oz) rump steak, sliced
1 tbsp vegetable oil
3 small pak choi, chopped
1 bunch of spring onions, sliced
egg noodles or tagliatelle to serve

1 Put the soy and Worcestershire sauces, tomato purée, lemon juice, sesame seeds and garlic into a bowl and mix well. Add the steak and toss to coat.

2 Heat the oil in a large wok or non-stick frying pan until hot. Add the steak and sear well. Remove from the wok and put to one side.

3 Add any sauce from the bowl to the wok and heat for 1 minute. Add the pak choi, spring onions and steak and stir-fry for 5 minutes. Add freshly cooked and drained noodles, toss and serve immediately.

★ TRY SOMETHING DIFFERENT
Use 400g (14oz) pork escalope cut into strips instead of beef. Cook for 5 minutes before removing from the pan at step 2.

Pork and Noodle Stir-fry

Preparation Time 10 minutes, plus marinating • Cooking Time 7–8 minutes • Serves 4 • Per Serving 500 calories, 9g fat (of which 2g saturates), 67g carbohydrate, 3.4g salt • Gluten Free • Dairy Free • Easy

1 tbsp sesame oil
5cm (2in) piece fresh root ginger, peeled and grated
2 tbsp soy sauce
1 tbsp fish sauce
½ red chilli, seeded and finely chopped (see page 13)
450g (1lb) stir-fry pork strips
2 red peppers, halved, seeded and roughly chopped
250g (9oz) baby sweetcorn, halved lengthways
200g (7oz) sugarsnap peas, halved
300g (11oz) bean sprouts
250g (9oz) rice noodles

1 Put the oil into a large bowl. Add the ginger, soy sauce, fish sauce, chilli and pork strips. Mix well and leave to marinate for 10 minutes.

2 Heat a large wok until hot. Lift the pork out of the marinade with a slotted spoon and add to the pan. Stir-fry over a high heat for 5 minutes. Add the red peppers, sweetcorn, sugarsnap peas, bean sprouts and remaining marinade and stir-fry for a further 2–3 minutes until the pork is cooked.

3 Meanwhile, cook the noodles in boiling water according to the pack instructions.

4 Drain the noodles, tip into the wok and toss together with the pork mixture, then serve immediately.

★ TRY SOMETHING DIFFERENT
Use 450g (1lb) chicken or turkey strips instead of pork.

Stir-fried Pork with Chinese Greens

Preparation Time 15 minutes, plus marinating • Cooking Time about 15 minutes • Serves 4 • Per Serving 234 calories, 15g fat (of which 2g saturates), 6g carbohydrate, 1.8g salt • **Dairy Free • Easy**

200g (7oz) pork tenderloin or fillet, cut into strips
2 tbsp finely chopped fresh root ginger
3 tbsp soy sauce
2 garlic cloves, crushed
700g (1½lb) mixed vegetables, such as pak choi, broccoli, carrots, bean sprouts and sugarsnap peas
3 tbsp vegetable oil
5 spring onions, cut into four lengthways
1 red chilli, seeded and sliced (see page 13)
1 tbsp sesame oil
2 tbsp dry sherry
2 tbsp oyster sauce
salt and ground black pepper

1 Put the pork into a non-metallic dish with the ginger, 2 tbsp soy sauce and the garlic. Put to one side to marinate for at least 30 minutes.

2 Meanwhile, prepare the vegetables. Cut the pak choi into quarters, separate the broccoli into florets and cut the carrot into ribbons, using a vegetable peeler.

3 Heat a wok or large frying pan over a high heat and add the vegetable oil. Stir-fry the pork in two batches, cooking each batch for 2–3 minutes until the meat is browned. Season the pork with salt and pepper, then put to one side and keep warm.

4 Add the spring onions and chilli to the pan and cook for 30 seconds. Add all the vegetables and stir-fry for 4–5 minutes. Return the pork to the pan. Add the remaining soy sauce, the sesame oil, sherry and oyster sauce and stir-fry for 2 minutes or until the sauce is syrupy. Serve immediately.

 GET AHEAD
To prepare ahead *Complete the recipe to the end of step 3, then cool, wrap and chill the pork and vegetables separately for up to four hours.*
To use *Complete the recipe. Make sure the pork is piping hot.*

Pork Stir-fry with Chilli and Mango

Preparation Time 5 minutes • **Cooking Time** 10 minutes • **Serves 1** • **Per Serving** 550 calories, 15g fat (of which 4g saturates), 67g carbohydrate, 3.1g salt • **Dairy Free** • **Easy**

75g (3oz) medium egg noodles
1 tsp groundnut oil
½ red chilli, seeded and finely chopped (see Cook's Tip and page 13)
125g (4oz) pork stir-fry strips
1 head pak choi, roughly chopped
1 tbsp soy sauce
½ ripe mango, peeled, stoned and sliced

1 Cook the egg noodles in boiling water according to the pack instructions. Drain, then plunge into cold water and put to one side.

2 Meanwhile, put the oil into a wok or large frying pan and heat until very hot. Add the chilli and pork and stir-fry for 3–4 minutes. Add the pak choi and soy sauce and cook for a further 2–3 minutes. Add the mango and toss to combine.

3 Drain the noodles and add to the pan. Toss well and cook for 1–2 minutes until heated through. Serve immediately.

 COOK'S TIP
The smaller the chilli, the hotter it is.

Five-minute Stir-fry

Preparation Time 2 minutes • **Cooking Time** 5 minutes • **Serves 2** • **Per Serving** 170 calories, 7g fat (of which 1g saturates), 11g carbohydrate, 1.6g salt • **Gluten Free** • **Dairy Free** • **Easy**

1 tbsp sesame oil

175g (6oz) raw peeled tiger prawns, deveined (see Cook's Tip)

50ml (2fl oz) ready-made sweet chilli and ginger sauce

225g (8oz) ready-prepared mixed stir-fry vegetables, such as sliced courgettes, broccoli and green beans

1 Heat the oil in a large wok or frying pan, add the prawns and sweet chilli and ginger sauce and stir-fry for 2 minutes.

2 Add the mixed vegetables and stir-fry for a further 2–3 minutes until the prawns are cooked and the vegetables are heated through. Serve immediately.

★ TRY SOMETHING DIFFERENT
Instead of prawns, try chicken cut into strips: stir-fry for 5 minutes in step 1.

★ COOK'S TIP
To devein prawns, pull off the head and discard (or put to one side and use later for making stock). Using pointed scissors, cut through the soft shell on the belly side. Prise off the shell, leaving the tail attached. (The shell can also be used later for making stock.) Using a small sharp knife, make a shallow cut along the back of the prawn. Using the point of the knife, remove and discard the black vein (the intestinal tract) that runs along the back of the prawn.

Prawn and Peanut Noodles

Preparation Time 10 minutes, plus soaking • **Serves 4** • **Per Serving** 579 calories, 24g fat (of which 7g saturates), 67g carbohydrate, 0.7g salt • **Dairy Free** • **Easy**

300g (11oz) straight-to-wok noodles
360g pack stir-fry vegetables
4 tbsp coconut cream
4 tbsp smooth peanut butter
1 tbsp Thai red or green curry paste
juice of ½ lime
225g (8oz) cooked and peeled king prawns
a small handful of freshly chopped coriander
25g (1oz) peanuts, chopped

1 Put the noodles and stir-fry vegetables into a large bowl or wok and cover with boiling water. Cover with clingfilm and leave for 5 minutes.

2 Meanwhile, mix the coconut cream with the peanut butter, curry paste and lime juice in a bowl.

3 Drain the noodles and vegetables in a colander. Put back into the bowl and toss with the prawns, coriander and half the dressing. Sprinkle with the peanuts and serve with the remaining dressing.

★ COOK'S TIP
Ready-prepared stir-fry vegetables make this extra-quick, but if you can't find them, try a mixture of three or four of the following: strips of red, orange or yellow peppers, baby sweetcorn, mangetouts or sugarsnaps, carrots cut into matchsticks, or bean sprouts.

Thai Noodles with Prawns

Preparation Time 10 minutes • Cooking Time 5 minutes • Serves 4 • Per Serving 343 calories, 11g fat (of which 2g saturates), 40g carbohydrate, 1g salt • **Dairy Free** • **Easy**

4–6 tsp Thai red curry paste
175g (6oz) medium egg noodles (wholewheat if possible)
2 small red onions, chopped
1 lemongrass stalk, trimmed and sliced
1 fresh red bird's-eye chilli, seeded and finely chopped (see page 13)
300ml (½ pint) reduced-fat coconut milk
400g (14oz) raw tiger prawns, peeled and deveined (see page 93)
4 tbsp freshly chopped coriander, plus extra freshly torn coriander to garnish
salt and ground black pepper

1 Pour 2 litres (3½ pints) water into a large pan and bring to the boil. Add the curry paste, noodles, onions, lemongrass, chilli and coconut milk and bring back to the boil.

2 Add the prawns and chopped coriander, reduce the heat and simmer for 2–3 minutes until the prawns turn pink. Season with salt and pepper.

3 Divide the prawns and noodles among four large bowls and sprinkle with the torn coriander.

★ COOK'S TIP
Don't overcook this dish or the noodles will be soggy and the prawns tough.

Squid and Vegetables in Black Bean Sauce

Preparation Time 35 minutes • Cooking Time 10–15 minutes • Serves 4 • Per Serving 274 calories, 15g fat (of which 2g saturates), 12g carbohydrate, 1g salt • Gluten Free • Dairy Free • A Little Effort

450g (1lb) cleaned squid
2 tbsp sesame seeds
2 tbsp sunflower oil
1 tbsp sesame oil
2 garlic cloves
2 dried red chillies
50g (2oz) broccoli, cut into florets
50g (2oz) mangetouts, trimmed
50g (2oz) carrots, thinly sliced
75g (3oz) cauliflower, cut into small florets
1 small green or red pepper, seeded and thinly sliced
50g (2oz) Chinese cabbage or pak choi, shredded

25g (1oz) bean sprouts
2 tbsp fresh coriander, roughly torn

FOR THE SAUCE
2 tbsp black bean sauce
1 tbsp Thai fish sauce
2–3 tsp clear honey
75ml (2½fl oz) fish or vegetable stock
1 tbsp tamarind juice
2 tsp cornflour

1 First, prepare the sauce. Put the black bean sauce, fish sauce, honey and stock into a small bowl and mix well. Add the tamarind juice and cornflour and whisk until smooth. Put to one side.

2 Wash and dry the squid and halve the tentacles if large. Open out the body pouches, score diagonally, then cut into large squares. Put to one side.

3 Toast the sesame seeds in a dry wok or large frying pan over a medium heat, stirring until they turn golden. Tip on to a plate.

4 Heat the sunflower and sesame oils in the same pan. Add the garlic and chillies and fry gently for 5 minutes, then remove with a slotted spoon and discard.

5 Add all the vegetables to the pan and stir-fry for 3 minutes. Add the squid, increase the heat and stir-fry for a further 2 minutes or until the squid curls up and turns opaque. Add the sauce and allow to simmer for 1 minute.

6 Scatter the sesame seeds and coriander over the squid and vegetables and serve immediately.

★ TRY SOMETHING DIFFERENT
Instead of squid, try 400g (14oz) rump steak, cut into thin strips.

Stir-fried Salmon and Broccoli

Preparation Time 10 minutes • Cooking Time 5–6 minutes • Serves 2 • Per Serving 90 calories, 4g fat (of which 1g saturates), 9g carbohydrate, 2.7g salt • **Dairy Free** • **Easy**

2 tsp sesame oil
1 red pepper, seeded and thinly
   sliced
½ red chilli, seeded and thinly
   sliced (see page 13)
1 garlic clove, crushed
125g (4oz) broccoli florets
2 spring onions, sliced
2 salmon fillets, about 125g (4oz)
   each, cut into strips
1 tsp Thai fish sauce
2 tsp soy sauce
wholewheat noodles to serve

1 Heat the oil in a wok or large frying pan. Add the red pepper, chilli, garlic, broccoli and spring onions and stir-fry over a high heat for 3–4 minutes.

2 Add the salmon, fish sauce and soy sauce and cook for 2 minutes, stirring gently. Serve immediately with wholewheat noodles.

Teriyaki Salmon with Spinach

Preparation Time 10 minutes, plus marinating • **Cooking Time** 6 minutes • **Serves 4** • **Per Serving** 672 calories, 30g fat (of which 4g saturates), 66g carbohydrate, 2.9g salt • **Dairy Free** • **Easy**

550g (1¼lb) salmon fillet, cut into 1cm (½in) slices
3 tbsp teriyaki sauce
3 tbsp tamari (see Cook's Tips) or light soy sauce
2 tbsp vegetable oil
1 tbsp sesame oil
1 tbsp freshly chopped chives
2 tsp peeled and grated fresh root ginger
2 garlic cloves, crushed
350g (12oz) soba noodles (see Cook's Tips)
350g (12oz) baby spinach leaves
furikake seasoning (see Cook's Tips)

1 Gently mix the salmon slices with the teriyaki sauce, then cover, chill and leave to marinate for 1 hour.

2 Mix together the tamari or soy sauce, 1 tbsp vegetable oil, the sesame oil, chives, ginger and garlic. Put to one side.

3 Cook the noodles in boiling water according to the pack instructions. Drain and put to one side.

4 Heat the remaining vegetable oil in a wok or large frying pan. Remove the salmon from the marinade and add it to the pan. Cook over a high heat until it turns opaque – about 30 seconds. Remove from the pan and put to one side.

5 Add the drained noodles to the pan and stir until warmed through. Stir in the spinach and cook for 1–2 minutes until the leaves have wilted. Add the soy sauce mixture and stir to combine. Divide the noodles among four deep bowls, then top with the salmon. Sprinkle with furikake seasoning and serve.

★ COOK'S TIPS
● *Tamari is a wheat-free Japanese soy sauce.*
● *Soba noodles are made from bucwheat and are gluten free. If you have a wheat allergy or gluten intoleance, check that the pack specifies '100% soba'.*
● *Furikake seasoning is a Japanese condiment consisting of sesame seeds and chopped dried seaweed; it can be found in supermarkets and Asian food shops.*

Chickpea and Chilli Stir-fry

Preparation Time 10 minutes • **Cooking Time** 15–20 minutes • **Serves** 4 • **Per Serving** 258 calories, 11g fat (of which 1g saturates), 30g carbohydrate, 1g salt • **Vegetarian** • **Gluten Free** • **Dairy Free** • **Easy**

2 tbsp olive oil
1 tsp ground cumin
1 red onion, sliced
2 garlic cloves, finely chopped
1 red chilli, seeded and finely
   chopped (see page 13)
2 × 400g cans chickpeas, drained
   and rinsed
400g (14oz) cherry tomatoes
125g (4oz) baby spinach leaves
salt and ground black pepper
brown rice or pasta to serve

1 Heat the oil in a wok or large frying pan. Add the cumin and fry for 1–2 minutes. Add the onion and stir-fry for 5–7 minutes.

2 Add the garlic and chilli and stir-fry for 2 minutes.

3 Add the chickpeas to the wok with the tomatoes. Reduce the heat and simmer until the chickpeas are hot. Season with salt and pepper. Add the spinach and cook for 1–2 minutes until the leaves have wilted. Serve with brown rice or pasta.

Rice and Red Pepper Stir-fry

★

Preparation Time 5 minutes • **Cooking Time** 15 minutes • **Serves** 1 • **Per Serving** 584 calories, 20g fat (of which 5g saturates), 82g carbohydrate, 1.7g salt • **Dairy Free** • **Easy**

75g (3oz) long-grain rice
200ml (7fl oz) hot vegetable stock
2 tsp vegetable oil
½ onion, sliced
2 rashers streaky bacon
1 small red pepper, halved, seeded and cut into chunks
a handful of frozen peas
a dash of Worcestershire sauce

1 Put the rice into a pan and pour in the hot stock. Cover and bring to the boil, then reduce the heat and simmer for 10 minutes or until the rice is tender and the liquid has been absorbed.

2 Heat the oil in a frying pan over a medium heat. Add the onion and fry for 5 minutes, then add the bacon and red pepper. Fry for 5 minutes or until the bacon is crisp. Stir in the cooked rice and the peas. Cook, stirring occasionally, for 2–3 minutes until the rice is hot and the peas are tender. Add a dash of Worcestershire sauce and serve.

Chilli Vegetable and Coconut Stir-fry

Preparation Time 25 minutes • Cooking Time about 10 minutes • Serves 4 • Per Serving 200 calories, 11g fat (of which 2g saturates), 21g carbohydrate, 1.4g salt • **Vegetarian** • **Dairy Free** • **Easy**

2 tbsp sesame oil
2 green chillies, seeded and finely chopped (see page 13)
2.5cm (1in) piece fresh root ginger, peeled and finely grated
2 garlic cloves, crushed
1 tbsp Thai green curry paste
125g (4oz) carrots, cut into fine matchsticks
125g (4oz) baby sweetcorn, halved
125g (4oz) mangetouts, halved on the diagonal
2 large red peppers, seeded and finely sliced
2 small pak choi, quartered
4 spring onions, finely chopped
300ml (½ pint) coconut milk
2 tbsp peanut satay sauce
2 tbsp light soy sauce
1 tsp soft brown sugar
4 tbsp freshly chopped coriander, plus extra sprigs to garnish
ground black pepper
roasted peanuts to garnish
rice or noodles to serve

1 Heat the oil in a wok or large non-stick frying pan over a medium heat, add the chillies, ginger and garlic and stir-fry for 1 minute. Add the curry paste and fry for a further 30 seconds.

2 Add the carrots, sweetcorn, mangetouts and red peppers. Stir-fry over a high heat for 3–4 minutes, then add the pak choi and spring onions. Cook, stirring, for a further 1–2 minutes.

3 Pour in the coconut milk, satay sauce, soy sauce and sugar. Season with pepper, bring to the boil and cook for 1–2 minutes, then add the chopped coriander. Garnish with the peanuts and coriander sprigs and serve with rice or noodles.

★ COOK'S TIP
Check the ingredients in the Thai curry paste: some contain shrimp and are therefore not suitable for vegetarians.

Thai Egg Noodles

Preparation Time 15 minutes, plus soaking • Cooking Time 12–15 minutes • Serves 4 • Per Serving 289 calories, 18g fat (of which 3g saturates), 24g carbohydrate, 2.9g salt • Dairy Free • Easy

1 lemongrass stalk, inner leaves
   only, finely chopped
100g (3½oz) medium egg noodles
100g (3½oz) sugarsnap peas,
   halved diagonally
4 tbsp vegetable oil
4 garlic cloves, crushed
3 large eggs, beaten
juice of 2 lemons
3 tbsp Thai fish sauce
2 tbsp light soy sauce
½ tsp caster sugar
50g (2oz) roasted salted peanuts
½ tsp chilli powder
12 spring onions, roughly chopped

150g (5oz) bean sprouts
2 tbsp freshly chopped coriander,
   plus extra to garnish
salt and ground black pepper

1 Put the lemongrass into a heatproof bowl with the noodles. Pour in 600ml (1 pint) boiling water and put to one side for 20 minutes, stirring from time to time.

2 Cook the sugarsnap peas in lightly salted boiling water for 1 minute, then drain and plunge them into ice-cold water.

3 Heat the oil in a wok or large frying pan, add the garlic and fry for 30 seconds. Add the beaten eggs and cook gently until lightly scrambled. Add the lemon juice, fish sauce, soy sauce, sugar, peanuts, chilli powder, spring onions and bean sprouts to the eggs. Pour the noodles, lemongrass and soaking liquid into the pan. Bring to the boil and bubble for 4–5 minutes, stirring from time to time.

4 Drain the sugarsnap peas, then add them to the noodle mixture with the chopped coriander. Heat through and season with salt and pepper. Garnish with coriander and serve immediately.

Crispy Noodles with Hot Sweet and Sour Sauce

★

Preparation Time 10 minutes • Cooking Time 15 minutes • Serves 4 • Per Serving 317 calories, 14g fat (of which 2g saturates), 43g carbohydrate, 1.7g salt • Vegetarian • Dairy Free • A Little Effort

vegetable oil for deep-frying
125g (4oz) rice or egg noodles
frisée leaves to serve

FOR THE SAUCE
2 tbsp vegetable oil
1 garlic clove, crushed
1cm (½in) piece fresh root ginger, peeled and grated
6 spring onions, sliced
½ red pepper, seeded and finely chopped
2 tbsp sugar
2 tbsp malt vinegar
2 tbsp tomato ketchup
2 tbsp dark soy sauce
2 tbsp dry sherry
1 tbsp cornflour
1 tbsp seeded and sliced green chillies (see page 13)

1 First, make the sauce. Heat the oil in a wok or large frying pan and stir-fry the garlic, ginger, spring onions and red pepper for 1 minute. Stir in the sugar, vinegar, ketchup, soy sauce and sherry. Blend the cornflour with 8 tbsp water and stir it into the sauce. Cook for 2 minutes, stirring. Add the chillies, cover and keep the sauce warm.

2 Heat the oil in a deep-fryer to 190°C (test by frying a small cube of bread: it should brown in 20 seconds). Divide the noodles into four portions and fry, a batch at a time, very briefly until lightly golden (take care as the hot oil rises up quickly).

3 Drain the noodles on kitchen paper and keep them warm while you cook the remainder.

4 Arrange the noodles on a bed of frisée leaves and serve immediately, with the sauce served separately.

Curries and Rice Dishes

Curried Tofu Burgers

Preparation Time 20 minutes • **Cooking Time** 6–8 minutes • **Serves 4** • **Per Serving** 253 calories, 18g fat (of which 3g saturates), 15g carbohydrate, 0.2g salt • **Dairy Free** • **Easy**

1 tbsp sunflower oil, plus extra
  to fry
1 large carrot, finely grated
1 large onion, finely grated
2 tsp coriander seeds, finely
  crushed (optional)
1 garlic clove, crushed
1 tsp curry paste
1 tsp tomato purée
225g pack firm tofu
25g (1oz) fresh wholemeal
  breadcrumbs
25g (1oz) mixed nuts, finely
  chopped
plain flour to dust

salt and ground black pepper
rice and green vegetables to serve

1 Heat the oil in a large frying pan. Add the carrot and onion and fry for 3–4 minutes until the vegetables are softened, stirring all the time. Add the coriander seeds, if using, the garlic, curry paste and tomato purée. Increase the heat and cook for 2 minutes, stirring all the time.

2 Put the tofu into a bowl and mash with a potato masher. Stir in the vegetables, breadcrumbs and nuts and season with salt and pepper. Beat thoroughly until the mixture starts to stick together. With floured hands, shape the mixture into eight burgers.

3 Heat some oil in a frying pan and fry the burgers for 3–4 minutes on each side until golden brown. Alternatively, brush lightly with oil and cook under a hot grill for about 3 minutes on each side or until golden brown. Drain on kitchen paper and serve hot, with rice and green vegetables.

Curried Lamb with Lentils

★

Preparation Time 15 minutes, plus marinating • Cooking Time 1 hour 50 minutes • Serves 4 • Per Serving 433 calories, 16g fat (of which 7g saturates), 38g carbohydrate, 0.3g salt • **Gluten Free** • **Dairy Free** • **Easy**

500g (1lb 2oz) lean stewing lamb on the bone, cut into eight pieces (ask your butcher to do this), trimmed of fat
1 tsp ground cumin
1 tsp ground turmeric
2 garlic cloves, crushed
1 medium red chilli, seeded and chopped (see page 13)
2.5cm (1in) piece fresh root ginger, peeled and grated
2 tbsp rapeseed oil
1 onion, chopped
400g can chopped tomatoes
2 tbsp vinegar
175g (6oz) red lentils, rinsed
salt and ground black pepper
coriander sprigs to garnish
rocket salad to serve

1 Put the lamb into a shallow sealable container, add the spices, garlic, chilli, ginger, salt and pepper. Stir well to mix, then cover and chill for at least 30 minutes.

2 Heat the oil in a large flameproof casserole dish, add the onion and cook over a low heat for 5 minutes. Add the lamb and cook for 10 minutes, turning regularly, or until the meat is evenly browned.

3 Add the tomatoes, vinegar, 450ml (¾ pint) boiling water and the lentils and bring to the boil. Reduce the heat, cover the pan and simmer for 1 hour. Remove the lid and cook for 30 minutes, stirring occasionally, or until the sauce is thick and the lamb is tender. Serve hot, garnished with coriander, with a rocket salad.

Lamb and Bamboo Shoot Red Curry

Preparation Time 10 minutes • Cooking Time 45 minutes • Serves 4 • Per Serving 397 calories, 25g fat (of which 8g saturates), 17g carbohydrate, 0.4g salt • Gluten Free • Dairy Free • Easy

2 tbsp sunflower oil

1 large onion, cut into wedges

2 garlic cloves, finely chopped

450g (1lb) lean boneless lamb, cut into 3cm (1¼in) cubes

2 tbsp Thai red curry paste

150ml (¼ pint) lamb or beef stock

2 tbsp Thai fish sauce

2 tsp soft brown sugar

200g can bamboo shoots, drained and thinly sliced

1 red pepper, seeded and thinly sliced

2 tbsp freshly chopped mint

1 tbsp freshly chopped basil

25g (1oz) unsalted peanuts, toasted

rice to serve

1 Heat the oil in a wok or large frying pan, add the onion and garlic and fry over a medium heat for 5 minutes.

2 Add the lamb and curry paste and stir-fry for 5 minutes. Add the stock, fish sauce and sugar and bring to the boil, then reduce the heat, cover the pan and simmer gently for 20 minutes.

3 Stir the bamboo shoots, red pepper and herbs into the curry and cook, uncovered, for a further 10 minutes. Stir in the peanuts and serve immediately, with rice.

Thai Green Curry

Preparation Time 10 minutes • **Cooking Time** 15 minutes • **Serves 6** • **Per Serving** 132 calories, 2g fat (of which 0g saturates), 4g carbohydrate, 1.4g salt • **Dairy Free** • **Easy**

2 tsp vegetable oil
1 green chilli, seeded and finely chopped (see page 13)
4cm (1½in) piece fresh root ginger, peeled and finely grated
1 lemongrass stalk, trimmed and cut into three pieces
225g (8oz) brown-cap or oyster mushrooms
1 tbsp Thai green curry paste
300ml (½ pint) coconut milk
150ml (¼ pint) chicken stock
1 tbsp Thai fish sauce
1 tsp light soy sauce
350g (12oz) boneless, skinless chicken breasts, cut into bite-size pieces
350g (12oz) cooked peeled large prawns
fresh coriander sprigs to garnish
Thai fragrant rice to serve

1 Heat the oil in a wok or large frying pan, add the chilli, ginger, lemongrass and mushrooms and stir-fry for about 3 minutes or until the mushrooms begin to turn golden. Add the curry paste and fry for a further 1 minute.

2 Pour in the coconut milk, stock, fish sauce and soy sauce and bring to the boil. Stir in the chicken, then reduce the heat and simmer for about 8 minutes or until the chicken is cooked.

3 Add the prawns and cook for a further 1 minute. Garnish with coriander sprigs and serve immediately, with Thai fragrant rice.

Salmon Laksa Curry

Preparation Time 10 minutes • Cooking Time 25 minutes • Serves 4 • Per Serving 607 calories, 22g fat (of which 3g saturates), 62g carbohydrate, 3.1g salt • **Gluten Free** • **Dairy Free** • **Easy**

1 tbsp olive oil
1 onion, finely sliced
3 tbsp laksa paste (see Cook's Tip)
200ml (7fl oz) coconut milk
900ml (1½ pints) hot vegetable stock
200g (7oz) baby sweetcorn, halved lengthways
600g (1lb 5oz) piece skinless salmon fillet, cut into 1cm (½in) slices
225g (8oz) baby leaf spinach
250g (9oz) medium rice noodles
salt and ground black pepper

FOR THE GARNISH
2 spring onions, sliced diagonally
2 tbsp freshly chopped coriander
2 limes, halved

1 Heat the oil in a wok or large frying pan, then add the onion and fry over a medium heat for 10 minutes, stirring, or until golden. Add the laksa paste and cook for 2 minutes.

2 Add the coconut milk, hot stock and sweetcorn and season. Bring to the boil, then reduce the heat and simmer for 5 minutes.

3 Add the salmon slices and spinach, stirring to immerse them in the liquid. Cook for 4 minutes or until the fish is opaque all the way through.

4 Meanwhile, put the noodles into a large heatproof bowl, pour boiling water over to cover and soak for 30 seconds. Drain well, then stir into the curry. Pour the curry into warmed bowls and garnish with the spring onion and coriander. Serve immediately with the lime.

⭐ COOK'S TIP
Laksa paste is a hot and spicy paste; you could use Thai curry paste instead.

⭐ TRY SOMETHING DIFFERENT
Instead of the medium rice noodles try using rice vermicelli, or leave out the noodles and serve with basmati rice.

Thai Green Shellfish Curry

Preparation Time 10 minutes • Cooking Time 10–15 minutes • Serves 6 • Per Serving 156 calories, 5g fat (of which 1g saturates), 6g carbohydrate, 0.8g salt • **Gluten Free** • **Dairy Free** • **Easy**

1 tbsp vegetable oil

1 lemongrass stalk, trimmed and chopped

2 small red chillies, seeded and chopped (see page 13)

a handful of coriander leaves, chopped, plus extra to serve

2 kaffir lime leaves, chopped

1–2 tbsp Thai green curry paste

400ml can coconut milk

450ml (¾ pint) vegetable stock

375g (13oz) queen scallops with corals

250g (9oz) raw tiger prawns, peeled and deveined (see page 93), with tails intact

salt and ground black pepper

jasmine rice to serve

1 Heat the oil in a wok or large frying pan. Add the lemongrass, chillies, coriander and lime leaves and stir-fry for 30 seconds. Add the curry paste and fry for 1 minute.

2 Add the coconut milk and stock and bring to the boil, then reduce the heat and simmer for 5–10 minutes until slightly reduced. Season well with salt and pepper.

3 Add the scallops and tiger prawns and bring to the boil, then reduce the heat and simmer gently for 2–3 minutes until cooked.

4 Divide the rice among six serving bowls and spoon the curry on top. Sprinkle with coriander and serve immediately.

★ TRY SOMETHING DIFFERENT
Use cleaned squid or mussels instead of scallops and prawns.

Szechuan Beef

★

Preparation Time 15 minutes, plus marinating • **Cooking Time** 5–10 minutes • **Serves 4** • **Per Serving** 298 calories, 14g fat (of which 4g saturates), 15g carbohydrate, 0.6g salt • **Dairy Free** • **Easy**

350g (12oz) beef skirt or rump
   steak, cut into thin strips
5 tbsp hoisin sauce
4 tbsp dry sherry
2 tbsp vegetable oil
2 red or green chillies, seeded and
   finely chopped (see page 13)
1 large onion, thinly sliced
2 garlic cloves, crushed
2 red peppers, seeded and cut into
   diamond shapes
2.5cm (1in) piece fresh root ginger,
   peeled and grated
225g can bamboo shoots, drained
   and sliced
1 tbsp sesame oil

1 Put the beef into a bowl, add the hoisin sauce and sherry and stir to coat. Cover and leave to marinate for 30 minutes.

2 Heat the vegetable oil in a wok or large frying pan until smoking hot. Add the chillies, onion and garlic and stir-fry over a medium heat for 3–4 minutes until softened. Remove with a slotted spoon and put to one side. Add the red peppers, increase the heat and stir-fry for a few seconds. Remove and put to one side.

3 Add the steak and marinade to the pan in batches. Stir-fry each batch over a high heat for about 1 minute, then remove with a slotted spoon.

4 Return the vegetables to the pan. Add the ginger and bamboo shoots, then the beef, and stir-fry for a further 1 minute or until heated through. Transfer to a warmed serving dish, sprinkle the sesame oil over the top and serve immediately.

Thai Beef Curry

Preparation Time 20 minutes, plus cooling • **Cooking Time** about 30 minutes • **Serves 4** • **Per Serving** 443 calories, 26g fat (of which 7g saturates), 23g carbohydrate, 1.2g salt • **Dairy Free** • **A Little Effort**

4 cloves
1 tsp coriander seeds
1 tsp cumin seeds
seeds from 3 cardamom pods
2 garlic cloves, roughly chopped
2.5cm (1in) piece fresh root ginger, peeled and roughly chopped
1 small onion, roughly chopped
2 tbsp sunflower oil
1 tbsp sesame oil
1 tbsp Thai red curry paste
1 tsp turmeric
450g (1lb) sirloin steak, cut into 3cm (1¼in) cubes
225g (8oz) potatoes, quartered
4 tomatoes, quartered
1 tsp sugar
1 tbsp light soy sauce
300ml (½ pint) coconut milk
150ml (¼ pint) beef stock
4 small red chillies, bruised (see page 13)
50g (2oz) cashew nuts
rice and stir-fried green vegetables to serve

1 Put the cloves, coriander, cumin and cardamom seeds into a small heavy-based frying pan and fry over a high heat for 1–2 minutes until the spices release their aroma. Be careful that they do not burn. Leave to cool slightly, then grind to a powder in a spice grinder or blender.

2 Put the garlic, ginger and onion into a blender or food processor and whiz to form a smooth paste. Heat the sunflower and sesame oils in a wok or deep frying pan. Add the onion purée and the curry paste and stir-fry for 5 minutes, then add the ground roasted spices and the turmeric and fry for a further 5 minutes.

3 Add the beef to the pan and fry for 5 minutes or until browned on all sides. Add the potatoes, tomatoes, sugar, soy sauce, coconut milk, stock and chillies. Bring to the boil, then reduce the heat, cover the pan and simmer gently for about 15 minutes or until the beef is tender and the potatoes are cooked.

4 Stir in the cashew nuts and serve the curry with rice and stir-fried vegetables.

Chicken Curry with Rice

Preparation Time 20 minutes • **Cooking Time** 25 minutes, plus standing • **Serves 4** • **Per Serving** 453 calories, 12g fat (of which 2g saturates), 49g carbohydrate, 2.4g salt • **Gluten Free** • **Dairy Free** • **Easy**

2 tbsp vegetable oil
1 onion, finely sliced
2 garlic cloves, crushed
6 boneless, skinless chicken thighs,
   cut into strips
2 tbsp tikka masala curry paste
200g can chopped tomatoes
450ml (¾ pint) hot vegetable stock
200g (7oz) basmati rice
1 tsp salt
225g (8oz) baby leaf spinach
poppadums and mango chutney
   to serve

1 Heat the oil in a large pan, add the onion and fry over a medium heat for about 5 minutes or until golden. Add the garlic and chicken and stir-fry for about 5 minutes or until golden.

2 Add the curry paste, tomatoes and hot stock. Stir and bring to the boil, then reduce the heat, cover the pan and simmer on a low heat for 15 minutes or until the chicken is cooked (cut a piece in half to check that it's white all the way through).

3 Meanwhile, cook the rice. Put 600ml (1 pint) water into a medium pan, cover and bring to the boil. Add the rice and salt and stir. Replace the lid and reduce the heat to its lowest setting. Cook for the time stated on the pack. Once cooked, cover with a teatowel and the lid. Leave for 5 minutes to absorb the steam.

4 Add the spinach to the curry and cook until it has just wilted.

5 Spoon the rice into bowls, add the curry and serve with poppadums and mango chutney.

Chicken Tikka Masala

★

Preparation Time 15 minutes • Cooking Time 30 minutes • Serves 4 • Per Serving 297 calories, 17g fat (of which 4g saturates), 4g carbohydrate, 0.6g salt • **Dairy Free** • **Easy**

2 tbsp vegetable oil
1 onion, finely sliced
2 garlic cloves, crushed
6 boneless, skinless chicken thighs, cut into strips
2 tbsp tikka masala curry paste
200g can chopped tomatoes
450ml (¾ pint) hot vegetable stock
225g (8oz) baby spinach leaves
fresh coriander leaves to garnish
rice, mango chutney and poppadoms to serve

1 Heat the oil in a large pan, add the onion and fry over a medium heat for 5–7 minutes until golden. Add the garlic and chicken and stir-fry for about 5 minutes or until golden.

2 Stir in the curry paste, then add the tomatoes and hot stock. Bring to the boil, then reduce the heat, cover the pan and simmer over a low heat for 15 minutes or until the chicken is cooked through.

3 Add the spinach to the curry, stir and cook until the leaves have just wilted. Garnish with coriander and serve with rice, mango chutney and poppadoms.

Aubergines in a Hot Sweet and Sour Sauce

Preparation Time 10 minutes • Cooking Time 35 minutes • Serves 4 • Per Serving 136 calories, 7g fat (of which 1g saturates), 17g carbohydrate, 2.5g salt • **Vegetarian** • **Gluten Free** • **Dairy Free** • **Easy**

3 tbsp vegetable oil
200g (7oz) onions, thinly sliced
2.5cm (1in) piece fresh root ginger, peeled and finely chopped
2 red chillies, finely chopped (see page 13), plus extra whole red chillies to garnish (optional)
1½ tsp cumin seeds
1½ tsp coriander seeds
3 cloves
5cm (2in) cinnamon stick
1 tbsp paprika
juice of 2 limes
3–4 tbsp dark muscovado sugar
1–2 tsp salt

450g (1lb) aubergines, cut into 2.5cm (1in) pieces
rice to serve

1 Heat the oil in a wok or large frying pan, add the onions, ginger and chopped chillies and stir-fry for about 4 minutes or until softened. Add the cumin and coriander seeds, cloves and cinnamon and cook for 2–3 minutes.

2 Add 300ml (½ pint) water to the pan, then stir in the paprika, lime juice, sugar, salt and aubergines. Bring to the boil, then cover the pan, reduce the heat and simmer for about 20 minutes or until the aubergines are tender.

3 Uncover the pan and bring the sauce back to the boil. Bubble for 3–4 minutes until the liquid is thick enough to coat the aubergine pieces. Garnish with whole red chillies, if you like, and serve with rice.

★ TRY SOMETHING DIFFERENT
Braised Aubergines
Omit the cumin, coriander, cloves, cinnamon and paprika. Add the aubergines to the onion mixture at the end of step 1 and stir-fry for 1–2 minutes. Add 1 tbsp sugar, 1 tsp salt, 3–4 tbsp yellow bean sauce and the water; complete the recipe.

Mauritian Vegetable Curry

Preparation Time 15 minutes • Cooking Time 30 minutes • Serves 4 • Per Serving 184 calories, 11g fat
(of which 1g saturates), 18g carbohydrate, 1.7g salt • Vegetarian • Dairy Free • Easy

3 tbsp vegetable oil
1 onion, finely sliced
4 garlic cloves, crushed
2.5cm (1in) piece fresh root ginger,
   peeled and grated
3 tbsp medium curry powder
6 fresh curry leaves
150g (5oz) potato, cut into 1cm
   (½in) cubes
125g (4oz) aubergine, cut into 2cm
   (1in) sticks, 5mm (¼in) wide
150g (5oz) carrots, cut into 5mm
   (¼in) dice
900ml (1½ pints) hot vegetable
   stock
a pinch of saffron threads
1 tsp salt
150g (5oz) green beans, trimmed
75g (3oz) frozen peas
ground black pepper
3 tbsp freshly chopped coriander
   to garnish

1 Heat the oil in a large heavy-based
pan over a low heat. Add the onion
and fry for 5–10 minutes until
golden. Add the garlic, ginger, curry
powder and curry leaves and fry for
a further minute.

2 Add the potato and aubergine
to the pan and fry, stirring, for
2 minutes. Add the carrots, hot
stock, saffron and salt and season
with plenty of pepper. Cover and
cook for 10 minutes or until the
vegetables are almost tender.

3 Add the beans and peas to
the pan and cook for a further
4 minutes. Sprinkle with the
chopped coriander and serve.

★ GET AHEAD
To prepare ahead *Complete the recipe,*
without the garnish, and chill quickly. It
will keep, in the fridge, for up to two days.
To use *Put into a pan, cover and bring to*
the boil, then simmer for 10–15 minutes.
Complete the recipe.

Lentil Chilli

Preparation Time 10 minutes • **Cooking Time** 30 minutes • **Serves 6** • **Per Serving** 195 calories, 2g fat (of which trace saturates), 32g carbohydrate, 0.1g salt • **Gluten Free** • **Dairy Free** • **Easy**

oil-water spray (see Cook's Tip, page 60)
2 red onions, chopped
1½ tsp each ground coriander and ground cumin
½ tsp ground paprika
2 garlic cloves, crushed
2 sun-dried tomatoes, chopped
¼ tsp crushed dried chilli flakes
125ml (4fl oz) red wine
300ml (½ pint) hot vegetable stock
2 × 400g cans brown or green lentils, drained and rinsed
2 × 400g cans chopped tomatoes

sugar to taste
salt and ground black pepper
natural low-fat yogurt and rice to serve

1 Spray a saucepan with the oil-water spray and cook the onions for 5 minutes or until softened. Add the coriander, cumin and paprika. Combine the garlic, sun-dried tomatoes, chilli, wine and stock and add to the pan. Cover and simmer for 5–7 minutes. Uncover and simmer until the onions are very tender and the liquid has almost gone.

2 Stir in the lentils and canned tomatoes and season with salt and pepper. Simmer, uncovered, for 15 minutes or until thick. Stir in sugar to taste. Remove from the heat.

3 Ladle out a quarter of the mixture and whiz in a food processor or blender. Combine the puréed and unpuréed portions. Serve with yogurt and rice.

Wild Mushroom Risotto

Preparation Time 10 minutes • **Cooking Time** 30 minutes • **Serves 6** • **Per Serving** 341 calories, 12g fat (of which 2g saturates), 48g carbohydrate, 0g salt • **Vegetarian** • **Gluten Free** • **Dairy Free** • **Easy**

900ml (1½ pints) vegetable stock
6 tbsp olive oil
2 shallots, finely chopped
2 garlic cloves, finely chopped
2 tsp freshly chopped thyme, plus
    sprigs to garnish
1 tsp grated lemon zest
350g (12oz) risotto (arborio) rice
150ml (¼ pint) dry white wine
450g (1lb) mixed fresh mushrooms,
    such as oyster, shiitake and cep,
    sliced if large
1 tbsp freshly chopped flat-leafed
    parsley
salt and ground black pepper

★ DOS AND DON'TS FOR THE PERFECT RISOTTO

● *Always use risotto (arborio) rice: the grains are thicker and shorter than long-grain rice and have a high starch content. They absorb more liquid slowly, producing a creamy-textured risotto.*
● *Stock should be hot when added: this swells the grains, yet keeps them firm. Keep stock simmering in a pan. Add it ladle by ladle to the risotto, allowing it to be absorbed by the rice after each addition.*
● *The correct heat is vital. If the risotto gets too hot, the liquid evaporates too quickly and the rice won't cook evenly. If the heat is too low, the risotto will go gluey. Over a medium heat, the rice should cook in about 25 minutes.*
● *Don't leave risotto – stir constantly to loosen the rice from the bottom of the pan.*
● *The quantity of liquid given is approximate – adjust it so that, when cooked, the rice is tender but firm to the bite. It should be creamily bound together, neither runny nor dry.*

1 Heat the stock in a pan to a steady, low simmer.

2 Meanwhile, heat half the oil in a heavy-based pan. Add the shallots, garlic, chopped thyme and lemon zest and fry gently for 5 minutes or until the shallots are softened. Add the rice and stir for 1 minute or until the grains are glossy. Add the wine, bring to the boil and let bubble until almost totally evaporated.

3 Gradually add the stock to the rice, a ladleful at a time, stirring with each addition and allowing it to be absorbed before adding more. Continue adding the stock slowly until the rice is tender. This should take about 25 minutes.

4 About 5 minutes before the rice is ready, heat the remaining oil in a large frying pan and stir-fry the mushrooms over a high heat for 4–5 minutes. Add to the rice with the parsley. The risotto should still be moist: if necessary add a little more stock. Check the seasoning and serve at once, garnished with thyme sprigs.

Saffron Risotto with Lemon Chicken

Preparation Time 20 minutes • Cooking Time 30 minutes • Serves 4 • Per Serving 830 calories, 44g fat (of which 15g saturates), 50g carbohydrate, 0.9g salt • **Gluten Free** • **Easy**

zest and juice of 1 lemon
a small handful of fresh parsley
25g (1oz) blanched almonds
1 tbsp dried thyme
1 garlic clove
75ml (2½fl oz) olive oil
450ml (¾ pint) chicken stock
4 boneless chicken breasts, skin on
50g (2oz) butter
225g (8oz) onions, finely chopped
a small pinch of saffron threads
225g (8oz) risotto (arborio) rice
125ml (4fl oz) white wine
50g (2oz) freshly grated Parmesan
salt and ground black pepper
fresh thyme sprigs to garnish

1 Preheat the oven to 200°C (180°C fan oven) mark 6. Whiz the lemon zest, parsley, almonds, thyme and garlic in a food processor for a few seconds, then slowly add the oil and whiz until combined. Season with salt and pepper. Heat the stock in a pan to a steady low simmer.

2 Spread the lemon and herb mixture under the skin of the chicken. Put the chicken into a roasting tin, brush with 25g (1oz) melted butter and pour the lemon juice over it. Cook in the oven for 25 minutes, basting occasionally.

3 Heat the remaining butter in a pan. Add the onions and fry until soft. Stir in the saffron and rice. Add the wine to the rice. Gradually add the hot stock, a ladleful at a time, stirring with each addition and allowing it to be absorbed before adding more. This will take about 25 minutes. Take the pan off the heat and stir in the Parmesan. Serve with the chicken, pouring any juices from the roasting tin over it. Garnish with thyme sprigs and lemon wedges.

★ COOK'S TIP
For how to make the perfect risotto, see page 119.

Special Prawn Fried Rice

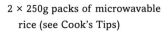

Preparation Time 5 minutes • Cooking Time 10–15 minutes • Serves 4 • Per Serving 412 calories, 18g fat (of which 3g saturates), 46g carbohydrate, 1.9g salt • **Dairy Free** • **Easy**

2 × 250g packs of microwavable rice (see Cook's Tips)
1 tbsp sesame oil
6 tbsp nasi goreng paste (see Cook's Tips)
200g (7oz) green cabbage, shredded
250g (9oz) cooked and peeled large prawns
2 tbsp light soy sauce
1 tbsp sunflower oil
2 medium eggs, beaten
2 spring onions, thinly sliced
1 lime, cut into wedges, to serve

1 Cook the rice according to the pack instructions.

2 Heat the sesame oil in a wok and fry the nasi goreng paste for 1–2 minutes. Add the cabbage and stir-fry for 2–3 minutes. Add the prawns and stir briefly, then add the rice and soy sauce and cook for a further 5 minutes, stirring occasionally.

3 To make the omelette, heat the sunflower oil in a non-stick frying pan (about 25.5cm/10in in diameter) and add the eggs. Swirl around to cover the base of the pan in a thin layer and cook for 2–3 minutes until set.

3 Roll up the omelette and cut it into strips. Serve the rice scattered with strips of omelette and spring onions and pass round the lime wedges to squeeze over it.

 COOK'S TIPS
● *Nasi goreng is a spicy Indonesian dish traditionally eaten for breakfast. Nasi goreng paste can be bought at large supermarkets and Asian food shops.*
● *If you can't find microwavable rice, use 200g (7oz) long-grain rice, cooked according to the pack instructions – but do not overcook. Rinse in cold water and drain well before you begin the recipe.*

Simple Paella

Preparation Time 15 minutes, plus infusing • **Cooking Time** 50 minutes • **Serves 6** • **Per Serving** 554 calories, 16g fat (of which 3g saturates), 58g carbohydrate, 0.5g salt • **Gluten Free** • **Dairy Free** • **A Little Effort**

1 litre (1¾ pints) chicken stock
½ tsp saffron threads
5 tbsp extra virgin olive oil
6 boneless, skinless chicken thighs, each cut into three pieces
1 large onion, chopped
4 large garlic cloves, crushed
1 tsp paprika
2 red peppers, seeded and sliced
400g can chopped tomatoes
350g (12oz) long-grain rice
200ml (7fl oz) dry sherry
500g (1lb 2oz) cooked mussels (see Cook's Tip)
200g (7oz) cooked and peeled tiger prawns
juice of ½ lemon
salt and ground black pepper
lemon wedges and fresh flat-leafed parsley to serve

1 Heat the stock, then add the saffron and leave to infuse for 30 minutes.

2 Heat half the oil in a frying pan and fry the chicken in batches for 3–5 minutes until golden brown. Set the chicken aside. Reduce the heat slightly. Add the remaining oil. Fry the onion for 5 minutes or until soft. Add the garlic and paprika and stir for 1 minute. Add the chicken, red peppers and tomatoes. Stir in the rice. Add one-third of the stock and bring to the boil. Season with salt and pepper. Reduce the heat to a simmer, then cook, uncovered, stirring continuously, until most of the liquid has been absorbed. Add the remaining stock a little at a time, letting the rice absorb it before adding more. (This should take about 25 minutes.)

3 Add the sherry and cook for 2 minutes – the rice should be quite wet, as it will continue to absorb liquid. Add the mussels and prawns, with their juices, and the lemon juice. Stir in and cook for 5 minutes to heat through. Adjust the seasoning and serve with lemon wedges and parsley.

★ COOK'S TIP
Ready-cooked mussels are available vacuum-packed from supermarkets. Alternatively, to cook from fresh, tap the mussels on the worksurface and discard any that do not close or have broken shells. Scrub the mussels and remove any beard, then rinse and put them into a large pan with 50ml (2fl oz) water. Cover with a tight-fitting lid and cook for 3–4 minutes, shaking the pan occasionally, until the mussels open. Transfer to a bowl, discard any unopened mussels, and reserve the cooking liquid.

Marinated Pork with Vegetable Rice

Preparation Time 10 minutes • **Cooking Time** 20–25 minutes • **Serves 4** • **Per Serving** 462 calories, 11g fat (of which 4g saturates), 41g carbohydrate, 2.2g salt • **Gluten Free** • **Dairy Free** • **Easy**

1 tsp peeled and grated fresh root ginger

2 tbsp soy sauce

2 tbsp freshly chopped rosemary

4 rindless pork steaks

150g (5oz) brown rice

450ml (¾ pint) hot vegetable stock

1 tbsp, plus 1 tsp olive oil

1 red onion, chopped

1 red pepper, chopped

a handful of shredded Savoy cabbage

1 Mix the ginger, soy sauce and rosemary in a shallow dish. Add the pork steaks, turn to coat, then put to one side.

2 Put the rice in a pan and pour in the hot stock. Cover and bring to the boil, then simmer over a low heat for 20 minutes or until the rice is tender and the liquid has been absorbed.

3 Meanwhile, heat 1 tbsp oil in a frying pan. Add the onion, red pepper and cabbage and fry for 10 minutes. Heat 1 tsp oil in a separate frying pan and fry the steaks for 4–5 minutes on each side. Stir the vegetables through the rice, then serve with the pork.

Spiced Egg Pilau

Preparation Time 5 minutes • **Cooking Time** 15 minutes • **Serves 4** • **Per Serving** 331 calories, 9g fat (of which 12g saturates), 50g carbohydrate, 0.6g salt • **Vegetarian** • **Gluten Free** • **Dairy Free** • **Easy**

200g (7oz) basmati or wild rice
150g (5oz) frozen peas
4 medium eggs
200ml (7fl oz) coconut cream
1 tsp mild curry paste
1 tbsp sweet chilli sauce
1 tbsp smooth peanut butter
1 large bunch of fresh coriander, roughly chopped
mini poppadums and mango chutney to serve

1 Put the rice into a pan with 450ml (¾ pint) boiling water over a low heat and cook for 15 minutes or until just tender. Add the peas for the last 5 minutes of cooking time.

2 Meanwhile, put the eggs into a large pan of boiling water, then reduce the heat and simmer for 6 minutes. Drain and shell.

3 Put the coconut cream, curry paste, chilli sauce and peanut butter into a small pan and whisk together. Heat the sauce gently, stirring, without allowing it to boil.

4 Drain the rice and stir in the chopped coriander and 2 tbsp of the sauce.

5 Divide the rice among four bowls. Cut the eggs into halves and serve on the rice, spooning the remaining coconut sauce over the top. Serve with the poppadums and chutney.

Coconut Fish Pilau

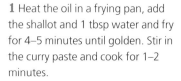

Preparation Time 15 minutes • **Cooking Time** 30 minutes • **Serves 4** • **Per Serving** 398 calories, 7g fat
(of which 1g saturates), 53g carbohydrate, 0.4g salt • **Gluten Free** • **Dairy Free** • **Easy**

2 tsp olive oil

1 shallot, chopped

1 tbsp Thai green curry paste

225g (8oz) brown basmati rice

600ml (1 pint) hot fish or vegetable
   stock

150ml (¼ pint) reduced-fat coconut
   milk

350g (12oz) skinless white fish fillet,
   cut into bite-size pieces

350g (12oz) sugarsnap peas

125g (4oz) cooked and peeled
   prawns

25g (1oz) flaked almonds, toasted

a squeeze of lemon juice

salt and ground black pepper

2 tbsp freshly chopped coriander
   to garnish

1 Heat the oil in a frying pan, add the shallot and 1 tbsp water and fry for 4–5 minutes until golden. Stir in the curry paste and cook for 1–2 minutes.

2 Add the rice, hot stock and coconut milk and bring to the boil. Cover the pan, reduce the heat and simmer for 15–20 minutes until all the liquid has been absorbed.

3 Add the fish and cook for 3–5 minutes. Add the sugarsnap peas, prawns, almonds and lemon juice and stir over the heat for 3–4 minutes until heated through. Check the seasoning and serve immediately, garnished with coriander.

★ TRY SOMETHING DIFFERENT
There are plenty of alternatives to cod: try coley (saithe), sea bass or pollack.

Salmon Kedgeree

Preparation Time 15 minutes, plus soaking • Cooking Time 55 minutes • Serves 4 • Per Serving 490 calories, 15g fat (of which 2g saturates), 62g carbohydrate, 0.1g salt • **Gluten Free** • **Easy**

50g (2oz) butter
700g (1½lb) onions, sliced
2 tsp garam masala
1 garlic clove, crushed
75g (3oz) split green lentils, soaked in 300ml (½ pint) boiling water for 15 minutes, then drained
750ml (1¼ pints) hot vegetable stock
225g (8oz) basmati rice
1 green chilli, seeded and finely chopped (see page 13)
350g (12oz) salmon fillet
salt and ground black pepper

1 Melt the butter in a flameproof casserole over a medium heat. Add the onions and cook for 5 minutes or until soft. Remove a third of the onions and put to one side. Increase the heat and cook the remaining onions for 10 minutes to caramelise. Remove and put to one side.

2 Put the first batch of onions back in the casserole, add the garam masala and garlic and cook, stirring, for 1 minute. Add the drained lentils and hot stock, cover the pan and cook for 15 minutes. Add the rice and chilli and season with salt and pepper. Bring to the boil, then cover the pan, reduce the heat and simmer for 5 minutes.

3 Put the salmon fillet on top of the rice, cover and continue to cook gently for 15 minutes or until the rice is cooked, the stock has been absorbed and the salmon is opaque.

4 Lift off the salmon and divide into flakes. Put it back in the casserole, and fork through the rice. Garnish with the reserved caramelised onion and serve.

★ TRY SOMETHING DIFFERENT
Instead of salmon, use undyed smoked haddock fillet.

Tuna with Coriander Rice

Preparation Time 5 minutes • **Cooking Time** 10 minutes • **Serves 4** • **Per Serving** 451 calories, 10g fat (of which 2g saturates), 54g carbohydrate, 0.4g salt • **Gluten Free** • **Dairy Free** • **Easy**

250g (9oz) basmati rice
8 × 125g (4oz) tuna steaks
5cm (2in) piece fresh root ginger,
    peeled and grated
1 tbsp olive oil
100ml (3½fl oz) orange juice
300g (11oz) pak choi, roughly
    chopped
a small handful of freshly chopped
    coriander
ground black pepper
lime wedges to garnish

1 Cook the rice according to the pack instructions.

2 Meanwhile, put the tuna steaks in a shallow dish. Add the ginger, oil and orange juice and season well with pepper. Turn the tuna over to coat.

3 Heat a non-stick frying pan until really hot. Add four tuna steaks and half the marinade and cook for 1–2 minutes on each side until just cooked. Repeat with the remaining tuna and marinade. Remove the fish from the pan and keep warm.

4 Add the pak choi to the frying pan and cook for 1–2 minutes until wilted. When the rice is cooked, drain and stir the coriander through it. Serve the tuna with the pak choi, rice and pan juices and garnish with lime wedges.

 COOK'S TIP
Basmati rice should be washed before cooking to remove excess starch and to give really light, fluffy results.

Warm Spiced Rice Salad

Preparation Time 10 minutes • **Cooking Time** 20–30 minutes • **Serves 4** • **Per Serving** 700 calories, 27g fat (of which 6g saturates), 88g carbohydrate, 0.7g salt • **Gluten Free** • **Easy**

½ tbsp ground cumin
½ tsp ground cinnamon
2 tbsp sunflower oil
2 large red onions, sliced
250g (9oz) basmati rice
600ml (1 pint) hot vegetable stock
400g can lentils, drained and rinsed
salt and ground black pepper

FOR THE SALAD
75g (3oz) watercress
250g (9oz) broccoli, steamed and
    chopped into 2.5cm (1in) pieces
25g (1oz) sultanas
75g (3oz) dried apricots, chopped
75g (3oz) mixed nuts and seeds
2 tbsp freshly chopped flat-leafed
    parsley
100g (3½oz) goat's cheese,
    crumbled

1 Put the cumin and cinnamon into a large deep frying pan and heat gently for 1–2 minutes. Add the oil and onions and fry over a low heat for 8–10 minutes until the onions are soft and golden.

2 Add the rice, toss to coat in the spices and onions, then add the hot stock. Cover and cook for 12–15 minutes until the stock has been absorbed and the rice is cooked. Season, tip into a serving bowl and add the lentils.

3 To make the salad, add the watercress, broccoli, sultanas, apricots and mixed nuts and seeds to the bowl. Scatter with the parsley, then toss together, top with the cheese and serve immediately.

★TRY SOMETHING DIFFERENT
Replace the goat's cheese with two roasted, skinless chicken breasts, which have been shredded.

Fish and Seafood

Fish and Chips

Preparation Time 30 minutes • **Cooking Time** 40–50 minutes • **Serves 4** • **Per Serving** 993 calories, 67g fat (of which 9g saturates), 64g carbohydrate, 1.6g salt • **Dairy Free** • **Easy**

900g (2lb) Desiree, Maris Piper or
   King Edward potatoes, peeled
2–3 tbsp olive oil
sea salt flakes
sunflower oil to deep-fry
2 × 128g packs batter mix
1 tsp baking powder
¼ tsp salt
330ml bottle of lager
4 plaice fillets, about 225g (8oz)
   each, with skin on, trimmed and
   cut in half
plain flour to dust
salt and ground black pepper
lemon wedges and chives to
   garnish

**FOR THE GARLIC
   MAYONNAISE**
2 garlic cloves, crushed
8 tbsp mayonnaise
1 tsp lemon juice

1 Preheat the oven to 240°C (220°C fan oven) mark 9. Cut the potatoes into chips. Put them in a pan of lightly salted boiling water, cover and bring to the boil. Boil for 2 minutes, then drain well and turn on to kitchen paper to remove the excess moisture. Tip into a large non-stick roasting tin, toss with the olive oil and season with sea salt. Roast for 40–50 minutes until golden and cooked, turning from time to time.

2 Meanwhile, half-fill a deep-fat fryer with sunflower oil and heat to 190°C. Put the batter mix into a bowl with the baking powder and salt and gradually whisk in the lager. Season the plaice and lightly dust with flour. Dip two of the fillets into the batter and deep-fry in the hot oil until golden. Transfer to a warmed plate and cover lightly with foil to keep warm while you deep-fry the remaining plaice fillets.

3 Mix the garlic, mayonnaise and lemon juice together in a bowl and season well. Serve the garlic mayonnaise with the plaice and chips, garnished with lemon wedges and chives.

★ TRY SOMETHING
DIFFERENT
Instead of garlic mayonnaise, serve with one of the following.
Simple Tartare Sauce
Mix 8 tbsp mayonnaise with 1 tbsp each chopped capers and gherkins, 1 tbsp freshly chopped tarragon or chives and 2 tsp lemon juice.
Herby Lemon Mayonnaise
Fold 2 tbsp finely chopped parsley, grated zest of ½ lemon and 2 tsp lemon juice into 8 tbsp mayonnaise.

Crispy Crumbed Fish

Preparation Time 5 minutes • Cooking Time 10–15 minutes • Serves 4 • Per Serving 171 calories, 1g fat (of which trace saturates), 10g carbohydrate, 0.8g salt • **Dairy Free** • **Easy**

50g (2oz) fresh breadcrumbs
a small handful of freshly chopped
    flat-leafed parsley
2 tbsp capers, chopped
zest of 1 lemon
4 × 150g (5oz) haddock or pollack
    fillets
½ tbsp Dijon mustard
juice of ½ lemon
salt and ground black pepper

1 Preheat the oven to 180°C (160°C fan oven) mark 4. Put the breadcrumbs into a bowl with the parsley, capers and lemon zest. Mix well, then put to one side.

2 Put the fish fillets on a non-stick baking tray. Mix the mustard and half the lemon juice in a bowl with a little salt and pepper, then spread over the top of each piece of fish. Spoon the breadcrumb mixture over the top – don't worry if some falls off.

3 Cook in the oven for 10–15 minutes until the fish is cooked and the breadcrumbs are golden. Pour the remaining lemon juice over it and serve with new potatoes and a mixed salad.

★ COOK'S TIP
To store fish, remove from its original wrapping, rinse in cold water, pat dry, cover and place towards the bottom of the fridge. Most varieties of fish can be stored for a day or two. Always check the use-by date on packaged fish, or ask the fishmonger how long it will keep.

Crusted Trout

Preparation Time 10 minutes • Cooking Time 10–13 minutes • Serves 4 • Per Serving 259 calories, 15g fat (of which 3g saturates), 1g carbohydrate, 0.8g salt • **Gluten Free** • **Dairy Free** • **Easy**

1 tbsp sesame oil
1 tbsp soy sauce
juice of 1 lime
4 × 150g (5oz) trout fillets
2 tbsp sesame seeds
lime wedges, herb salad and fennel
   to serve

1 Preheat the grill. Put the oil in a bowl. Add the soy sauce and lime juice and whisk together.

2 Put the trout fillets on a baking sheet, pour the soy mixture over them and grill for 8–10 minutes. Sprinkle with the sesame seeds and grill for a further 2–3 minutes until the seeds are golden. Serve with lime wedges, a herb salad and some finely sliced fennel.

★ COOK'S TIP
Sesame seeds are deliciously nutty and highly nutritious. They are a valuable source of protein, omega fats and vitamin E. Lightly toasted sesame seeds, crushed with a little salt and stirred into 1–2 tbsp of olive oil, make an excellent dressing for cooked green beans, broccoli and carrots.

Simple Smoked Haddock

★

Preparation Time 10 minutes • **Cooking Time** about 10 minutes • **Serves 4** • **Per Serving** 217 calories, 9g fat (of which 4g saturates), 1g carbohydrate, 3.4g salt • **Gluten Free** • **Easy**

25g (1oz) unsalted butter
1 tbsp olive oil
1 garlic clove, thinly sliced
4 thick smoked haddock or cod
    fillets, about 175g (6oz) each
a small handful of freshly chopped
    parsley (optional)
finely grated zest of 1 small lemon,
    plus lemon wedges to serve
    (optional)
romanesco, cauliflower or broccoli
    to serve

1 Heat the butter, oil and garlic in a large non-stick pan over a high heat until the mixture starts to foam and sizzle. Put the fish into the pan, skin side down, and fry for 10 minutes – this will give a golden crust underneath the fish.

2 Carefully turn the fish over. Scatter the parsley, if using, and lemon zest over each fillet, then fry for a further 30 seconds.

3 Put a cooked fillet on each of four warmed plates and spoon some of the buttery juices over each. Serve with the lemon wedges, if using, and steamed romanesco, cauliflower or broccoli.

★ COOK'S TIP
Smoked fish is quite salty, so always taste the sauce before seasoning with any extra salt.

Plaice with Herb and Polenta Crust

Preparation Time 15 minutes • Cooking Time 4–6 minutes • Serves 2 • Per Serving 376 calories, 17g fat (of which 3g saturates), 19g carbohydrate, 0.6g salt • **Gluten Free** • **Dairy Free** • **Easy**

1 tsp finely chopped rosemary or
   1 tsp finely snipped chives
1 tsp finely chopped thyme
2 garlic cloves, very finely chopped
50g (2oz) polenta
finely grated zest and juice of
   2 small lemons
2 plaice fillets, about 175g (6oz)
   each, skinned
1 large egg
2 tbsp olive oil
salt and ground black pepper
roasted tomatoes, green beans and
   lemon wedges to serve

1 Combine the herbs, garlic and polenta on a flat plate. Add the lemon zest, salt and pepper and mix well. Wipe the plaice fillets with kitchen paper.

2 Beat the egg in a shallow dish, dip the fish fillets in the egg and coat them with the polenta mixture, pressing it on well.

3 Heat the oil in a very large frying pan over a high heat. When hot, add the fish, reduce the heat to medium and cook for 2–3 minutes on each side, depending on the thickness of the fillets. Drain on kitchen paper. Serve with lemon juice poured over them, with roasted tomatoes, green beans and extra lemon wedges.

Salmon with a Spicy Yogurt Crust

Preparation Time 10 minutes • Cooking Time 10 minutes • Serves 4 • Per Serving 250 calories, 14g fat (of which 3g saturates), 3g carbohydrate, 0.2g salt • Gluten Free • Easy

3 tbsp freshly chopped coriander

1 garlic clove, crushed

2.5cm (1in) piece fresh root ginger, peeled and grated

½ tsp each ground cumin and coriander

¼ tsp cayenne pepper

150g (5oz) natural yogurt

4 × 125g (4oz) salmon fillets

salt

lime wedges and herb salad to serve

1 Preheat the grill. Mix together the chopped coriander, garlic, ginger, ground cumin and coriander, the cayenne, yogurt and a pinch of salt. Add the salmon and turn to coat.

2 Grill the fish for 7–10 minutes until cooked through. Serve with lime wedges to squeeze over the fish and a herb salad.

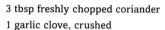 TRY SOMETHING DIFFERENT
Use another fish instead of salmon; try trout or plump mackerel fillets.

Trout and Dill Fishcakes

Preparation Time 15 minutes • Cooking Time 25 minutes • Serves 4 • Per Serving 196 calories, 5g fat (of which 1g saturates), 27g carbohydrate, 0.1g salt • Gluten Free • Dairy Free • Easy

4 medium potatoes, roughly chopped
2 trout fillets
3 spring onions, finely chopped
2 dill sprigs, finely chopped
zest of 1 lemon
1 tbsp olive oil
a little plain gluten-free flour
salt
watercress to serve

1 Cook the potatoes in a pan of lightly salted boiling water for 6–8 minutes until tender. Drain, return to the pan and mash.

2 Preheat the grill to high. Grill the trout fillets for 8–10 minutes until cooked through and firm to the touch. Skin the fish, flake into pieces, removing any bones, then put into the pan with the mashed potato.

3 Add the spring onions, dill and lemon zest to the pan with the oil, season with salt and mix well.

4 Shape the mixture into eight small patties. Dust with flour and put on a non-stick baking sheet, then grill for 3 minutes on each side. Serve the fishcakes hot, with watercress.

★ TRY SOMETHING DIFFERENT
Replace the trout with 225g (8oz) cooked salmon, haddock or smoked haddock: skin, flake and add at step 2.

Peppered Mackerel

★

Preparation Time 10 minutes • **Cooking Time** 15 minutes • **Serves 4** • **Per Serving** 764 calories, 63g fat (of which 22g saturates), 1g carbohydrate, 0.4g salt • **Gluten Free** • **Easy**

4 tsp whole mixed peppercorns
4 fresh mackerel, gutted, about
   250g (9oz) each
1 tbsp sunflower oil
200ml (7fl oz) crème fraîche
lemon wedges to garnish
asparagus and sugarsnap peas
   to serve

1 Lightly crush 2 tsp peppercorns using a pestle and mortar. Sprinkle one side of each mackerel with half the crushed peppercorns.

2 Heat the oil in a frying pan over a medium-high heat. Add the fish, peppered side down, and cook for 5–7 minutes. Sprinkle the mackerel with the remaining crushed peppercorns, turn the fish over and continue to fry for 5–7 minutes until cooked (see Cook's Tips). Remove and keep warm.

3 Wipe out the pan, add the crème fraîche and bring to the boil. Stir in the remaining whole peppercorns. (If the sauce becomes too thick, add some boiling water.)

4 To serve, spoon the sauce over the mackerel, garnish with lemon wedges and serve with asparagus and sugarsnap peas.

★ COOK'S TIPS
● *If the mackerel are large, make three shallow slashes on either side of the fish.*
● *To test whether the fish is cooked, prise the flesh from the backbone with a knife: it should be opaque and come away easily.*

Peppered Tuna with Olive and Herb Salsa

★

Preparation Time 15 minutes • Cooking Time 8–12 minutes • Serves 4 • Per Serving 398 calories, 32g fat (of which 12g saturates), 1g carbohydrate, 1.9g salt • Gluten Free • Dairy Free • Easy

1 tsp olive oil

zest and juice of 1 lime, plus lime
  wedges to serve

1 tbsp cracked mixed peppercorns

4 × 150g (5oz) tuna steaks

grilled tomatoes to serve

**FOR THE OLIVE AND HERB
  SALSA**

1 tbsp extra virgin olive oil

1 tbsp each pitted black and green
  olives, roughly chopped

zest and juice of ½ lemon

2 tbsp freshly chopped parsley

1 tbsp freshly chopped coriander

1 tbsp capers, roughly chopped

salt and ground black pepper

1 Put the olive oil into a large shallow bowl, add the lime zest and juice and peppercorns and stir to mix. Add the tuna and turn to coat in the oil.

2 Heat a non-stick griddle pan until hot. Cook the tuna steaks, two at a time, for 2–3 minutes on each side.

3 Meanwhile, put all the ingredients for the salsa into a bowl and stir to combine. Season to taste and mix well. Serve the tuna with the salsa, some grilled tomatoes, and lime wedges to squeeze over.

★ TRY SOMETHING
DIFFERENT
Use swordfish instead of tuna.

Grilled Sardines with Harissa

Preparation Time 10 minutes • Cooking Time 10–20 minutes • Serves 2 • Per Serving 292 calories, 21g fat (of which 4g saturates), 2g carbohydrate, 0.3g salt • **Gluten Free** • **Dairy Free** • **Easy**

1 garlic clove, crushed
2 tbsp olive oil
1–2 tsp harissa paste
4 whole sardines
salt and ground black pepper
tomato salad, watercress and lime
  wedges to serve

1 Preheat the grill to high. Put the garlic into a bowl. Add the oil and harissa, season to taste with salt and pepper and mix well.

2 Slash the sardines a couple of times on each side, then brush the harissa and oil mixture all over them. Grill for 5–10 minutes on each side until cooked through.

3 Serve with tomato salad and watercress, with lime wedges to squeeze over the sardines.

★ COOK'S TIP
Oily fish such as sardines are one of the best sources of essential heart-protecting omega-3 oils. Eat them at least once a week. Fresh Cornish sardines, when they are available, are a treat and are cheap. Look out for them at the fishmonger's or on the fresh fish counter at the supermarket.

Moules Marinière

★

Preparation Time 15 minutes • Cooking Time 20 minutes • Serves 4 • Per Serving 262 calories, 13g fat (of which 7g saturates), 2g carbohydrate, 0.9g salt • **Easy**

2kg (4½lb) fresh mussels, scrubbed, rinsed and beards removed (see page 122)
25g (1oz) butter
4 shallots, finely chopped
2 garlic cloves, crushed
200ml (7fl oz) dry white wine
2 tbsp freshly chopped flat-leafed parsley
100ml (3½fl oz) single cream
salt and ground black pepper
crusty bread to serve

1 Tap the mussels on the worksurface and discard any that do not close or have broken shells. Heat the butter in a large non-stick lidded frying pan and sauté the shallots over a medium-high heat for about 10 minutes or until soft.

2 Add the garlic, wine and half the parsley to the pan and bring to the boil. Tip in the mussels and reduce the heat a little. Cover and cook for about 5 minutes or until all the shells have opened; discard any mussels that don't open.

3 Lift out the mussels with a slotted spoon and put into serving bowls, then cover with foil to keep warm. Add the cream to the pan, season with salt and pepper and cook for 1–2 minutes to heat through.

4 Pour a little sauce over the mussels and sprinkle with the rest of the parsley. Serve immediately with crusty bread.

Clams with Chilli

★

Preparation Time 15 minutes • **Cooking Time** about 10 minutes • **Serves 4** • **Per Serving** 405 calories, 8g fat (of which 1g saturates), 60g carbohydrate, 2.3g salt • **Dairy Free** • **Easy**

300g (11oz) linguine pasta
2 tbsp olive oil
1 garlic clove, crushed
1 red chilli, seeded and finely
    chopped (see page 13)
4 tomatoes, seeded and chopped
900g (2lb) clams in their shells,
    washed and scrubbed
150ml (¼ pint) light dry white wine
2 tbsp freshly chopped parsley

1 Cook the linguine in lightly salted boiling water according to the pack instructions.

2 Meanwhile, heat the oil in a large pan. Add the garlic, chilli and tomatoes and fry for 4 minutes, stirring gently. Add the clams and wine. Cover the pan with a lid and cook over a high heat for 3–4 minutes until the clam shells spring open – discard any that remain closed.

3 Drain the pasta and return to the pan, then add the clams with the sauce and the parsley. Toss together gently and serve immediately.

Red Mullet with Cherry Tomatoes and Basil Oil

Preparation Time 10 minutes • Cooking Time about 40 minutes • Serves 6 • Per Serving (without potatoes) 282 calories, 17g fat (of which 2g saturates), 4g carbohydrates, 0.4g salt • **Dairy Free** • **Easy**

450g (1lb) cherry tomatoes,
  mixture of red and yellow
2 tbsp green peppercorns in brine,
  drained
8 garlic cloves, bruised not peeled
zest and juice of 1 small lemon
75ml (2½fl oz) basil oil
12 × 50g (2oz) red mullet fillets,
  descaled
a small handful of fresh basil leaves
salt and ground black pepper

1 Preheat the oven to 180°C (160°C fan oven) mark 4. Halve the larger tomatoes, then put them all into a shallow roasting tin. Add the peppercorns, garlic and lemon zest, drizzle with half the oil and bake for 20 minutes.

2 Add the fish to the tin and drizzle with the remaining oil. Cook for a further 15–20 minutes until golden and cooked through.

3 Pour the lemon juice over the fish and sprinkle with basil leaves, salt and pepper. Serve with steamed new potatoes.

Gurnard with a Summer Vegetable Broth

Preparation Time 20 minutes • Cooking Time about 20 minutes • Serves 6 • Per Serving 483 calories, 26g fat (of which 13g saturates), 38g carbohydrate, 1.6g salt • **Easy**

3–4 tbsp plain flour
zest of 1 lemon
6 × 200g (7oz) gurnard fillets
25g (1oz) butter
1 tsp oil
salt and ground black pepper

FOR THE VEGETABLE BROTH
a handful each peas in their pods,
   runner beans and baby leeks
1 tomato, seeded and chopped
18 cherry tomatoes
2 shallots, finely chopped
1 thyme sprig

1 bay leaf
450ml (¾ pint) light vegetable
   stock
leaves picked from 8 tarragon
   sprigs

1 Start the vegetable broth: pod the peas and put into a large bowl. Thickly slice the runner beans and leeks. Add both to the bowl with the chopped tomato and cherry tomatoes.

2 Put the flour on to a large plate. Add the lemon zest and season with salt and pepper. Toss the fish in the mixture and put to one side.

3 Heat the butter and oil in a large sauté pan for 1–2 minutes. Add the fish and fry in batches, skin side down, until crisp. Set aside.

4 Add the shallots to the pan and cook for 3–4 minutes until just golden. Add the thyme, bay leaf and stock and bring to the boil, then reduce the heat and simmer for 3–4 minutes.

5 Add the mixed vegetables. Roughly chop the tarragon leaves, add to the mixture and stir well, then cover and cook for 5 minutes or until the vegetables are tender. Add the fish and cook gently for 3–4 minutes to heat through, then serve.

Salmon and Bulgur Wheat Pilau

Preparation Time 5 minutes • Cooking Time 20 minutes • Serves 4 • Per Serving 323 calories, 11g fat (of which 2g saturates), 30g carbohydrate, 1.5g salt • Dairy Free • Easy

1 tbsp olive oil
1 onion, chopped
175g (6oz) bulgur wheat
450ml (¾ pint) vegetable stock
400g can pink salmon, drained and flaked
125g (4oz) spinach, roughly chopped
225g (8oz) frozen peas
zest and juice of 1 lemon
salt and ground black pepper

1 Heat the oil in a large pan, add the onion and cook until softened. Stir in the bulgur wheat to coat in the oil, then stir in the stock and bring to the boil. Cover the pan, reduce the heat and simmer for 10–15 minutes until the stock has been fully absorbed.

2 Stir in the salmon, spinach, peas and lemon juice and cook until the spinach has wilted and the salmon and peas are heated through. Season to taste with salt and pepper and sprinkle with lemon zest before serving.

★ TRY SOMETHING DIFFERENT
Instead of salmon, use 200g (7oz) cooked peeled prawns and 200g (7oz) cherry tomatoes.

Roasted Salmon

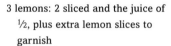

Preparation Time 20 minutes, plus cooling and chilling • Cooking Time about 30 minutes • Serves 20 •
Per Serving 366 calories, 27g fat (of which 10g saturates), 3g carbohydrate, 0.4g salt • Gluten Free • Easy

3 lemons: 2 sliced and the juice of
   ½, plus extra lemon slices to
   garnish
2 salmon sides, filleted, each 1.4kg
   (3lb), with skin on, boned and
   trimmed
2 tbsp dry white wine
salt and ground black pepper
cucumber slices and 2 large
   bunches of watercress to garnish

FOR THE DRESSING
500g carton crème fraîche
500g carton natural yogurt
2 tbsp horseradish sauce

3 tbsp freshly chopped tarragon
4 tbsp capers, roughly chopped,
   plus extra to garnish
¼ cucumber, halved lengthways,
   seeded and finely chopped, to
   garnish

1 Preheat the oven to 190°C (170°C
fan oven) mark 5. Take two pieces of
foil, each large enough to wrap one
side of salmon, and put a piece of
greaseproof paper on top of each.
Divide the lemon slices between
each piece of greaseproof paper and

lay the salmon on top, skin side up.
Season with salt and pepper, then
pour the lemon juice and wine over.

2 Score the skin of each salmon
fillet at 4cm (1½ in) intervals to mark
10 portions. Scrunch the foil loosely
around each fillet. Cook for
25 minutes or until the flesh is just
opaque. Unwrap the foil and cook
for a further 5 minutes or until the
skin is crisp. Leave the fish to cool
quickly in a cold place. Re-wrap
and chill.

3 Put all the dressing ingredients,
except the garnishes, into a bowl
and season with salt and pepper.
Mix well, then cover and chill.

4 Serve the salmon on a platter
garnished with lemon and
cucumber slices and watercress.
Garnish the dressing with capers
and chopped cucumber and serve
separately.

 COOK'S TIPS
● *There'll be a lot of hot liquid in the
parcel of salmon, so ask someone to
help you lift it out of the oven.*
● *To check the fish is cooked, ease a
knife into one of the slashes in the skin.
The flesh should look opaque and the
knife should come out hot.*
● *If you like, you can complete the
recipe to the end of step 3, then keep the
salmon wrapped and chilled for up to
one day. Garnish the salmon and
dressing before serving.*

Smoked Haddock Rarebit

Preparation Time 5 minutes • Cooking Time 10–15 minutes • Serves 4 • Per Serving 481 calories, 32g fat (of which 21g saturates), 16g carbohydrate, 3.4g salt • **Easy**

- 4 × 150g (5oz) smoked haddock fillets, skinned
- 4 slices bread
- 200g (7oz) spinach
- 2 large tomatoes, sliced
- 300g (11oz) low-fat crème fraîche
- salt and ground black pepper

1 Preheat the grill. Season the haddock fillets with salt and pepper and put into a shallow ovenproof dish. Grill for 6–8 minutes until opaque and cooked through.

2 Toast the bread on both sides until golden.

3 Wash the spinach, squeeze out the water and put into a pan. Cover and cook for 1–2 minutes until starting to wilt. Tip into a bowl.

4 Top each piece of toast with a piece of fish, then add the tomato slices and spinach. Spoon the crème fraîche over it and grill for 2–3 minutes to heat through. Season with pepper and serve immediately.

Cod Steaks with Fennel

Preparation Time 10 minutes, plus marinating • **Cooking Time** 30 minutes • **Serves 4** • **Per Serving** 209 calories, 6g fat (of which 1g saturates), 6g carbohydrate, 1.4g salt • **Dairy Free** • **Easy**

1 tbsp hoisin sauce
4 tbsp light soy sauce
4 tbsp dry vermouth
4 tbsp orange juice
½ tsp Chinese five-spice powder
½ tsp ground cumin
1 garlic clove, crushed
4 × 150g (5oz) thick cod fillets or steaks (see Cook's Tip)
1 tbsp vegetable oil
2 fennel bulbs, about 700g (1½lb), thinly sliced and tops put to one side
2 tsp sesame seeds

1 For the marinade, combine the hoisin sauce, soy sauce, vermouth, orange juice, five-spice powder, cumin and garlic. Put the cod into a shallow dish and pour the marinade over it. Cover and leave to marinate in a cool place for at least 1 hour.

2 Preheat the grill or a lightly oiled griddle. Remove the fish and put the marinade to one side. Cook the fish under the hot grill or on the hot griddle for 4 minutes, then turn over and cook for 3–4 minutes until cooked.

3 Heat the oil in a sauté pan. Add the fennel and cook briskly for 5–7 minutes until brown and beginning to soften. Add the marinade, bring to the boil and bubble until reduced and sticky.

4 Put the fish on a bed of fennel, spoon any pan juices around it and sprinkle with the sesame seeds. Garnish with the reserved fennel tops.

 COOK'S TIP
Ask your fishmonger to remove the scales from the cod's skin. When grilled, the skin will be crisp and delicious to eat.

Cod with Cherry Tomatoes

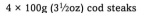

Preparation Time 15 minutes • **Cooking Time** 20–25 minutes • **Serves 4** • **Per Serving** 168 calories, 7g fat (of which 1g saturates), 8g carbohydrate, 0.2g salt • **Dairy Free** • **Easy**

4 × 100g (3½oz) cod steaks
1 tbsp plain flour
2 tbsp olive oil
1 small onion, sliced
1 large red chilli, seeded and
   chopped (see page 13)
1 garlic clove, crushed
250g (9oz) cherry tomatoes, halved
4 spring onions, chopped
2 tbsp freshly chopped coriander
salt and ground black pepper

1 Season the cod with salt and pepper, then dust lightly with the flour. Heat 1 tbsp oil in a large frying pan, add the onion and fry for 5–10 minutes until golden.

2 Pour the remaining oil into the pan. Add the cod and fry for 3 minutes on each side. Add the chilli, garlic, cherry tomatoes, spring onions and coriander and season with salt and pepper. Cover and continue to cook for 5–10 minutes until everything is heated through. Serve immediately.

★ TRY SOMETHING DIFFERENT
Use another white fish such as sea bass or pollack fillets instead of the cod.

Cod with Sweet Chilli Glaze

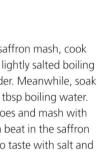

Preparation Time 10 minutes • Cooking Time 20 minutes • Serves 4 • Per Serving 193 calories, 1g fat
(of which trace saturates), 13g carbohydrate, 0.7g salt • Gluten Free • Easy

1 red chilli, seeded and finely
   chopped (see page 13)
2 tsp dark soy sauce
grated zest and juice of 1 lime
¼ tsp ground allspice or 6 allspice
   berries, crushed
50g (2oz) light muscovado sugar
4 thick cod fillets, with skin on,
   about 175g (6oz) each
finely sliced red chilli, finely sliced
   lime zest and lime wedges to
   garnish

FOR THE SAFFRON MASH
900g (2lb) potatoes, roughly
   chopped
a pinch of saffron threads
50g (2oz) butter
salt and ground black pepper

1 To make the saffron mash, cook
the potatoes in lightly salted boiling
water until tender. Meanwhile, soak
the saffron in 2 tbsp boiling water.
Drain the potatoes and mash with
the butter, then beat in the saffron
liquid. Season to taste with salt and
pepper.

2 Meanwhile, preheat the grill or
griddle pan until hot. Stir the
chopped chilli, soy sauce, lime zest
and juice, allspice and sugar
together.

3 Grill the cod for about 1 minute
on the flesh side. Turn skin side up
and grill for 1 minute. Spoon the
chilli glaze over it and grill for a
further 2–3 minutes until the skin
is crisp and golden.

4 Garnish with finely sliced chilli and
lime zest and the lime wedges.
Serve with the saffron mash.

Luxury Smoked Fish Pie

Preparation Time 30 minutes • Cooking Time 1 hour 20 minutes • Serves 4 • Per Serving 1057 calories, 63g fat (of which 34g saturates), 66g carbohydrate, 3.8g salt • **Easy**

1.1kg (2½lb) Desirée potatoes, cut into rough chunks
450ml (¾ pint) milk
125g (4oz) butter
125g (4oz) Cheddar, grated
75ml (2½fl oz) dry white wine
150ml (¼ pint) fish stock
450g (1lb) skinless smoked haddock fillet, undyed if possible, cut into wide strips
350g (12oz) skinless salmon fillet, cut into wide strips
40g (1½oz) plain flour
75ml (2½fl oz) double cream
1 tbsp capers, drained, rinsed and chopped
1½ tbsp freshly chopped flat-leafed parsley
2 medium eggs, hard-boiled
salt and ground black pepper

1 Preheat the oven to 180°C (160°C fan oven) mark 4. Put the potatoes into a pan of lightly salted water and bring to the boil, then cover the pan, reduce the heat and simmer until tender.

2 Warm 100ml (3½fl oz) milk. Drain the potatoes, then put back into the pan over a low heat for 2 minutes. Mash until smooth. Stir in 75g (3oz) butter, half the cheese and the warmed milk, then season with salt and pepper. Cover and put to one side.

3 Meanwhile, bring the wine, stock and remaining milk to the boil in a large wide pan. Add the haddock and salmon and return the liquid to the boil, then reduce the heat to poach the fish gently for 5 minutes or until it flakes easily. Lift the fish with a draining spoon into a 1.4 litre (2½ pint) deep ovenproof dish and flake with a fork if necessary. Put the cooking liquid to one side.

4 Melt the remaining butter in another pan, add the flour and stir until smooth, then cook for 2 minutes. Gradually add the fish liquid, whisking until smooth. Bring to the boil, stirring, and cook for 2 minutes or until thickened. Stir in the cream, capers and parsley and season to taste with salt and pepper.

5 Shell the eggs and chop roughly. Scatter over the fish, then pour in the sauce. Spoon the potato mixture on top, then sprinkle with the remaining cheese.

6 Bake the pie for 35–40 minutes until golden and bubbling at the edges. Serve hot.

Fish Stew

Preparation Time 15 minutes • Cooking Time about 30 minutes • Serves 4 • Per Serving 280 calories, 7g fat (of which 1g saturates), 34g carbohydrate, 0.3g salt • **Gluten Free** • **Dairy Free** • **Easy**

2 tbsp olive oil
1 onion, chopped
1 leek, trimmed and chopped
2 tsp smoked paprika
2 tbsp tomato purée
450g (1lb) cod or haddock, roughly chopped
125g (4oz) basmati rice
175ml (6fl oz) white wine
450ml (¾ pint) hot fish stock
200g (7oz) cooked and peeled king prawns
a large handful of spinach leaves
crusty bread to serve

1 Heat the oil in a large pan. Add the onion and leek and fry for 8–10 minutes until they start to soften. Add the smoked paprika and tomato purée and cook for 1–2 minutes.

2 Add the fish, rice, wine and hot stock. Bring to the boil, then cover the pan, reduce the heat and simmer for 10 minutes or until the fish is cooked through and the rice is tender. Add the prawns and cook for 1 minute or until heated through. Stir in the spinach until it wilts, then serve with chunks of bread.

★ TRY SOMETHING DIFFERENT
There are lots of alternatives to cod and haddock: try sea bass, gurnard, coley (saithe) or pollack.

Chinese-style Fish

Preparation Time 5 minutes • **Cooking Time** 10 minutes • **Serves 4** • **Per Serving** 150 calories, 3g fat (of which 1g saturates), 10g carbohydrate, 0.7g salt • **Dairy Free** • **Easy**

2 tsp sunflower oil
1 small onion, finely chopped
1 green chilli, seeded and finely
   chopped (see page 13)
2 courgettes, thinly sliced
125g (4oz) frozen peas, thawed
350g (12oz) skinless haddock fillet,
   cut into bite-size pieces
2 tsp lemon juice
4 tbsp hoisin sauce
lime wedges to serve

1 Heat the oil in a large non-stick frying pan. Add the onion, chilli, courgettes and peas and stir-fry over a high heat for 5 minutes or until the onion and courgettes begin to soften.

2 Add the fish to the pan with the lemon juice, hoisin sauce and 150ml (¼ pint) water. Bring to the boil, then reduce the heat and simmer, uncovered, for 2–3 minutes until the fish is cooked through. Serve with lime wedges.

★ TRY SOMETHING DIFFERENT
There are plenty of alternatives to haddock: try sea bass, sea bream or gurnard.

Poultry and Meat

Lemon Chicken

Preparation Time 2 minutes • **Cooking Time** 6–8 minutes • **Serves 4** • **Per Serving** 231 calories, 7g fat (of which 1g saturates), 13g carbohydrate. 0.2g salt • **Gluten Free** • **Easy**

4 small boneless, skinless chicken breasts, about 125g (4oz) each, cut into chunky strips
juice of 2 lemons
2 tbsp olive oil
4–6 tbsp demerara sugar
salt
green salad to serve

1 Put the chicken into a large bowl and season with salt. Add the lemon juice and oil and stir to mix.

2 Preheat the grill to medium. Spread out the chicken strips on a large flat baking sheet and sprinkle with half the sugar. Grill for 3–4 minutes until caramelised, then turn the chicken over, sprinkle with the remaining sugar and grill until the chicken is cooked through and golden.

3 Divide the chicken among four warmed plates and serve with a green salad.

⭐ TRY SOMETHING DIFFERENT
Instead of lemons, use limes. Knead them on the worktop for 30 seconds before squeezing so they give as much juice as possible.

Spiced One-pot Chicken

Preparation Time 10 minutes, plus marinating • Cooking Time 1 hour 10 minutes • Serves 6 • Per Serving 604 calories, 36g fat (of which 10g saturates), 20g carbohydrate, 0.5g salt • Dairy Free • Easy

3 tbsp Thai red curry paste

150ml (¼ pint) orange juice

2 garlic cloves, crushed

6 chicken pieces, 2.3kg (5lb) total
   weight, with bone in

700g (1½lb) squash or pumpkin,
   peeled and cut into 5cm (2in)
   cubes

5 red onions, quartered

2 tbsp capers, drained and chopped

salt and ground black pepper

1 Combine the curry paste, orange juice and garlic in a bowl. Put the chicken pieces in the marinade and leave to marinate for 15 minutes.

2 Preheat the oven to 220°C (200°C fan oven) mark 7. Put the vegetables into a large roasting tin, then remove the chicken from the marinade and arrange on top of the vegetables. Pour the marinade over it and season with salt and pepper. Mix everything together, so that it's covered with the marinade, then scatter with the capers.

3 Cook for 1 hour 10 minutes, turning from time to time, or until the chicken is cooked through and the skin is golden.

★ GET AHEAD

To prepare ahead Complete the recipe to the end of step 2. Cover and chill for up to one day.

To use Complete the recipe, but cook for a further 5–10 minutes.

Coronation Chicken

Preparation Time 20 minutes • Cooking Time about 50 minutes • Serves 6 • Per Serving 425 calories, 26g fat
(of which 4g saturates), 14g carbohydrate, 0.6g salt • **Easy**

1 tbsp vegetable oil
1 onion, chopped
1 tbsp ground coriander
1 tbsp ground cumin
1½ tsp ground turmeric
1½ tsp paprika
150ml (¼ pint) dry white wine
500ml (18fl oz) chicken stock
6 boneless, skinless chicken breasts
   or thighs
2 bay leaves
2 fresh thyme sprigs
2 fresh parsley sprigs
salt and ground black pepper
3–4 tbsp freshly chopped flat-leafed
   parsley to garnish

mixed leaf salad and French bread
   to serve

FOR THE DRESSING
150ml (¼ pint) mayonnaise
5 tbsp natural yogurt
2 tbsp mango chutney
125g (4oz) ready-to-eat dried
   apricots, chopped
juice of ½ lemon

1 Heat the oil in a large heavy-based pan, add the onion and fry for 5–10 minutes until softened and golden. Add the spices and cook, stirring, for 1–2 minutes.

2 Pour in the wine, bring to the boil and let it bubble for 5 minutes to reduce right down. Add the stock and bring to the boil again.

3 Season the chicken with salt and pepper, then add to the pan with the bay leaves and herb sprigs. Cover and bring to the boil. Reduce the heat to low and poach the chicken for 25 minutes or until cooked through. Cool quickly by plunging the base of the pan into a sink of cold water, replacing the water as it warms up.

4 Meanwhile, to make the dressing, mix the mayonnaise, yogurt and mango chutney in a bowl. Drain the cooled stock from the chicken and whisk 200ml (7fl oz) into the mayonnaise mixture. Add the apricots and lemon juice and season well.

5 Stir the chicken into the curried mayonnaise, then cover and chill until required. Scatter with chopped parsley and serve with a mixed leaf salad and French bread.

Coq au Vin

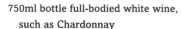

Preparation Time 45 minutes • Cooking Time about 1 hour • Serves 4 • Per Serving 787 calories, 51g fat (of which 22g saturates), 24g carbohydrate, 1.5g salt • **A Little Effort**

750ml bottle full-bodied white wine, such as Chardonnay
4 tbsp brandy
2 bouquet garni (see page 10)
1 garlic clove, bruised
flour to coat
1 chicken, about 1.4kg (3lb), jointed, or 2 boneless breasts, halved, plus 2 drumsticks and 2 thighs
125g (4oz) butter
125g (4oz) rindless unsmoked bacon rashers, cut into strips
225g (8oz) baby onions, peeled with root ends intact
225g (8oz) brown-cap mushrooms, halved, or quartered if large
25g (1oz) butter mixed with 25g (1oz) plain flour (beurre manié)
salt and ground black pepper
buttered noodles or rice to serve

1 Preheat the oven to 180°C (160°C fan oven) mark 4. Pour the wine and brandy into a pan. Add 1 bouquet garni and the garlic. Bring to the boil, then reduce the heat and simmer until reduced by half. Cool.

2 Season the flour with salt and pepper and use to coat the chicken joints lightly. Melt half the butter in a large frying pan. When foaming, add the chicken joints and brown all over (in batches if necessary). Transfer to a flameproof casserole. Add the bacon to the frying pan and fry until golden. Remove with a slotted spoon and add to the chicken.

3 Strain the cooled reduced wine mixture over the chicken and add the other bouquet garni. Bring to the boil, cover and cook in the oven for 30 minutes.

4 Meanwhile, melt the remaining butter in a frying pan and fry the onions until tender and lightly browned. Add the mushrooms and fry until softened.

5 Add the mushrooms and onions to the casserole, cover and cook for a further 10 minutes or until the chicken is tender. Lift out the chicken and vegetables with a slotted spoon and put into a warmed serving dish. Cover and keep warm.

6 Bring the cooking liquid in the casserole to the boil. Whisk in the beurre manié, a piece at a time, until the sauce is shiny and syrupy. Check the seasoning.

7 Pour the sauce over the chicken. Serve with buttered noodles or rice.

Chicken and Leek Pie

Preparation Time 15 minutes • **Cooking Time** 40–45 minutes • **Serves 4** • **Per Serving** 591 calories, 23g fat (of which 15g saturates), 54g carbohydrate, 0.3g salt • **Gluten Free** • **Easy**

5 large potatoes, chopped into
  chunks
200g (7oz) crème fraîche
3 boneless chicken breasts, with
  skin on, about 125g (4oz) each
3 large leeks, trimmed and chopped
  into chunks
about 10 fresh tarragon leaves,
  finely chopped
salt and ground black pepper

1 Preheat the oven to 200°C (180°C fan oven) mark 6. Put the potatoes into a pan of lightly salted cold water. Cover the pan and bring to the boil, then reduce the heat and simmer for 10–12 minutes until soft. Drain and put back into the pan. Add 1 tbsp crème fraîche, season with salt and pepper and mash well.

2 Meanwhile, heat a frying pan, add the chicken, skin side down, and fry gently for 5 minutes or until the skin is golden. Turn the chicken over and fry for 6–8 minutes. Remove the chicken from the pan and put on to a board. Tip the leeks into the pan and cook in the juices over a low heat for 5 minutes to soften.

3 Discard the chicken skin and cut the flesh into bite-size pieces (don't worry if it is not quite cooked through). Put the chicken back into the pan, stir in the remaining crème fraîche and heat for 2–3 minutes until bubbling. Stir in the tarragon and season with salt and pepper, then spoon into a 1.7 litre (3 pint) ovenproof dish and spread the mash on top.

4 Cook in the oven for 20–25 minutes until golden and heated through. Serve hot.

★ TRY SOMETHING DIFFERENT

● *To use leftover chicken or turkey, don't fry the meat at step 2. Add it to the pan with the crème fraîche at step 3. Cook the leeks in 2 tsp olive oil.*
● *For a different flavour, make the mash with 2 large potatoes and a small celeriac, that has been peeled, cut into chunks and cooked with the potato.*

Spanish Chicken Parcels

Preparation Time 15 minutes • Cooking Time about 30 minutes • Serves 6 • Per Serving 444 calories, 29g fat (of which 9g saturates), 4g carbohydrate, 3.1g salt • **Gluten Free** • **Dairy Free** • **Easy**

12 boneless, skinless chicken thighs, about 900g (2lb)
180g jar pimientos or roasted red peppers, drained
12 thin slices chorizo sausage
2 tbsp olive oil
1 onion, finely chopped
4 garlic cloves, crushed
225g can chopped tomatoes
4 tbsp dry sherry
18 queen green olives (see Cook's Tip)
salt and ground black pepper
rice or crusty bread to serve

1 Put the chicken thighs on a board, season well with salt and pepper and put a piece of pimiento or roasted pepper inside each one. Wrap a slice of chorizo around the outside and secure with two cocktail sticks. Put to one side.

2 Heat the oil in a pan over a medium heat and fry the onion for 10 minutes. Add the garlic and cook for 1 minute. Put the chicken parcels, chorizo side down, into the pan and brown them all over for 10–15 minutes.

3 Add the tomatoes and sherry to the pan and bring to the boil. Reduce the heat and simmer for 5 minutes or until the juices run clear when the chicken is pierced with a skewer. Add the olives and warm through. Remove the cocktail sticks and serve with rice or crusty bread.

★ COOK'S TIP
Queen green olives are large meaty olives with a mild flavour. Remember to tell people the olives still have stones.

Mediterranean Chicken

Preparation Time 5 minutes • Cooking Time 20 minutes • Serves 4 • Per Serving 223 calories, 7g fat (of which 1g saturates), 3g carbohydrate, 0.2g salt • **Gluten Free** • **Dairy Free** • **Easy**

1 red pepper, seeded and chopped
2 tbsp capers
2 tbsp freshly chopped rosemary
2 tbsp olive oil
4 skinless chicken breasts, about
    125g (4oz) each
salt and ground black pepper
rice or new potatoes to serve

1 Preheat the oven to 200°C (180°C fan oven) mark 6. Put the red pepper into a bowl with the capers, rosemary and oil. Season with salt and pepper and mix well.

2 Put the chicken breasts into an ovenproof dish and spoon the pepper mixture over the top. Roast for 15–20 minutes until the chicken is cooked through and the topping is hot. Serve with rice or new potatoes.

★ TRY SOMETHING DIFFERENT
Use chopped black olives instead of capers.

Chicken Tabbouleh with Tomato Dressing

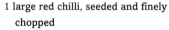

Preparation Time 50 minutes, plus marinating and soaking • Cooking Time 45 minutes • Serves 4 •
Per Serving 777 calories, 33g fat (of which 6g saturates), 50g carbohydrate, 0.6g salt • Dairy Free • Easy

1 large red chilli, seeded and finely
   chopped
3 garlic cloves, crushed
juice of 4 limes: about 8 tbsp juice
½ tsp ground turmeric
4 chicken breast quarters (breast
   and wing), about 300g (11oz)
   each, lightly scored
450g (1lb) tomatoes, preferably
   plum, chopped
2 tbsp capers
1 tbsp sugar
225g (8oz) bulgur wheat
125g (4oz) cucumber, chopped
50g (2oz) pinenuts, toasted
3 tbsp freshly chopped parsley
3 tbsp freshly chopped chives
50g (2oz) raisins
5 tbsp olive oil
225g (8oz) onions, thinly sliced
salt and ground black pepper
lime slices and fresh flat-leafed
   parsley to garnish

1 Put the chilli into a non-metallic bowl with the garlic, 3 tbsp lime juice and the turmeric. Add the chicken and stir well to coat. Cover the bowl, chill and leave to marinate for at least 3 hours.

2 Mix the tomatoes with the capers, 2 tbsp lime juice, the sugar and seasoning.

3 Put the bulgur wheat into a bowl, cover with 600ml (1 pint) boiling water and leave to soak for 30 minutes. Drain, then stir in the cucumber, pinenuts, herbs, raisins, remaining lime juice and 3 tbsp oil. Season.

4 Preheat the oven to 240°C (220°C fan oven) mark 9. Drain the chicken, putting the marinade to one side. Put, skin side up, in a roasting tin with the remaining oil and onions. Cook in the oven for 30–35 minutes until done. Put to one side. Add the tomato mixture and remaining marinade to the roasting tin and put back in the oven for 5 minutes.

5 Spoon the dressing over the chicken. Garnish with lime slices and parsley, if you like, and serve at room temperature with the tabbouleh.

★ COOK'S TIP
Bulgur wheat is grains of wheat that have been boiled until they crack, and then dried. It is reconstituted in water.

Tandoori Chicken with Cucumber Raita

Preparation Time 45 minutes, plus marinating • Cooking Time 20 minutes • Serves 4 • Per Serving 399 calories, 20g fat (of which 4g saturates), 15g carbohydrate, 2g salt • **Gluten Free** • **Easy**

4 tbsp groundnut oil, plus extra to oil
3 × 150g cartons natural yogurt
juice of ½ lemon
4 boneless, skinless chicken breasts, about 600g (1lb 5oz), cut into finger-width pieces
½ cucumber
salt and ground black pepper
mint leaves to garnish

FOR THE TANDOORI PASTE
24 garlic cloves, about 125g (4oz), crushed
5cm (2in) piece fresh root ginger, peeled and chopped
3 tbsp each coriander seeds, cumin seeds, ground fenugreek and paprika
3 red chillies, seeded and chopped (see page 13)
3 tsp English mustard
2 tbsp tomato purée
1 tsp salt

1 Put all the ingredients for the tandoori paste into a food processor with 8 tbsp water and blend to a paste. Divide the paste into three equal portions, freeze two (see Freezing Tip) and put the other in a large bowl.

2 To make the tandoori chicken, add 2 tbsp oil, 2 cartons of yogurt and the lemon juice to the paste. Add the chicken and stir well to coat. Cover the bowl, chill and leave to marinate for at least 4 hours.

3 Preheat the oven to 220°C (200°C fan oven) mark 7. Oil a roasting tin. Put the chicken in it, drizzle the remaining oil over the chicken and roast for 20 minutes or until cooked through.

4 Meanwhile, prepare the raita. Whisk the remaining carton of yogurt. Using a vegetable peeler, scrape the cucumber into very thin strips. Put the strips in a bowl and pour the whisked yogurt over them. Season, then chill until ready to serve. Garnish the cucumber raita with mint sprigs. Sprinkle the chicken with mint and serve with the raita.

★ FREEZING TIP
To freeze the paste At the end of step 1, put two of the portions of tandoori paste into separate freezer bags and freeze. They will keep for up to three months.
To use the frozen paste Put the paste in a microwave and cook on Defrost for 1 minute 20 seconds (based on 900W oven), or thaw at a cool room temperature for 1 hour.

Crispy Duck with Hot and Sweet Dip

Preparation Time 10 minutes • Cooking Time 1 hour • Serves 4 • Per Serving 504 calories, 29g fat (of which 6g saturates), 42g carbohydrate, 0.5g salt • **Gluten Free** • **Dairy Free** • **Easy**

8 small duck legs
2 pieces star anise
4 fat garlic cloves, sliced
1 dried red chilli
grated zest and juice of 1 orange
1 tbsp tamarind paste or lemon juice
fried garlic slivers, fried chilli pieces and star anise to garnish

FOR THE HOT AND SWEET DIP
200ml (7fl oz) white wine vinegar
150g (5oz) golden caster sugar
75g (3oz) each cucumber, spring onion and mango, cut into fine shreds
1 dried red chilli or ¼ tsp seeded and shredded red chilli (see page 13)

1 To make the hot and sweet dip, boil the vinegar and sugar together in a pan for 2 minutes, then stir in the cucumber, spring onion, mango and chilli. Transfer to a serving bowl and leave to cool.

2 Prick the duck legs all over with a skewer or fork. Put them into a large pan, cover with cold water and bring to the boil, then reduce the heat and simmer for 45 minutes.

3 Meanwhile, put the 2 star anise, garlic, chilli, orange zest and juice and tamarind paste or lemon juice in a blender and whiz to a paste. Preheat the grill.

4 Drain the duck and put, skin side down, on a foil-lined grill pan. Brush half the spice paste over the duck. Grill for 5 minutes, then turn skin side up and brush the remaining paste over it. Grill for a further 5–7 minutes until the duck skin is well charred and crisp.

5 Garnish with the fried garlic slivers, fried chilli pieces and star anise and serve with the hot and sweet dip.

Turkey, Pepper and Haricot Bean Casserole

Preparation Time 20 minutes, plus soaking • Cooking Time 1 hour 20 minutes • Serves 6 • Per Serving 326 calories, 6g fat (of which 1g saturates), 41g carbohydrate, 0.1g salt • Gluten Free • Dairy Free • Easy

350g (12oz) dried haricot beans, soaked in cold water overnight
2 large onions
2 small carrots, cut into chunks
1 bouquet garni (see page 10)
1 tbsp olive oil
2 red chillies, seeded and chopped (see page 13)
2 garlic cloves, crushed
350g (12oz) lean turkey meat, cut into bite-size pieces
1 large red pepper and 1 large orange pepper, both seeded and finely diced
2 courgettes, finely diced
400g can chopped tomatoes
1 tbsp sun-dried tomato paste
large handful of basil leaves
salt and ground black pepper

1 Drain the soaked haricot beans, put them into a large flameproof casserole and cover with fresh water. Quarter 1 onion and add to the casserole with the carrots and bouquet garni. Bring to the boil, then cover, reduce the heat and simmer for 45 minutes or until the beans are tender. Drain the beans, reserving 150ml (¼ pint) of the cooking liquid; discard the flavouring vegetables. Spoon the beans into a bowl and put to one side. Wipe out the casserole.

2 Finely slice the remaining onion. Heat the oil in the casserole, add the onion and cook gently for 5 minutes. Add the chillies and garlic and cook for 1 minute or until softened.

3 Add the turkey to the pan and stir-fry for 5 minutes, then add the diced peppers and courgettes and season well. Cover the casserole and cook for 5 minutes or until the vegetables are slightly softened.

4 Add the tomatoes and tomato paste, cover and bring to the boil. Add the haricot beans and reserved cooking liquid, then stir and season well. Cover the pan, reduce the heat and simmer for 15 minutes. Stir in the basil leaves just before serving.

Quick Steak Supper

Preparation Time 10 minutes • **Cooking Time** 10 minutes • **Serves 4** • **Per Serving** 452 calories, 17g fat (of which 6g saturates), 44g carbohydrate, 1.6g salt • **Easy**

2 sirloin steaks
3 tsp olive oil
4 large mushrooms, sliced
1 red onion, sliced
1 tbsp Dijon mustard
25g (1oz) butter
2 ciabattas, halved lengthways, then quartered, to make eight pieces
salt and ground black pepper
green salad to serve

1 Heat a griddle or large frying pan until very hot. Rub the steaks with 1 tsp oil, season with salt and pepper and fry for about 2 minutes on each side if you like your steak rare, or 3 minutes each side for medium-rare. Remove from the pan and leave to rest.

2 Heat the remaining oil in the pan. Add the mushrooms and onion and fry, stirring, for 5 minutes or until softened. Stir in the Dijon mustard and butter and take off the heat.

3 Toast the ciabatta pieces on both sides. Thinly slice the steaks and divide among four pieces of ciabatta. Top with the mushrooms, onion and remaining ciabatta and serve with a green salad.

★ TRY SOMETHING DIFFERENT
Instead of ciabatta, serve the steak with tagliatelle or other pasta.

Steak and Chips

Preparation Time 10 minutes • **Cooking Time** 35–45 minutes • **Serves 4** • **Per Serving** 318 calories, 13g fat (of which 5g saturates), 18g carbohydrate, 0.4g salt • **Gluten Free** • **Easy**

2 large potatoes, cut into chips
2 tbsp olive oil
4 sirloin steaks, 125g (4oz) each, fat trimmed
25g (1oz) Roquefort cheese, cut into four small pieces
salt and ground black pepper
watercress to garnish

1 Preheat the oven to 220°C (200°C fan oven) mark 7. Put the potato chips into a pan of lightly salted water. Bring to the boil, then reduce the heat and simmer for 4–5 minutes. Drain well.

2 Put the chips into a roasting tin, toss with 1 tbsp oil and cook in the oven, turning once, for 30–40 minutes until cooked through and golden.

3 When the chips are nearly done, heat a non-stick frying pan until really hot. Brush the remaining oil over the steaks and season with salt and pepper. Add to the pan and fry for 3 minutes on each side for medium-rare, or 2 minutes more if you prefer the meat well done. Put on to warmed plates, top each steak with a small piece of Roquefort while still hot and serve with the chips. Garnish with watercress.

Speedy Burgers

★

Preparation Time 10 minutes • Cooking Time 8–12 minutes • Serves 4 • Per Serving 80 calories, 20g fat (of which 8g saturates), 2g carbohydrate, 0.3g salt • **Gluten Free** • **Dairy Free** • **Easy**

450g (1lb) top-quality lean minced beef
1 onion, very finely chopped
1 tbsp dried Herbes de Provence
2 tsp sun-dried tomato paste
1 medium egg, beaten
ground black pepper
Chilli Coleslaw to serve (see Cook's Tip)

1 Put the minced beef, onion, herbs, tomato paste and beaten egg into a bowl and stir to combine. Season with pepper, then shape the mixture into four round burgers about 2cm (¾in) thick.

2 Preheat the grill or griddle pan. Cook the burgers for 4–6 minutes on each side. Serve with chilli coleslaw.

★ COOK'S TIP
Chilli Coleslaw
Put 3 peeled and finely shredded carrots into a large bowl. Add ½ finely shredded white cabbage, 1 finely sliced, seeded red pepper and ½ chopped cucumber. In a small bowl, mix together ½ tsp harissa, 100g (3½oz) natural yogurt and 1 tbsp white wine vinegar. Add to the vegetables and toss well.

Chilli Steak and Corn on the Cob

Preparation Time 5 minutes • Cooking Time 15 minutes • Serves 4 • Per Serving 564 calories, 31g fat (of which 14g saturates), 33g carbohydrate, 1.4g salt • **Gluten Free** • **Easy**

50g (2oz) butter, softened
1 large red chilli, seeded and finely
   chopped (see page 13)
1 garlic clove, crushed
25g (1oz) freshly grated Parmesan
1 tbsp finely chopped fresh basil
4 corn on the cob, each cut into
   three pieces
1 tbsp olive oil
4 sirloin steaks, about 150g (5oz)
   each
mixed green salad to serve

1 Put the butter into a bowl and beat with a wooden spoon. Add the chilli, garlic, Parmesan and basil and mix everything together. Cover and chill to firm up.

2 Meanwhile, bring a large pan of water to the boil. Add the corn, cover to bring back to the boil, then reduce the heat and simmer, half-covered, for about 10 minutes or until tender. Drain well.

3 Heat the oil in a large frying pan or griddle over a medium heat. Cook the steaks for 2–3 minutes on each side for medium-rare, 3–4 minutes for medium.

4 Divide the corn and steaks among four warmed plates and top with the chilled butter. Serve immediately, with a mixed green salad.

Beef Stroganoff

Preparation Time 10 minutes • Cooking Time about 20 minutes • Serves 4 • Per Serving 750 calories, 60g fat (of which 35g saturates), 3g carbohydrate, 0.5g salt • Gluten Free • Easy

700g (1½lb) rump or fillet steak, trimmed
50g (2oz) unsalted butter or 4 tbsp olive oil
1 onion, thinly sliced
225g (8oz) brown-cap mushrooms, sliced
3 tbsp brandy
1 tsp French mustard
200ml (7fl oz) crème fraîche
100ml (3½fl oz) double cream
3 tbsp freshly chopped flat-leafed parsley
salt and ground black pepper
rice or noodles to serve

1 Cut the steak into strips about 5mm (¼in) wide and 5cm (2in) long.

2 Heat half the butter or oil in a large heavy frying pan over a medium heat. Add the onion and cook gently for 10 minutes or until soft and golden. Remove with a slotted spoon and put to one side. Add the mushrooms to the pan and cook, stirring, for 2–3 minutes until golden brown; remove and put to one side.

3 Increase the heat and add the remaining butter or oil to the pan. Quickly fry the meat, in two or three batches, for 2–3 minutes, stirring constantly to ensure even browning. Remove from the pan. Add the brandy to the pan and allow it to bubble to reduce.

4 Put all the meat, onion and mushrooms back into the pan. Reduce the heat and stir in the mustard, crème fraîche and cream. Heat through, stir in most of the parsley and season with salt and pepper. Serve with rice or noodles, with the remaining parsley scattered over the top.

★ FREEZING TIP
To freeze *Complete the recipe, transfer to a freezerproof container, cool, label and freeze for up to three months.*
To use *Thaw overnight in the fridge. Put in a pan, cover and bring to the boil; reduce the heat to low and simmer until piping hot.*

Braised Beef with Bacon and Mushrooms

Preparation Time 20 minutes • Cooking Time about 3½ hours • Serves 4 • Per Serving 535 calories, 25g fat (of which 9g saturates), 29g carbohydrate, 1.6g salt • **Dairy Free** • **Easy**

175g (6oz) smoked pancetta or smoked streaky bacon, cut into cubes
2 medium leeks, trimmed and thickly sliced
1 tbsp olive oil
450g (1lb) braising steak, cut into 5cm (2in) pieces
1 large onion, finely chopped
2 carrots and 2 parsnips, thickly sliced
1 tbsp plain flour
300ml (½ pint) red wine
1–2 tbsp redcurrant jelly
125g (4oz) chestnut mushrooms, halved
salt and ground black pepper
freshly chopped flat-leafed parsley to garnish

1 Preheat the oven to 170°C (150°C fan oven) mark 3. Fry the pancetta or bacon in a shallow flameproof casserole for 2–3 minutes until golden. Add the leeks and cook for 2 minutes or until the leeks are just beginning to colour. Remove with a slotted spoon and put to one side.

2 Heat the oil in the casserole and fry the beef in batches for 2–3 minutes until a rich golden colour on all sides. Remove from the casserole and put to one side. Add the onion and fry over a gentle heat for 5 minutes or until golden. Stir in the carrots and parsnips and fry for 1–2 minutes.

3 Put the beef back into the casserole and stir in the flour to soak up the juices. Gradually add the red wine and 300ml (½ pint) water, then stir in the redcurrant jelly. Season with pepper and bring to the boil. Cover with a tight-fitting lid and cook in the oven for 2 hours.

4 Stir in the fried leeks, pancetta and mushrooms, re-cover and cook for a further 1 hour or until everything is tender. Serve scattered with chopped flat-leafed parsley.

★ FREEZING TIP
To freeze *Put into a freezerproof container, cool and freeze for up to three months.*
To use *Thaw overnight at cool room temperature. Preheat the oven to 180°C (160°C fan oven) mark 4. Bring to the boil on the hob, cover tightly and reheat in the oven for 30 minutes or until piping hot.*

★ COOK'S TIP
Leeks can trap a lot of fine soil, so need to be washed thoroughly: trim the ends of the leaves, then cut a cross about 7.5cm (3in) into the white part and hold under cold running water.

Beef with Beer and Mushrooms

★

Preparation Time 15 minutes • Cooking Time 2¾–3 hours • Serves 4 • Per Serving 450 calories, 22g fat
(of which 8g saturates), 21g carbohydrate, 0.6g salt • **Gluten Free** • **Dairy Free** • **Easy**

700g (1½lb) braising steak, cut into
    large chunks about 5cm (2in)
    across
2 tsp plain gluten-free flour
2 tbsp oil
25g (1oz) butter
2 large onions, finely sliced
225g (8oz) carrots, cut into large
    sticks
200ml (7fl oz) Guinness
300ml (½ pint) vegetable stock
2 tsp tomato purée
2 tsp English mustard
2 tsp light muscovado sugar
225g (8oz) large field mushrooms

salt and ground black pepper
mashed potatoes and rocket leaves
    to serve

1 Preheat the oven to 150°C (130°C fan oven) mark 2. Toss the meat in the flour. Heat the oil and butter in a large casserole dish over a medium heat and sear the meat, a few pieces at a time, until brown all over. Lift out each batch as soon as it is browned and put to one side. The flavour and colour of the finished casserole depend on the meat taking on a good deep colour now. Stir the onions into the casserole and cook for about 10 minutes.

2 Return all the meat to the casserole, add the carrots, then stir in the Guinness, stock, tomato purée, mustard, sugar and plenty of seasoning. Bring to the boil and stir well, then cover tightly with foil or a lid and simmer gently in the oven for 1½ hours.

3 Stir the whole mushrooms into the casserole and return to the oven for a further 45 minutes–1 hour until the meat is meltingly tender. Serve with mashed potatoes and rocket leaves.

Braised Beef with Mustard and Capers

Preparation Time 15 minutes • Cooking Time 2 hours 20 minutes, plus cooling • Serves 4 • Per Serving 391 calories, 19g fat (of which 7g saturates), 10g carbohydrate, 1.5g salt • **Easy**

50g (2oz) can anchovy fillets in oil, drained, chopped and oil put to one side
olive oil
700g (1½lb) braising steak, cut into small strips
2 large Spanish onions, thinly sliced
2 tbsp capers
1 tsp English mustard
6 fresh thyme sprigs
20g pack fresh flat-leafed parsley, roughly chopped
salt and ground black pepper
mashed potato or green salad and crusty bread to serve

1 Preheat the oven to 170°C (150°C fan oven) mark 3. Measure the anchovy oil into a deep flameproof casserole, then make up to 3 tbsp with the olive oil. Heat the oil and sear the meat, a few pieces at a time, until brown all over. Lift out each batch as soon as it is browned and put to one side. When all the meat has been browned, pour 4 tbsp cold water into the empty casserole and stir to loosen any bits on the bottom.

2 Put the meat back into the pan and add the onions, anchovies, capers, mustard, half the thyme and all but 1 tbsp parsley. Stir until thoroughly mixed.

3 Tear off a sheet of greaseproof paper big enough to cover the pan. Crumple it up and wet it under the cold tap. Squeeze out most of the water, open it out and press down over the surface of the meat.

4 Cover with a tight-fitting lid and cook in the oven for 2 hours or until the beef is meltingly tender. Check the casserole after 1 hour to make sure it's still moist. If it looks dry, add a little water.

5 Adjust for seasoning, then stir in the remaining parsley and thyme. Serve with mashed potato or a green salad and crusty bread.

★ COOK'S TIP
To make a deliciously easy mash, put four baking potatoes into the oven when you put in the casserole. Leave to bake for 2 hours. Cut each potato in half and use a fork to scrape out the flesh into a bowl. Add 50g (2oz) butter and season well with salt and pepper – the potato will be soft enough to mash with the fork.

Steak and Onion Puff Pie

Preparation Time 30 minutes • Cooking Time about 2½ hours • Serves 4 • Per Serving 1036 calories, 67g fat (of which 10g saturates), 65g carbohydrate, 1.4g salt • **Easy**

3 tbsp vegetable oil
2 onions, sliced
900g (2lb) casserole beef, cut into chunks
3 tbsp plain flour
500ml (17fl oz) hot beef stock
2 fresh rosemary sprigs, bruised
flour to dust
500g pack puff pastry
1 medium egg, beaten, to glaze
salt and ground black pepper

1 Preheat the oven to 170°C (150°C fan oven) mark 3.

2 Heat 1 tbsp oil in a large flameproof casserole and sauté the onions for 10 minutes or until golden. Lift out and put to one side. Sear the meat in the same casserole, in batches, using more oil as necessary, until brown all over. Lift out each batch as soon as it is browned and put to one side. Add the flour to the casserole and cook for 1–2 minutes to brown. Return the onions and beef to the casserole and add the hot stock and the rosemary. Season well with salt and pepper. Cover and bring to the boil, then cook in the oven for 1½ hours or until the meat is tender.

3 About 30 minutes before the end of the cooking time, lightly dust a worksurface with flour and roll out the pastry. Cut out a lid using a 1.1 litre (2 pint) pie dish as a template, or use four 300ml (½ pint) dishes and cut out four lids. Put on a baking sheet and chill.

4 Remove the casserole from the oven. Increase the heat to 220°C (200°C fan oven) mark 7. Pour the casserole into the pie dish (or dishes), brush the edge with water and put on the pastry lid. Press lightly to seal. Lightly score the top and brush with the egg. Put the dish back on the baking sheet. Bake for 30 minutes or until the pastry is risen and golden. Serve immediately.

★ FREEZING TIP
To freeze *Complete the recipe to the end of step 3. Cool the casserole quickly. Roll out the pastry as step 4. Put the beef mixture into a pie dish. Brush the dish edge with water, put on the pastry and press down lightly to seal. Score the pastry. Cover with clingfilm and freeze for up to three months.*
To use *Thaw overnight at cool room temperature or in the fridge. Lightly score the pastry, brush with beaten egg and cook at 220°C (200°C fan oven) mark 7 for 35 minutes or until the pastry is brown and the filling piping hot.*

Steak and Kidney Pie

Preparation Time 40 minutes, plus cooling • Cooking Time about 1½ hours • Serves 6 • Per Serving 565 calories, 36g fat (of which 8g saturates), 26g carbohydrate, 0.9g salt • Easy

700g (1½lb) stewing steak, cut into cubes and seasoned
2 tbsp plain flour, plus extra to dust
3 tbsp vegetable oil
25g (1oz) butter
1 small onion, finely chopped
175g (6oz) ox kidney, cut into small pieces
150g (5oz) flat mushrooms, cut into large chunks
a small pinch of cayenne pepper
1 tsp anchovy essence
350g (12oz) puff pastry, thawed if frozen
1 large egg, beaten with a pinch of salt, to glaze
salt and ground black pepper

1 Preheat the oven to 170°C (150°C fan oven) mark 3. Toss half the steak with half the flour. Heat the oil in a flameproof non-stick casserole and add the butter. Fry the steak in batches until brown. Lift out each batch as soon as it is browned and put to one side.

2 Add the onion and cook gently until soft. Return the steak to the casserole with 200ml (7fl oz) water, the kidney, mushrooms, cayenne and anchovy essence. Bring to the boil, then cover the pan, reduce the heat and simmer for 5 minutes.

3 Transfer to the oven and cook for 1 hour or until tender. The sauce should be syrupy. If not, transfer the casserole to the hob, remove the lid,

bring to the boil and bubble for 5 minutes to reduce the liquid. Leave the steak mixture to cool.

4 Preheat the oven to 200°C (180°C fan oven) mark 6. Put the steak and kidney mixture into a 900ml (1½ pint) pie dish. Pile it high to support the pastry lid.

5 Roll out the pastry on a lightly floured surface to 5mm (¼in) thick. Cut off four to six strips, 1cm (½in) wide. Dampen the edge of the dish with cold water, then press the pastry strips on to the edge.

Dampen the pastry rim and lay the sheet of pastry on top. Press the surfaces together, trim the edge and press down with the back of a knife to seal. Brush the pastry with the glaze and score with the back of a knife. Put the pie dish on a baking sheet and cook for 30 minutes or until the pastry is golden brown and the filling is hot to the centre.

Calf's Liver with Fried Sage and Balsamic Vinegar

Preparation Time 5 minutes • **Cooking Time** 5 minutes • **Serves 4** • **Per Serving** 88 calories, 6g fat (of which 3g saturates), trace carbohydrate, 0.1g salt • **Gluten Free** • **Dairy Free** • **Easy**

15g (½oz) butter plus a little olive
    oil for frying
12 sage leaves
4 thin slices of calf's liver
1–2 tbsp balsamic vinegar
rice, with freshly chopped parsley
    stirred through, or grilled polenta
    to serve

1 Preheat the oven to a low setting. Melt the butter with a little oil in a heavy-based frying pan and when hot add the sage leaves. Cook briefly for 1 minute or so until crisp. Remove, put in a single layer in a shallow dish and keep hot in the oven.

2 Add a little extra oil to the pan, put in two slices of calf's liver and cook quickly for 30 seconds on each side over a high heat. Remove and place on a plate while you quickly cook the remaining two slices.

3 Return all four slices to the pan, splash the balsamic vinegar over the top and cook for another minute or so. Serve immediately with rice or grilled polenta.

American Sticky Ribs

Preparation Time 10 minutes • **Cooking Time** about 1 hour • **Serves 4** • **Per Serving** 485 calories, 30g fat (of which 12g saturates), 12g carbohydrate, 1.3g salt • **Dairy Free** • **Easy**

900g (2lb) lean pork spare ribs
125g (4oz) hoisin sauce
2 tbsp mild clear honey
2 tsp English mustard
3 tsp white wine or cider vinegar
4 tbsp tomato ketchup
2 garlic cloves, crushed
4 tbsp fresh apple or orange juice
coleslaw, onion rings and orange
   wedges to serve

1 Preheat the oven to 200°C (180°C fan oven) mark 6. Line a large tin with a double layer of foil and spread the ribs over the base.

2 Whisk together the remaining ingredients in a bowl, then spoon over the pork – it may look as though there isn't enough liquid but the ribs will release plenty of juices as they cook.

3 Cover with foil and cook for 20 minutes. Turn the ribs over, then put back in the oven, uncovered. Cook for 40–45 minutes, basting occasionally, until they are dark golden and sticky, and most of the liquid has gone. Serve hot, with coleslaw, onion rings and orange wedges.

Sausages with Roasted Onions and Potatoes

Preparation Time 10 minutes • Cooking Time 1 hour 20 minutes • Serves 4 • Per Serving 640 calories, 40g fat (of which 12g saturates), 55g carbohydrate, 2.5g salt • **Dairy Free** • **Easy**

900g (2lb) Desiree potatoes, cut
   into wedges
4 tbsp olive oil
3–4 fresh rosemary sprigs
   (optional)
2 red onions, each cut into eight
   wedges
8 sausages
salt and ground black pepper

1 Preheat the oven to 220°C (200°C fan oven) mark 7. Put the potatoes in a roasting tin – they should sit in one layer. Drizzle with the oil and season with salt and pepper. Toss well to coat the potatoes in oil, then put the rosemary on top, if using, and roast in the oven for 20 minutes.

2 Remove the roasting tin from the oven and add the onion wedges. Toss again to coat the onions and turn the potatoes. Put the sausages

in between the potatoes and onions. Return the tin to the oven for 1 hour.

3 Divide among four plates and serve immediately.

 COOK'S TIP
If you can't find Desiree potatoes, use Maris Piper or King Edward instead.

Sausages with Red Onion Marmalade

Preparation Time 15 minutes • Cooking Time 35 minutes • Serves 6 • Per Serving 390 calories, 25g fat
(of which 10g saturates), 14g carbohydrate, 0.3g salt • **Gluten Free** • **Dairy Free** • **Easy**

12 gluten-free (100% meat) venison
   sausages
6 tsp redcurrant jelly
Colcannon (see Cook's Tip) or
   mashed potatoes to serve

**FOR THE RED ONION
   MARMALADE**
400g (14oz) red onions, chopped
2 tbsp olive oil
4 tbsp red wine vinegar
2 tbsp demerara sugar
1 tsp juniper berries, crushed

1 Preheat the oven to 220°C (200°C
fan oven) mark 7. Put the sausages
into a small roasting tin. Roast in the
oven for 35 minutes, turning once
(after 25 minutes, spoon the
redcurrant jelly over them and
continue to cook).

2 Meanwhile, make the red onion
marmalade. Gently fry the onions in
the oil for 15–20 minutes. Add the
vinegar, sugar and juniper berries
and cook for a further 5 minutes or
until the onions are very tender.
Serve the sausages with the red
onion marmalade and colcannon.

★ COOK'S TIP
Colcannon
*Cook 1.1kg (2½lb) floury potatoes in
lightly salted boiling water until tender.
Drain in a colander. Add 25g (1oz) butter
to the pan and gently fry 1 chopped leek
or 100g (3½oz) shredded cabbage until
soft. Return the potato to the pan with
another 25g (1oz) butter and a handful of
chopped herbs such as parsley, chives
and thyme. Heat through gently.*

Spicy Pork and Bean Stew

Preparation Time 15 minutes • **Cooking Time** 50–55 minutes • **Serves 4** • **Per Serving** 348 calories, 14g fat (of which 3g saturates), 27g carbohydrate, 1.5g salt • **Gluten Free** • **Dairy Free** • **Easy**

3 tbsp olive oil

400g (14oz) pork escalopes, cut into cubes

1 red onion, sliced

2 leeks, trimmed and cut into chunks

2 celery sticks, cut into chunks

1 tbsp harissa paste

1 tbsp tomato purée

400g (14oz) cherry tomatoes

300ml (½ pint) hot vegetable or chicken stock

400g can cannellini beans, drained and rinsed

1 marinated red pepper, sliced

salt and ground black pepper

freshly chopped flat-leafed parsley to garnish

Greek yogurt, lemon wedges and bread to serve

1 Preheat the oven to 180°C (160°C fan oven) mark 4. Heat 2 tbsp oil in a flameproof casserole and fry the pork in batches until golden. Remove from the pan and put to one side.

2 Heat the remaining oil in the pan and fry the onion for 5–10 minutes until softened. Add the leeks and celery and cook for about 5 minutes. Return the pork to the pan, and add the harissa and tomato purée. Cook for 1–2 minutes, stirring all the time. Add the tomatoes and hot stock and season well with salt and pepper. Bring to the boil, then transfer to the oven and cook for 25 minutes.

3 Add the drained beans and red pepper to the mixture and put back into the oven for 5 minutes to warm through. Garnish with parsley and serve with a dollop of Greek yogurt, lemon wedges for squeezing over the stew, and chunks of crusty baguette or wholegrain bread.

Winter Hotpot

Preparation Time 20 minutes, plus marinating • **Cooking Time** 2 hours 20 minutes • **Serves 8** • **Per Serving** 613 calories, 26g fat (of which 9g saturates), 42g carbohydrate, 1.7g salt • **Easy**

- **1.4kg (3lb) boned shoulder of pork, cut into 2.5cm (1in) cubes**
- **6 garlic cloves, crushed**
- **7 tbsp olive oil**
- **2 tbsp red wine vinegar**
- **4 tbsp soft brown sugar**
- **2 tsp minced chilli or a few drops of chilli sauce**
- **3 tsp dried oregano**
- **2 tsp dried thyme**
- **450g (1lb) onions, halved and sliced**
- **2 tbsp tomato purée**
- **2 × 400g cans haricot or flageolet beans, drained and juice put to one side**
- **2 × 400g cans chopped tomatoes**
- **300ml (½ pint) red wine**
- **4 bay leaves**
- **25g (1oz) butter**
- **125g (4oz) white breadcrumbs from French bread or ciabatta**
- **125g (4oz) grated Gruyère cheese**
- **fresh thyme sprigs to garnish**

1 Put the pork into a large bowl with the garlic, 2 tbsp oil, the vinegar, sugar, chilli, 2 tsp oregano, all the thyme and salt and pepper. Combine all the ingredients, then cover, chill and leave to marinate for at least 8 hours. Drain the pork, putting the marinade to one side.

2 Preheat the oven to 180°C (160°C fan oven) mark 4. Heat 3 tbsp oil in a large flameproof casserole and fry the pork in batches until well browned and sealed on all sides. Put to one side.

3 Add the remaining oil with the onions and cook for 10 minutes over a high heat, stirring occasionally, or until they are soft and caramelized. Add the tomato purée and cook for 1 minute. Put the meat back into the casserole with the drained bean juice, tomatoes, wine, bay leaves and the reserved marinade. Bring to the boil, stirring, then cover and cook in the oven for 2 hours or until the pork is very tender.

4 About 20 minutes before the end of the cooking time, stir in the beans. Increase the oven temperature to 200°C (180°C fan oven) mark 6 and move the pork to a lower shelf.

5 Heat the butter in a roasting tin, add the breadcrumbs, the remaining oregano and seasoning. Brown on the top shelf of the oven for 10 minutes. Sprinkle the hotpot with the breadcrumbs and grated cheese. Garnish with thyme sprigs and serve.

Braised Lamb Shanks with Cannellini Beans

Preparation Time 15 minutes • Cooking Time 3 hours • Serves 6 • Per Serving 382 calories, 18g fat (of which 6g saturates), 29g carbohydrate, 1.2g salt • Gluten Free • Dairy Free • Easy

3 tbsp olive oil
6 lamb shanks
1 large onion, chopped
3 carrots, sliced
3 celery sticks, sliced
2 garlic cloves, crushed
2 × 400g cans chopped tomatoes
125ml (4fl oz) balsamic vinegar
2 bay leaves
2 × 400g cans cannellini beans,
  drained and rinsed
salt and ground black pepper
steamed spinach to serve

1 Preheat the oven to 170°C (150°C fan oven) mark 3. Heat the oil in a large flameproof casserole and brown the lamb shanks, in two batches, all over. Remove and put to one side.

2 Add the onion, carrots, celery and garlic to the casserole and cook gently until softened and just beginning to colour.

3 Return the lamb to the casserole and add the tomatoes and vinegar, giving the mixture a good stir.

Season with salt and pepper and add the bay leaves. Bring to a simmer, then cover, reduce the heat and cook on the hob for 5 minutes.

4 Transfer to the oven and cook for 1½–2 hours until the lamb shanks are nearly tender.

5 Remove the casserole from the oven and add the cannellini beans. Cover and return to the oven for a further 30 minutes. Serve with steamed spinach.

Warming Winter Casserole

Preparation Time 20 minutes • Cooking Time 1 hour • Serves 4 • Per Serving 407 calories, 16g fat (of which 3g saturates), 32g carbohydrate, 1g salt • **Dairy Free** • **Easy**

2 tbsp olive oil

500g (1lb 2oz) pork fillet, cut into cubes

1 onion, finely chopped

2 garlic cloves, finely chopped

1 tsp ground cinnamon

1 tbsp ground coriander

1 tsp ground cumin

2.5cm (1in) piece fresh root ginger, peeled and grated

400g can mixed beans or chickpeas, drained

1 red pepper, seeded and sliced

50g (2oz) ready-to-eat dried apricots, roughly chopped

300ml (½ pint) chicken stock

25g (1oz) flaked almonds, toasted

salt and ground black pepper

freshly chopped flat-leafed parsley to garnish

brown basmati rice to serve

1 Heat 1 tbsp oil in a flameproof casserole, add the pork and fry, in batches, until brown all over. Remove and put to one side. Add the remaining oil, then add the onion and cook for 10 minutes or until softened. Return the pork to the casserole, add the garlic, spices and ginger and cook for 2 minutes.

2 Add the mixed beans, red pepper, apricots and stock. Season well with salt and pepper, then stir and bring to the boil. Reduce the heat to the lowest setting, cover the pan and simmer for 40 minutes, adding a little extra stock if it begins to looks dry.

3 Sprinkle with the almonds and parsley, check the seasoning and serve with brown basmati rice.

★ TRY SOMETHING DIFFERENT
Instead of pork, use the same quantity of lean lamb, such as leg, trimmed of excess fat and cut into cubes.

Lamb Chops with Crispy Garlic Potatoes

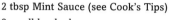

Preparation Time 10 minutes • Cooking Time 20 minutes • Serves 4 • Per Serving 835 calories, 45g fat
(of which 19g saturates), 22g carbohydrate, 0.7g salt • **Gluten Free** • **Dairy Free** • **Easy**

2 tbsp Mint Sauce (see Cook's Tips)
8 small lamb chops
3 medium potatoes, cut into 5mm
  (¼in) slices
2 tbsp Garlic-infused Olive Oil (see
  Cook's Tips)
1 tbsp olive oil
salt and ground black pepper
steamed green beans to serve

1 Spread the mint sauce over the lamb chops and leave to marinate while you prepare the potatoes.

2 Boil the potatoes in a pan of lightly salted water for 2 minutes or until just starting to soften. Drain, tip back into the pan and season, then add the garlic oil and toss to combine.

3 Meanwhile, heat the olive oil in a large frying pan and fry the chops for 4–5 minutes on each side until just cooked, adding a splash of

boiling water to the pan to make a sauce. Remove the chops and sauce from the pan and keep warm.

4 Add the potatoes to the pan. Fry over a medium heat for 10–12 minutes until crisp and golden. Divide the potatoes, chops and sauce among four warmed plates and serve with green beans.

★ COOK'S TIPS
Mint Sauce
Finely chop 20g (³⁄₄oz) fresh mint and mix with 1 tbsp each olive oil and white wine vinegar.
Garlic-infused Olive Oil
Gently heat 2 tbsp olive oil with peeled sliced garlic for 5 minutes and use immediately. Do not store.

Lamb Steaks with Mixed Bean Salad

★

Preparation Time 5 minutes • **Cooking Time** 10 minutes • **Serves 4** • **Per Serving** 545 calories, 20g fat (of which 7g saturates), 30g carbohydrate, 1.8g salt • **Gluten Free** • **Dairy Free** • **Easy**

150g (5oz) sunblush tomatoes in oil
1 garlic clove, crushed
2 rosemary sprigs
4 × 175g (6oz) leg of lamb steaks
½ small red onion, finely sliced
2 × 400g cans mixed beans, drained and rinsed
large handful of rocket
salt and ground black pepper

1 Preheat the grill to high. Drain the sunblush tomatoes, reserving the oil. Put the garlic into a large shallow dish with 1 tbsp oil from the tomatoes. Strip the leaves from the rosemary sprigs, snip into small pieces and add to the dish. Season with salt and pepper, then add the lamb and toss to coat.

2 Grill the lamb for 3–4 minutes on each side until cooked but still just pink. Meanwhile, roughly chop the tomatoes and put into a pan with the onion, beans, remaining rosemary, the rocket and a further 1 tbsp oil from the tomatoes. Warm through until the rocket starts to wilt. Serve the lamb steaks with the bean salad on warmed plates.

Spiced Lamb with Lentils

★

Preparation Time 10 minutes • Cooking Time 2 hours • Serves 4 • Per Serving 459 calories, 17g fat (of which 6g saturates), 36g carbohydrate, 1.1g salt • **Gluten Free** • **Dairy Free** • **Easy**

1 tbsp sunflower oil
8 lamb chops, trimmed of all fat
2 onions, sliced
1 tsp each paprika and ground
    cinnamon
400g can lentils, drained
400g can chickpeas, drained and
    rinsed
300ml (½ pint) lamb or chicken
    stock
salt and ground black pepper

1 Preheat the oven to 180°C (160°C fan oven) mark 4. Heat the oil in a large non-stick frying pan, add the chops and brown on both sides. Remove from the pan with a slotted spoon.

2 Add the onions, paprika and cinnamon and fry for 2–3 minutes. Stir in the lentils and chickpeas and season, then spoon into a shallow 2 litre (3½ pint) ovenproof dish.

3 Put the chops on top of the onion and lentil mixture and pour the stock over them.

4 Cover the dish tightly and cook in the oven for 1½ hours or until the chops are tender. Uncover and cook for 30 minutes or until lightly browned.

Italian Lamb Stew

Preparation Time 35 minutes • **Cooking Time** 3¾ hours • **Serves 6** • **Per Serving** 824 calories, 41g fat (of which 12g saturates), 25g carbohydrate, 1.8g salt • **Easy**

2 half legs of lamb (knuckle ends)
2 tbsp olive oil
75g (3oz) butter
275g (10oz) onions, finely chopped
175g (6oz) carrots, finely chopped
175g (6oz) celery, finely chopped
2 tbsp dried porcini pieces (see
    Cook's Tip) or 125g (4oz) brown-
    cap mushrooms, finely chopped
9 pieces sun-dried tomato, finely
    chopped
150g (5oz) Italian-style spicy
    sausage or salami, thickly sliced
600ml (1 pint) red wine
400g (14oz) passata
600ml (1 pint) vegetable stock
125g (4oz) pasta shapes
15g (½oz) freshly grated Parmesan
freshly chopped flat-leafed parsley
    to garnish

1 Preheat the oven to 240°C (220°C fan oven) mark 9. Put the lamb in a large roasting tin and drizzle 1 tbsp oil over it. Roast for 35 minutes.

2 Meanwhile, melt the butter with the remaining oil in a large flameproof casserole. Stir in the onions, carrots and celery and cook, stirring, for 10–15 minutes until golden and soft. Stir in the porcini pieces or mushrooms and cook for a further 2–3 minutes. Add the sun-dried tomatoes, sausage, wine, passata and stock to the pan and bring to the boil, then reduce the heat and simmer for 10 minutes.

3 Lift the lamb from the roasting tin, add to the tomato sauce and cover with a tight-fitting lid. Reduce the oven temperature to 170°C (150°C fan oven) mark 3. Put the casserole into the oven and cook the stew for 3 hours or until the lamb is falling off the bone.

4 Lift the lamb from the casserole and put on to a deep, heatproof serving dish. Cover loosely with foil and keep warm in a low oven.

5 Put the casserole on the hob, stir in the pasta and bring back to the boil. Reduce the heat and simmer for 10 minutes or until the pasta is tender. Stir in the Parmesan just before serving. Carve the lamb into large pieces and serve with the pasta sauce, garnished with parsley.

★ COOK'S TIP
Look out for bags of dried porcini pieces in supermarkets. These chopped dried mushrooms are ideal for adding a rich depth of flavour to stews or casseroles.

Irish Stew

Preparation Time 15 minutes • **Cooking Time** 2 hours • **Serves** 4 • **Per Serving** 419 calories, 20g fat (of which 9g saturates), 24g carbohydrate, 0.6g salt • **Dairy Free** • **Easy**

700g (1½lb) middle neck lamb
  cutlets, fat trimmed
2 onions, thinly sliced
450g (1lb) potatoes, thinly sliced
1 tbsp freshly chopped parsley, plus
  extra to garnish
1 tbsp dried thyme
300ml (½ pint) lamb stock

1 Preheat the oven to 170°C (150°C fan oven) mark 3. Layer the meat, onions and potatoes in a deep casserole dish, sprinkling some herbs and seasoning between each layer. Finish with a layer of potato, overlapping the slices neatly.

2 Pour the stock over the potatoes, then cover with greaseproof paper and a lid. Cook for about 2 hours or until the meat is tender.

3 Preheat the grill. Take the lid off the casserole and remove the paper. Put under the grill and brown the top. Sprinkle with parsley and serve immediately.

Shepherd's Pie

Preparation Time 20 minutes • **Cooking Time** about 55 minutes • **Serves 4** • **Per Serving** 513 calories, 27g fat (of which 11g saturates), 44g carbohydrate, 0.6g salt • **Easy**

2 tbsp sunflower oil
450g (1lb) lamb mince
1 large onion, chopped
50g (2oz) mushrooms, sliced
2 carrots, chopped
2 tbsp plain flour
1 tbsp tomato purée
1 bay leaf
300ml (½ pint) lamb stock
700g (1½lb) potatoes, cut into large
    chunks
25g (1oz) butter
75ml (2½fl oz) milk
50g (2oz) Lancashire cheese or
    Cheddar, crumbled (optional)
salt and ground black pepper

1 Heat half the oil in a large pan and brown the mince over a medium to high heat – do this in batches, otherwise the meat will steam rather than fry. Remove with a slotted spoon and put to one side.

2 Turn the heat to low and add the remaining oil. Gently fry the onion, mushrooms and carrots for 10 minutes or until softened. Stir in the flour and tomato purée and cook for 1 minute. Return the meat to the pan and add the bay leaf. Pour in the stock and bring to the boil, then cover the pan, reduce the heat and simmer for 25 minutes.

3 Preheat the oven to 200°C (180°C fan oven) mark 6. Cook the potatoes in lightly salted boiling water for 20 minutes or until tender. Drain and leave to stand in the colander for 2 minutes to steam dry. Melt the butter with the milk in the potato pan and add the cooked potatoes. Mash until smooth.

4 Spoon the lamb mixture into a 1.7 litre (3 pint) ovenproof casserole dish. Remove the bay leaf and check the seasoning. Cover with the mashed potato and sprinkle the

cheese over it, if using. Bake for 15–20 minutes until bubbling and golden. Serve immediately with green vegetables.

Roasts

Roast Chicken with Stuffing and Gravy

Preparation Time 30 minutes • Cooking Time about 1 hour 20 minutes, plus resting • Serves 5 • Per Serving 682 calories, 49g fat (of which 21g saturates), 17g carbohydrate, 1g salt • **Easy**

1.4kg (3lb) chicken
2 garlic cloves
1 onion, cut into wedges
2 tsp sea salt
2 tsp ground black pepper
4 sprigs each fresh parsley and
    tarragon
2 bay leaves
50g (2oz) butter, cut into cubes
salt and ground black pepper

FOR THE STUFFING
40g (1½oz) butter
1 small onion, chopped
1 garlic clove, crushed
75g (3oz) fresh white breadcrumbs
finely grated zest and juice of
    1 small lemon, halves reserved
    for the chicken
2 tbsp each freshly chopped
    flat-leafed parsley and tarragon
1 medium egg yolk

FOR THE GRAVY
200ml (7fl oz) white wine
1 tbsp Dijon mustard
450ml (¾ pint) hot chicken stock
25g (1oz) butter, mixed with 25g
    (1oz) plain flour (beurre manié)

1 Preheat the oven to 190°C (170°C fan oven) mark 5. To make the stuffing, melt the butter in a pan and fry the onion and garlic for 5–10 minutes until soft. Cool, then add the remaining ingredients, stirring in the egg yolk last. Season well with salt and pepper.

2 Put the chicken on a board, breast upwards, then put the garlic, onion, reserved lemon halves and half the salt, pepper and herb sprigs into the body cavity.

3 Lift the loose skin at the neck and fill the cavity with stuffing. Turn the bird on to its breast and pull the neck flap over the opening to cover the stuffing. Rest the wing tips across it and truss the chicken. Weigh the stuffed bird to calculate the cooking time, and allow 20 minutes per 450g (1lb), plus an extra 20 minutes.

4 Put the chicken on a rack in a roasting tin. Season, then add the remaining herbs and the bay leaves. Dot with the butter and roast, basting halfway through, until cooked and the juices run clear when the thickest part of the thigh is pierced with a skewer.

5 Put the chicken on a serving dish and cover with foil. Leave to rest while you make the gravy. Pour off all but about 3 tbsp fat from the tin, put the tin over a high heat, add the wine and boil for 2 minutes. Add the mustard and hot stock and bring back to the boil. Gradually whisk in knobs of the butter mixture until smooth, then season with salt and pepper. Carve the chicken and serve with the stuffing and gravy.

Herb Chicken with Roasted Vegetables

★

Preparation Time 15 minutes, plus marinating • Cooking Time 40 minutes • Serves 4 • Per Serving 453 calories, 29g fat (of which 7g saturates), 10g carbohydrate, 0.3g salt • **Gluten Free** • **Dairy Free** • **Easy**

2 garlic cloves
25g (1oz) fresh basil
25g (1oz) fresh mint
8 fresh lemon thyme sprigs
4 tbsp olive oil
4 whole chicken legs (drumsticks
    and thighs)
1 small aubergine, chopped
200g (7oz) baby plum tomatoes
2 red peppers, seeded and chopped
2 courgettes, sliced
juice of 1 lemon
salt and ground black pepper
green salad to serve

1 Whiz the garlic, two-thirds of the basil and mint and the leaves from 4 lemon thyme sprigs in a food processor, adding half the oil gradually until the mixture forms a thick paste. (Alternatively, use a mortar and pestle.)

2 Rub the paste over the chicken legs, then put into a bowl. Cover, then chill and leave to marinate for at least 30 minutes.

3 Preheat the oven to 200°C (180° fan oven) mark 6. Put the aubergine, plum tomatoes, red peppers and courgettes into a large roasting tin with the remaining oil and season with salt and pepper. Toss to coat. Add the chicken and roast for 30–40 minutes until the vegetables are tender and the chicken is cooked through.

4 Squeeze the lemon juice over the chicken and stir in the remaining herbs. Serve immediately with a crisp green salad.

Poussins with Pancetta, Artichoke and Potato Salad

Preparation Time 20 minutes, plus overnight marinating • **Cooking Time** 1 hour 40 minutes, plus resting • **Serves 6**
Per Serving 442 calories, 27g fat (of which 8g saturates), 13g carbohydrate, 1.5g salt • **Gluten Free** • **Dairy Free** • **Easy**

grated zest of 1 lemon

5 large fresh rosemary sprigs,
    leaves stripped

4 tbsp white wine vinegar

150ml (¼ pint) fruity white wine

4 garlic cloves, crushed

3 tbsp chopped fresh oregano or
    a pinch of dried oregano

290g jar marinated artichokes,
    drained, oil reserved

3 poussins, each weighing about
    450g (1lb)

½ tsp cayenne pepper

450g (1lb) new potatoes, quartered

225g (8oz) pancetta or prosciutto or
    streaky bacon, roughly chopped

350g (12oz) peppery salad leaves,
    such as watercress, mustard leaf
    and rocket, washed and dried

salt and ground black pepper

1 Put the lemon zest and rosemary leaves into a large bowl with the vinegar, wine, garlic, oregano and 4 tbsp oil from the artichokes. Stir well. Using a fork, pierce the skin of the poussins in five or six places, then season well with black pepper and the cayenne pepper. Put the birds, breast side down, in the bowl and spoon the marinade over them. Cover and chill overnight.

2 Cook the potatoes in lightly salted boiling water for 2 minutes. Drain. Preheat the oven to 200°C (180°C fan oven) mark 6.

3 Lift the poussins from the marinade and place, breast side up, in a large roasting tin. Scatter the potatoes, pancetta and artichokes around them and pour the marinade over. Cook for 1½ hours, basting occasionally, or until golden and cooked through.

4 Cut each poussin in half lengthways and keep warm. Toss the salad leaves with about 5 tbsp warm cooking juices. Arrange the leaves on warmed plates, then top with the potatoes, pancetta, artichokes and poussins.

 COOK'S TIP
Use the oil drained from the artichokes to make a salad dressing.

Spiced Roast Turkey

Preparation Time 30 minutes • Cooking Time 3 hours, plus resting • Serves 8 • Per Serving 611 calories, 40g fat (of which 16g saturates), 12g carbohydrate, 2.0g salt • **Easy**

4.5kg (10lb) oven-ready turkey
Pork, Spinach and Apple Stuffing
    (see Cook's Tip), cooled
2 tsp Cajun spice seasoning
150g (5oz) butter, softened
salt and ground black pepper
herbs to garnish

FOR THE SAUSAGES
8 sausages
16 thin rashers streaky bacon

1 Loosen the skin at the neck end of the turkey, ease your fingers up between the skin and the breast and, using a small, sharp knife, remove the wishbone.

2 Preheat the oven to 190°C (170°C fan oven) mark 5. Season the inside of the turkey, then spoon the cold stuffing into the neck end only. Neaten the shape, turn the bird over and secure the neck skin with skewers or cocktail sticks. Weigh the turkey to calculate the cooking time, and allow 20 minutes per 450g (1lb), plus an extra 20 minutes.

3 Put the turkey in a roasting tin. Mix the spice with the butter, smear it over the turkey and season. Cover with a tent of foil. Roast for about 3 hours, basting occasionally. If the legs were tied together, loosen after the first hour so that they cook more evenly.

4 Twist each sausage in half and cut to make two mini sausages. Stretch the bacon rashers by running the blunt side of a kitchen knife along each rasher (this stops them shrinking too much when they're cooked). Roll a rasher around each mini sausage. Put into a small roasting tin or around the turkey and cook for about 1 hour. Remove the foil from the turkey 45 minutes before the end of the cooking time.

5 When the turkey is cooked, tip the bird so the juices run into the tin, then put it on a warmed serving plate with the sausages. Cover loosely with foil and leave to rest for 20–30 minutes before carving. Garnish with herbs.

★ COOK'S TIP
Pork, Spinach and Apple Stuffing
Heat 2 tbsp olive oil in a frying pan, add 150g (5oz) finely chopped onion and cook for 10 minutes or until soft. Increase the heat, add 225g (8oz) fresh spinach, torn into pieces if the leaves are large, and cook until wilted. Add 2 sharp apples, such as Granny Smith's, peeled, cored and cut into chunks, and cook, stirring, for 2–3 minutes, then put to one side to cool. When the mixture is cold, add 400g (14oz) pork sausagemeat, the coarsely grated zest of 1 lemon, 1 tbsp freshly chopped thyme, 100g (3½oz) fresh white breadcrumbs and 2 large beaten eggs, then season with salt and ground black pepper and stir until evenly mixed. Serves 8.

Turkey Crown with Orange

Preparation Time 20 minutes • Cooking Time 2½ hours, plus resting • Serves 8 • Per Serving 181 calories, 6g fat (of which 3g saturates), 3g carbohydrate, 0.2g salt • Easy

2 onions, sliced

2 bay leaves, plus extra to garnish

2.7kg (6lb) oven-ready turkey crown

40g (1½oz) butter, softened

1 lemon, halved

2 tbsp chicken seasoning

2 oranges, halved

150ml (¼ pint) dry white wine or chicken stock

1 Preheat the oven to 190°C (170°C fan oven) mark 5. Spread the onions in a flameproof roasting tin, add the bay leaves and sit the turkey on top. Spread the butter over the turkey breast, then squeeze the lemon over it. Put the lemon halves in the tin. Sprinkle the chicken seasoning over the turkey and then put the orange halves in the tin, around the turkey.

2 Pour the wine or stock into the roasting tin, with 250ml (9fl oz) hot water. Cover the turkey loosely with a large sheet of foil. Make sure it's completely covered, but with enough space between the foil and the turkey for air to circulate.

3 Roast for 2 hours or until the turkey is cooked through and the juices run clear when the thickest part of the thigh is pierced with a skewer. Remove the foil and put back in the oven for 30 minutes or until golden.

4 Lift the turkey on to a warmed carving dish, cover loosely with foil and leave to rest for 15 minutes before carving.

Goose with Roasted Apples

Preparation Time 30 minutes • **Cooking Time** 4¼ hours, plus resting • **Serves 8** • **Per Serving** 646 calories, 41g fat (of which 12g saturates), 11g carbohydrate, 1g salt • **Dairy Free** • **Easy**

6 small red onions, halved

7 small red eating apples, unpeeled, halved

5kg (11lb) oven-ready goose, washed, dried and seasoned inside and out

1 small bunch of fresh sage

1 small bunch of fresh rosemary

1 bay leaf

salt and ground black pepper

FOR THE GRAVY

1 tbsp plain flour

300ml (½ pint) red wine

200ml (7fl oz) Giblet Stock (see Cook's Tip)

1 Preheat the oven to 230°C (210°C fan oven) mark 8. Put half an onion and half an apple inside the goose with half the sage and rosemary and the bay leaf. Tie the legs together with string. Push a long skewer through the wings to tuck them in. Put the goose, breast side up, on a rack in a roasting tin. Prick the breast all over and season with salt and pepper. Put the remaining onions around the bird, then cover with foil.

2 Roast for 30 minutes, then take the goose out of the oven and baste with the fat that has run off. Remove and reserve any excess fat. Reduce the oven temperature to 190°C (170°C fan oven) mark 5.

3 Put the goose back in the oven and roast for a further 1½ hours, removing any excess fat every 20–30 minutes. Remove the foil. Remove excess fat, then add the remaining apples. Sprinkle the goose with the remaining herbs and roast for a further 1 hour. Transfer to a warmed serving plate, cover with foil and leave to rest for 30 minutes. Remove the apples and onions and keep warm.

4 To make the gravy, pour out all but 1 tbsp of the fat from the tin, stir in the flour, then add the wine and stock. Bring to the boil and cook, stirring all the time, for 5 minutes. Carve the goose, cut the roast apples into wedges and serve with the goose, onions and gravy.

★ COOK'S TIP
Giblet Stock

Put the turkey giblets, 1 onion, quartered, 1 carrot, halved, 1 celery stick, halved, 6 black peppercorns and 1 bay leaf into a large pan and add 1.4 litres (2½ pints) cold water. Cover and bring to the boil, then reduce the heat and simmer for 30 minutes–1 hour, skimming occasionally. Strain through a sieve into a bowl and cool quickly. This can be made in advance: cover and chill for up to two days. Makes 1.3 litres (2¼ pints).

Roast Duck with Orange Sauce

Preparation Time 50 minutes • **Cooking Time** 1 hour 40 minutes, plus resting • **Serves 4** • **Per Serving** 561 calories, 38g fat (of which 9g saturates), 20g carbohydrate, 0.5g salt • **Dairy Free** • **Easy**

2 large oranges
2 large fresh thyme sprigs
2.3kg (5lb) duck, preferably with giblets
4 tbsp vegetable oil
2 shallots, chopped
1 tsp plain flour
600ml (1 pint) home-made chicken stock
25g (1oz) caster sugar
2 tbsp red wine vinegar
100ml (3½fl oz) fresh orange juice
100ml (3½fl oz) fruity German white wine
2 tbsp orange liqueur, such as Grand Marnier (optional)
1 tbsp lemon juice
salt and ground black pepper
glazed orange wedges (see Cook's Tip) to garnish
mangetouts and broccoli to serve

1 Preheat the oven to 200°C (180°C fan oven) mark 6. Using a zester, remove strips of zest from the oranges. Put half the zest into a pan of cold water, bring to the boil, drain and put to one side. Remove the pith from both oranges and cut the flesh into segments.

2 Put the thyme and unblanched orange zest inside the duck; season. Rub the skin with 2 tbsp oil, sprinkle with salt and place, breast side up, on a rack over a roasting tin. Roast, basting every 20 minutes, for 1¼–1½ hours until just cooked and the juices run clear when the thickest part of the thigh is pierced with a skewer. After 30 minutes, turn breast side down, then cook breast side up for the last 10 minutes.

3 Meanwhile, cut the gizzard, heart and neck into pieces. Heat the remaining 2 tbsp oil in a heavy-based pan, add the giblets and fry until dark brown. Add the chopped shallots and flour and cook for 1 minute. Pour in the stock and bring to the boil, then bubble until reduced by half. Strain.

4 Put the sugar and vinegar in a heavy-based pan over a low heat until the sugar dissolves. Increase the heat and cook until it forms a dark caramel. Pour in the orange juice and stir. Cool, cover and put to one side.

5 Lift the duck off the rack and keep it warm. Skim all the fat off the juices to leave about 3 tbsp sediment. Stir the wine into the sediment, bring to the boil and bubble for 5 minutes or until syrupy. Add the stock mixture and orange mixture and bring back to the boil, then bubble until syrupy, skimming if necessary. To serve the sauce, add the blanched orange zest and segments. Add Grand Marnier, if using, and lemon juice to taste.

6 Carve the duck and garnish with mint and glazed orange wedges. Serve with the orange sauce, mangetouts and broccoli.

★ COOK'S TIP
To glaze oranges, quarter them or cut into wedges, dust with a little caster sugar and grill until caramelised.

Fillet of Beef en Croûte

★

Preparation Time 1 hour, plus soaking and chilling • **Cooking Time** about 1 hour 20 minutes, plus resting • Serves 6 •
Per Serving 802 calories, 53g fat (of which 15g saturates), 27g carbohydrate, 2.4g salt • **For the Confident Cook**

1–1.4kg (2¼–3lb) fillet of beef,
   trimmed
50g (2oz) butter
2 shallots, chopped
15g (½oz) dried porcini
   mushrooms, soaked in 100ml
   (3½fl oz) boiling water
2 garlic cloves, chopped
225g (8oz) flat mushrooms, finely
   chopped
2 tsp freshly chopped thyme, plus
   extra sprigs to garnish
175g (6oz) chicken liver pâté
175g (6oz) thinly sliced Parma ham
375g ready-rolled puff pastry
plain flour to dust
1 medium egg, beaten
salt and ground black pepper
Red Wine Sauce (see Cook's Tip) to
   serve

1 Season the beef with salt and pepper. Melt 25g (1oz) butter in a large frying pan and, when foaming, add the beef and cook for 4–5 minutes to brown all over. Transfer to a plate and leave to cool.

2 Melt the remaining butter in a pan, add the shallots and cook for 1 minute. Drain the porcini mushrooms, reserving the liquid, and chop them. Add them to the pan with the garlic, the reserved liquid and the fresh mushrooms. Increase the heat and cook until the liquid has evaporated, then season with salt and pepper and add the thyme. Leave to cool.

3 Put the pâté into a bowl and beat until smooth. Add the mushroom mixture and stir well until thoroughly combined. Check the seasoning. Spread half the mushroom mixture evenly over one side of the beef. Lay half the Parma ham on a length of clingfilm, overlapping the slices. Invert the mushroom-topped beef on to the ham. Spread the remaining mushroom mixture on the other side of the beef, then lay the rest of the Parma ham, also overlapping, on top of the mushroom mixture. Wrap the beef in the clingfilm to form a firm sausage shape and chill for 30 minutes. Preheat the oven to 220°C (200°C fan oven) mark 7.

4 Cut off one-third of the pastry and roll out on a lightly floured surface to 3mm (⅛ in) thick and 2.5cm (1in) larger all around than the beef. Prick all over with a fork. Transfer to a baking sheet and bake for 12–15 minutes until brown and crisp. Cool on a wire rack, then trim to the size of the beef and place on a baking sheet. Remove the clingfilm from the beef, brush with the egg and place on the cooked pastry.

5 Roll out the remaining pastry to a 25.5 x 30.5cm (10 x 12in) rectangle. Roll a lattice pastry cutter over it and gently ease the lattice open. Cover the beef with the lattice, tuck the ends under and seal the edges. Brush with the beaten egg, then cook for 40 minutes for rare to medium-rare, 45 minutes for medium. Leave to rest for 10 minutes before carving. Garnish with thyme and serve with Red Wine Sauce.

★ COOK'S TIP
Red Wine Sauce
Soften 350g (12oz) finely chopped shallots in 2 tbsp olive oil for 5 minutes. Add 3 chopped garlic cloves and 3 tbsp tomato purée and cook for 1 minute, then add 2 tbsp balsamic vinegar. Simmer briskly until reduced to almost nothing, then add 200ml (7fl oz) red wine and reduce by half. Pour in 600ml (1 pint) beef stock and simmer until reduced by one-third.

Classic Roast Beef with Yorkshire Puddings

Preparation Time 20 minutes • **Cooking Time** about 1½ hours, plus resting • **Serves 8** • **Per Serving** 510 calories, 24g fat (of which 9g saturates), 16g carbohydrate, 0.5g salt • **Easy**

1 boned and rolled rib, sirloin, rump or topside of beef, about 1.8kg (4lb)
1 tbsp plain flour
1 tbsp mustard powder
salt and ground black pepper
fresh thyme sprigs to garnish
vegetables to serve

FOR THE YORKSHIRE PUDDING
125g (4oz) plain flour
½ tsp salt
300ml (½ pint) milk
2 eggs

FOR THE GRAVY
150ml (¼ pint) red wine
600ml (1 pint) beef stock

1 Preheat the oven to 230°C (210°C fan oven) mark 8. Put the beef in a roasting tin, thickest part of the fat uppermost. Mix the flour with the mustard powder, salt and pepper. Rub the mixture over the beef.

2 Roast the beef in the middle of the oven for 30 minutes.

3 Baste the beef and reduce the oven temperature to 190°C (170°C fan oven) mark 5. Cook for a further 1 hour, approximately, basting occasionally.

4 Meanwhile, prepare the Yorkshire pudding batter. Sift the flour and salt into a bowl. Mix in half the milk, then add the eggs and season with pepper. Beat until smooth, then whisk in the rest of the milk.

5 Put the beef on a warmed carving dish, cover loosely with foil and leave to rest in a warm place. Increase the oven temperature to 220°C (200°C fan oven) mark 7.

6 Pour off about 3 tbsp fat from the roasting tin and use to grease 8–12 individual Yorkshire pudding tins. Heat in the oven for 5 minutes or until the fat is almost smoking. Pour the Yorkshire batter into the tins. Bake for 15–20 minutes until well risen, golden and crisp.

7 Meanwhile, make the gravy. Skim off any remaining fat from the roasting tin. Put the tin on the hob, add the wine and boil until syrupy. Pour in the stock and, again, boil until syrupy – there should be about 450ml (¾ pint) gravy. Taste and adjust the seasoning.

8 Carve the beef into slices. Garnish with thyme, serve with the gravy, Yorkshire puddings and vegetables of your choice.

Roast Rib of Beef

★

Preparation Time 5 minutes • Cooking Time 2½ hours, plus resting • Serves 8 • Per Serving 807 calories, 53g fat
(of which 24g saturates), 2g carbohydrate, 0.5g salt • **Dairy Free** • **Easy**

2-bone rib of beef, about 2.5–2.7kg
   (5½–6lb)
1 tbsp plain flour
1 tbsp mustard powder
150ml ¼ pint) red wine
600ml (1 pint) beef stock
600ml (1 pint) water from parboiled
   potatoes
salt and ground black pepper
Yorkshire Puddings (see page 209),
   roasted root vegetables and a
   green vegetable to serve

1 Preheat the oven to 230°C (210°C fan oven) mark 8. Put the beef, fat side up, in a roasting tin just large enough to hold the joint. Mix the flour and mustard together in a small bowl and season with salt and pepper, then rub the mixture over the beef. Roast in the centre of the oven for 30 minutes.

2 Move the beef to a lower shelf, near the bottom of the oven. Turn the oven down to 220°C (200°C fan oven) mark 7 and continue to roast for a further 2 hours, basting occasionally.

3 Put the beef on a carving dish, cover loosely with foil and leave to rest while you make the gravy. Skim off most of the fat from the roasting tin. Put the roasting tin on the hob, pour in the wine and boil vigorously until very syrupy. Pour in the stock and, again, boil until syrupy. Add the vegetable water and boil until syrupy. There should be about 450ml (¾ pint) gravy. Taste and adjust the seasoning.

4 Remove the rib bone and carve the beef. Serve with gravy, Yorkshire puddings and vegetables.

Stuffed Topside of Beef

Preparation Time 35 minutes, plus marinating • **Cooking Time** 1–1¼ hours, plus resting • **Serves 6** •
Per Serving 535 calories, 29g fat (of which 10g saturates), 13g carbohydrate, 1.4g salt • **Gluten Free** • **Dairy Free** • **Easy**

1.4kg (3lb) topside or top rump of
   beef
1 tbsp balsamic vinegar
2 tbsp white wine vinegar
3 tbsp olive oil
3 tbsp freshly chopped marjoram or
   thyme
2 red peppers, cored, seeded and
   quartered
75g (3oz) fresh spinach, cooked and
   well drained
75g (3oz) pitted black olives,
   chopped
50g (2oz) smoked ham, chopped
75g (3oz) raisins or sultanas
salt and ground black pepper
roast potatoes and vegetables
   to serve

1 Make a deep cut along the beef to create a pocket and put the joint into a dish. Combine the vinegars, oil, marjoram or thyme and some black pepper. Pour over the beef and into the pocket. Marinate in a cool place for 4–6 hours, or overnight.

2 Grill the peppers, skin side up, under a hot grill until the skins are charred. Cool in a covered bowl, then remove the skins.

3 Squeeze excess water from the spinach, then chop and put into a bowl with the olives, ham and raisins or sultanas. Mix well and season with salt and pepper.

4 Preheat the oven to 190°C (170°C fan oven) mark 5. Line the pocket of the beef with the peppers, keeping back two pepper quarters for the gravy. Spoon the spinach mixture into the pocket and spread evenly. Reshape the meat and tie at intervals with string. Put the beef into a roasting tin just large enough to hold it and pour the marinade over it.

5 Roast for 1 hour for rare beef, or 1¼ hours for medium-rare, basting from time to time. Put the beef on a board, cover with foil and leave to rest in a warm place while you make the gravy.

6 Skim off the excess fat from the roasting tin. Put the tin on the hob and bring the pan juices to the boil. Add 125ml (4fl oz) water and bubble for 2–3 minutes. Finely chop the remaining pepper pieces and add to the gravy.

7 Carve the beef and serve with the gravy, roast potatoes and vegetables of your choice.

Spiced Silverside

Preparation Time 20 minutes, plus soaking • Cooking Time 4–5 hours • Serves 6 • Per Serving 339 calories, 8g fat
(of which 3g saturates), 28g carbohydrate, 4.2g salt • **Gluten Free** • **Dairy Free** • **Easy**

1.8kg (4lb) piece boned, salted
    silverside
1 onion, sliced
4 carrots, sliced
1 small turnip, sliced
1–2 celery sticks, chopped
8 cloves
125g (4oz) light muscovado sugar
½ tsp mustard powder
1 tsp ground cinnamon
juice of 1 orange

1 Soak the meat for several hours, or overnight, in enough cold water to cover it.

2 Rinse the meat and put into a large heavy-based pan with the vegetables. Add water to cover the meat and bring slowly to the boil. Skim off any scum, cover with a lid and simmer for 4 hours. Leave to cool in the liquid.

3 Drain the meat well, then put into a roasting tin and press the cloves into the fat. Mix together the sugar,

mustard, cinnamon and orange juice and spread over the meat. Preheat the oven to 180°C (160°C fan oven) mark 4.

4 Roast for 45 minutes to 1 hour, basting from time to time. Serve hot or cold (see Cook's Tip).

★ COOK'S TIP
This is equally good hot – with roast potatoes, carrots and green cabbage – or cold, with salad, mustardy mayonnaise, gherkins and bread.

Roast Pork Loin with Rosemary and Mustard

Preparation Time 5 minutes • **Cooking Time** 1 hour 35 minutes • **Serves 8** • **Per Serving** 354 calories, 13g fat (of which 4g saturates), 24g carbohydrate, 1.1g salt • **Dairy Free** • **Easy**

2 tbsp freshly chopped rosemary
4 tbsp Dijon mustard
50ml (2fl oz) lemon juice
50g (2oz) light muscovado sugar
175g (6oz) honey
1 tbsp soy sauce
1.4kg (3lb) loin of pork, chine bone (backbone) removed, rib bones cut off and separated into individual ribs (ask the butcher to do this for you)
lemon wedges and rosemary sprigs to serve

1 Preheat the oven to 200°C (180°C) mark 6. Mix together the rosemary, mustard, lemon juice, sugar, honey and soy sauce and put to one side.

2 Put the loin into a roasting tin and cook in the oven for 40 minutes.

3 Add the ribs to the roasting tin and cook the pork for a further 40 minutes.

4 Drain off any fat and brush the pork with the mustard glaze. Put back in the oven for about 15 minutes, basting occasionally with the glaze or until well browned and tender. Serve hot or cold, garnished with rosemary and lemon.

★ COOK'S TIP
The sweetness of buttered parsnips makes them an ideal accompaniment to pork. Cut about 700g (1½lb) scrubbed, unpeeled parsnips into chunky lengths from the stalk to the root end. Melt 50g (2oz) butter in a deep frying pan and add the parsnips. Stir over the heat for 5–7 minutes, shaking the pan occasionally, until the parsnips are tender and have a wonderful sticky glaze.

Crisp Roast Pork with Apple Sauce

Preparation Time 30 minutes, plus standing • **Cooking Time** 2 hours, plus resting • **Serves 6** • **Per Serving** 769 calories, 50g fat (of which 18g saturates), 22g carbohydrate, 0.4g salt • **Dairy Free** • **Easy**

1.6kg (3½lb) boned rolled loin
  of pork
olive oil
1kg (2¼lb) cooking apples, cored
  and roughly chopped
1–2 tbsp granulated sugar
1 tbsp plain flour
600ml (1 pint) chicken stock
salt and ground black pepper
roast potatoes and green vegetables
  to serve

1 Score the pork skin, sprinkle generously with salt and leave at room temperature for 1–2 hours.

2 Preheat the oven to 220°C (200°C fan oven) mark 7. Wipe the salt off the skin, rub with oil and sprinkle again with salt. Put half the apples in a small roasting tin, sit the pork on top and roast for 30 minutes. Turn the oven down to 190°C (170°C fan oven) mark 5 and roast for a further 1½ hours or until cooked.

3 Meanwhile, put the remaining apples in a pan with the sugar and 2 tbsp water, cover with a tight-fitting lid and cook until just soft. Set aside.

4 Remove the pork from the tin and leave to rest. Skim off most of the fat, leaving about 1 tbsp and the apples in the tin. Stir in the flour until smooth, then stir in the stock and bring to the boil. Bubble gently for 2–3 minutes, skimming if necessary. Strain the sauce through a sieve into a jug, pushing through as much of the apple as possible. Slice the pork and serve with the sauce, roast potatoes and green vegetables.

★ COOK'S TIP
Apples discolour quickly when exposed to air. Toss with lemon juice if you are not going to use the prepared fruit immediately.

Lemon-roasted Pork with Garlic and Basil

★

Preparation Time 20 minutes, plus marinating • **Cooking Time** 40 minutes • **Serves 6** • **Per Serving** 185 calories, 9g fat (of which 2g saturates), 1.5g carbohydrate, 0.2g salt • **Gluten Free** • **Dairy Free** • **Easy**

2 pork tenderloins, about 350g (12oz) each, trimmed

finely grated zest and juice of 2 lemons, sieved

6 tbsp freshly chopped basil or parsley

12 garlic cloves, blanched and halved if large

2–3 bay leaves

2 tbsp olive oil

fresh herbs and lemon slices to garnish

sautéed shallots to serve

1 Split the pork lengthways without cutting right through and open each piece out flat. Sprinkle with the lemon zest and basil or parsley. Lay the garlic cloves evenly along the middle of each fillet and season with salt and pepper.

2 Close the pork and tie loosely at 2.5cm (1in) intervals with string. Put in a shallow non-metallic dish with the bay leaves and sieved lemon juice. Cover, chill and leave to marinate overnight.

3 Preheat the oven to 200°C (180°C fan oven) mark 6. Remove the pork and put the marinade aside. Heat the oil in a sauté pan. Add the meat and fry until browned. Transfer to a shallow roasting tin with the marinade. Season the pork and cook in the oven for 35 minutes, basting frequently.

4 Serve sliced, garnished with herbs and lemon slices, and with sautéed shallots.

Honey Pork with Roast Potatoes and Apples

Preparation Time 20 minutes • Cooking Time 1 hour 40 minutes, plus resting • Serves 4 • Per Serving 830 calories, 55g fat (of which 19g saturates), 40g carbohydrate, 0.4g salt • **Gluten Free** • **Easy**

1kg (2¼lb) loin of pork, with skin and four bones
4 tbsp olive oil
25g (1oz) butter
700g (1½lb) Charlotte potatoes, scrubbed and halved
1 large onion, cut into eight wedges
1 tbsp clear honey mixed with 1 tbsp wholegrain mustard
2 Cox's Orange Pippin apples, cored and each cut into six wedges
12 fresh sage leaves
175ml (6fl oz) dry cider
salt and ground black pepper

1 Preheat the oven to 240°C (220°C fan oven) mark 9. Put the pork on a board and use a paring knife to score the skin into thin strips, cutting about halfway into the fat underneath. Rub 1 tsp salt and 2 tbsp oil over the skin and season well with pepper. Put the meat on a rack, skin side up, over a large roasting tin (or just put the pork in the tin). Roast for 25 minutes. Turn the oven down to 190°C (170°C fan oven) mark 5 and continue to roast for 15 minutes.

2 Add the remaining oil and the butter to the roasting tin. Scatter the potatoes and onion around the meat, season and continue to roast for 45 minutes.

3 Brush the meat with the honey and mustard mixture. Add the apples and sage leaves to the tin and roast for a further 15 minutes or until the pork is cooked.

4 Remove the pork from the tin and wrap completely with foil, then leave to rest for 10 minutes. Put the potatoes, onions and apples into a warmed serving dish and put back in the oven to keep warm.

5 Put the roasting tin on the hob, add the cider and stir well to make a thin gravy. Season.

6 Cut between each bone and cut the meat away from the bone. Pull the crackling away from the meat and cut into strips. Carve the joint, giving each person some crackling, and a bone to chew. Serve with the gravy and potatoes, onion and apples.

Belly of Pork with Cider and Rosemary

Preparation Time 30 minutes, plus cooling and chilling • **Cooking Time** about 4½ hours • **Serves 8** •
Per Serving 694 calories, 52g fat (of which 19g saturates), 9g carbohydrate, 0.5g salt • **Easy**

2kg (4½lb) piece pork belly roast,
   on the bone
500ml bottle medium cider
600ml (1 pint) hot chicken stock
6–8 fresh rosemary sprigs
3 fat garlic cloves, halved
2 tbsp olive oil
grated zest and juice of 1 large
   orange and 1 lemon
3 tbsp light muscovado sugar
25g (1oz) softened butter, mixed
   with 1 tbsp plain flour
salt and ground black pepper
mixed vegetables to serve

1 Preheat the oven to 150°C (130°C fan oven) mark 2. Put the pork, skin side up, in a roasting tin just large enough to hold it. Add the cider, hot stock and half the rosemary. Bring to the boil on the hob, then cover with foil and cook in the oven for 4 hours. Leave to cool in the cooking liquid.

2 Strip the leaves from the remaining rosemary and chop. Put into a pestle and mortar with the garlic, oil, orange and lemon zest, 1 tsp salt and 1 tbsp sugar. Pound for 3–4 minutes to make a rough paste.

3 Remove the pork from the tin (keep the cooking liquid) and slice off the rind from the top layer of fat. Put to one side. Score the fat into a diamond pattern and rub in the rosemary paste. Cover loosely with clingfilm and chill until required.

4 Pat the rind dry with kitchen paper and put it (fat side up) on a foil-lined baking sheet. Cook under a hot grill, about 10cm (4in) away from the heat, for 5 minutes. Turn over, sprinkle lightly with salt, then grill for 7–10 minutes until crisp. Cool, then cut the crackling into rough pieces.

5 Make the gravy. Strain the cooking liquid into a pan. Add the orange and lemon juice and the remaining 2 tbsp sugar, bring to the boil and bubble until reduced by half. Whisk the butter mixture into the liquid and boil for 4–5 minutes until thickened. Put to one side.

6 When almost ready to serve, preheat the oven to 220°C (200°C fan oven) mark 7. Cook the pork, uncovered, in a roasting tin for 20 minutes or until piping hot. Wrap the crackling in foil and warm in the oven for the last 5 minutes of the cooking time. Heat the gravy on the hob. Carve the pork into slices and serve with the crackling, gravy and vegetables.

Maple, Ginger and Soy-roasted Gammon

Preparation Time 10 minutes • Cooking Time 2 hours 10 minutes • Serves 18 • Per Serving 392 calories, 21g fat (of which 7g saturates), 2g carbohydrate, 6.1g salt • Dairy Free • Easy

2 x 2.5kg (5½lb) smoked boneless
   gammon joints
8 tbsp vegetable oil
7.5cm (3in) piece fresh root ginger,
   peeled and grated
8 tbsp maple syrup
6 tbsp dark soy sauce
12 star anise (optional)

1 If the gammon is salty (check with your butcher), soak it in cold water overnight. Alternatively, bring to the boil in a large pan of water and simmer for 10 minutes.

2 Preheat the oven to 200°C (180°C fan oven) mark 6. Put the joints in a roasting tin and pour 4 tbsp oil over them. Cover with foil and roast for 1 hour 50 minutes or 20 minutes per 450g (1lb).

3 Mix the ginger with the maple syrup, soy sauce and the remaining vegetable oil in a bowl.

4 Take the gammon out of the oven, remove the foil and allow to cool a little, then carefully peel away the skin and discard. Score the fat in a criss-cross pattern, stud with the star anise, if using, then pour the ginger sauce over the gammon. Continue to roast for another 20 minutes or until the glaze is golden brown. Slice and serve one joint warm. Cool the other, wrap in foil and chill until needed.

 COOK'S TIP
Home-cooked ham is great hot or cold, but cooking a large joint is often impractical. Roasting two medium joints at the same time means you can serve a hot joint and have plenty left to eat cold.

Roast Lamb with Orange

Preparation Time 20 minutes • **Cooking Time** 1 hour 25 minutes, plus resting • **Serves 4** • **Per Serving** 581 calories, 28g fat (of which 12g saturates), 14g carbohydrate, 0.4g salt • **Dairy Free** • **Easy**

grated zest and juice of 1 orange,
   plus extra wedges to garnish
2 garlic cloves, sliced
3 large fresh rosemary sprigs,
   leaves stripped
1 tbsp olive oil
1.4kg (3lb) leg of lamb
3 tbsp orange marmalade
1 tbsp plain flour
salt and ground black pepper
roasted vegetables to serve

1 Preheat the oven to 180°C (160°C fan oven) mark 4. Mix the orange zest with the garlic, the leaves from 2 rosemary sprigs and the oil, then season. Put the lamb on a board and make several slits all over it. Stuff the mixture into the slits. Put the lamb on a rack in a roasting tin and roast for 1¼ hours, basting with the juices from time to time.

2 About 10–15 minutes before the end of the cooking time, brush the lamb with the marmalade. Insert a few rosemary leaves into each slit in the meat.

3 Remove the lamb from the oven, wrap loosely in foil and leave to rest for 10–15 minutes.

4 Put the roasting tin on the hob, skim off and discard the fat and stir in the flour. Add 150ml (¼ pint) water and the orange juice and bring to the boil, then simmer, stirring occasionally, for 8 minutes or until thick. Season. Carve the lamb, garnish with orange wedges and serve with the gravy and vegetables.

Rack of Lamb with Balsamic Gravy

Preparation Time 5 minutes • **Cooking Time** 30–45 minutes • **Serves 8** • **Per Serving** 532 calories, 48g fat (of which 18g saturates), 0.2g carbohydrate, 0.2g salt • **Gluten Free** • **Dairy Free** • **Easy**

4 fat garlic cloves, crushed
2 tbsp Herbes de Provence
6 tbsp balsamic vinegar
12 tbsp olive oil
4 trimmed racks of lamb, each with about 6 bones
salt and ground black pepper

1 Preheat the oven to 220°C (200°C fan oven) mark 7. Put the garlic into a bowl along with the herbs, 2 tbsp vinegar and 4 tbsp oil. Season with salt and pepper.

2 Put the racks in a large flameproof roasting tin and rub the garlic mixture into both the fat and meat.

3 Roast for 25–30 minutes if you like your meat pink, or cook for a further 5–10 minutes if you like it well done. Lift the racks from the roasting tin and put to one side on a warm serving dish. Cover with foil and leave to rest.

4 Put the roasting tin on the hob over a medium heat and whisk in the remaining vinegar and oil, scraping up any sediment as the liquid bubbles. Season if needed. Pour into a small heatproof jug.

5 Serve the lamb in cutlets with the hot gravy.

Stuffed Leg of Lamb

Preparation Time 40 minutes • **Cooking Time** 3 hours–3 hours 40 minutes, plus resting • **Serves 8** •
Per Serving 632 calories, 47g fat (of which 15g saturates), 1g carbohydrate, 0.4g salt • **Gluten Free** • **Easy**

1 leg of lamb, about 2.7kg (6lb),
　knucklebone removed but end
　bone left in
2 garlic bulbs
salt and ground black pepper
Redcurrant Sauce (see Cook's Tip)
　to serve

FOR THE STUFFING
25g (1oz) butter
75ml (2½fl oz) olive oil
1 small red onion, finely chopped
450g (1lb) chestnut mushrooms,
　finely chopped
4 tbsp freshly chopped flat-leafed
　parsley, 1 tbsp freshly chopped
　oregano and 6–8 thyme sprigs,
　leaves stripped

1 First make the stuffing. Melt the
butter in a frying pan with 2 tbsp oil.
Fry the onion gently for 10–15
minutes until soft. Add the
mushrooms and cook for 15–20
minutes – the mixture will become
dryish – stirring all the time, until the
mushrooms begin to turn golden
brown. Add the herbs and cook for
1 minute. Season and leave to cool.

2 Preheat the oven to 190°C (170°C
fan oven) mark 5. Open out the
lamb and spread the stuffing over
the meat. Reshape the lamb and
secure with string. Put the lamb in a
roasting tin and season. Roast,
basting occasionally, for 2½–3
hours. About 1 hour before the end
of the cooking time, rub the whole

garlic bulbs with the remaining oil
and put them alongside the lamb
until very soft. When the lamb is
cooked to your liking, transfer to a
carving board, cover with a tent of
foil and leave to rest. Keep the garlic
warm until ready to serve.

3 Carve the lamb and garnish with
the roasted garlic, broken into
cloves. Serve with Redcurrant Sauce.

★ COOK'S TIP
Redcurrant Sauce
*Pour 600ml (1 pint) fruity red wine into a
small pan. Add 6 tbsp redcurrant jelly,
3 tbsp Worcestershire sauce and the juice of
1 lemon and 1 orange. Heat very gently
until the jelly melts. Pour off all but 2 tbsp
fat from the roasting tin. Put the tin on the
hob over a low heat and stir in 2 tbsp plain
flour and 2 tsp English mustard powder to
make a paste. Increase the heat and pour
in the wine mixture, a little at a time. Mix
with a wooden spoon after each addition,
scraping up any crusty bits from the
bottom of the tin. Once all the wine has
been incorporated, swap the spoon for a
whisk and whisk until the sauce is smooth.
Reduce the heat and bubble gently for
10 minutes, then pour into a warm jug
to serve. Serves 8.*

Rack of Lamb with Rosemary and Red Wine Sauce

★

Preparation Time 10 minutes, plus marinating • **Cooking Time** 15–20 minutes, plus resting • **Serves 6**
Per Serving 355 calories, 26g fat (of which 12g saturates), 5g carbohydrate, 0.2g salt • **Gluten Free** • **Easy**

2 garlic cloves, crushed
3 trimmed racks of lamb
300ml (½ pint) red wine
6 rosemary sprigs, roughly crushed
  to release the flavour
1 tbsp olive oil
300g carton fresh lamb stock
3 tbsp redcurrant jelly
knob of herb butter
salt and ground black pepper
green vegetables and potato and
  carrot mash to serve

1 Rub the garlic into the meat, then put into a shallow sealable container and add the wine and rosemary. Cover, chill and leave to marinate for at least 4 hours or overnight.

2 Preheat the oven to 200°C (180°C fan oven) mark 6. Drain off the marinade and put to one side. Pat the meat dry with kitchen paper and put into a roasting tin with the rosemary. Drizzle with oil, season with salt and pepper and roast for 15–20 minutes.

3 Meanwhile, put the marinade into a wide heavy-based pan, bring to the boil and reduce by half. Add the stock and redcurrant jelly and bring to the boil, then reduce the heat and simmer for 10–12 minutes to reduce to a syrupy sauce.

4 Take the lamb out of the oven and leave to rest for 5–10 minutes. Add the herb butter to the sauce, along with juices from the roasting tin. Whisk in and season to taste. Slice the lamb into cutlets, garnish with rosemary, drizzle with sauce and serve with vegetables and mash.

Lamb Boulangère

Preparation Time 40 minutes • **Cooking Time** about 2¼ hours, plus resting • **Serves 6** • **Per Serving** 998 calories, 61g fat (of which 24g saturates), 53g carbohydrate, 0.8g salt • **Gluten Free** • **Easy**

1.8kg (4lb) waxy potatoes such as
  King Edward, finely sliced
1 onion, sliced and blanched in
  boiling water for 2 minutes
600ml (1 pint) vegetable stock
5 garlic cloves, crushed
3 tbsp finely chopped fresh mint
2 tbsp finely chopped fresh
  rosemary
100g (3½oz) butter, at room
  temperature, plus extra to grease
1 leg of lamb, weighing around
  2.3kg (5lb)
salt and ground black pepper

FOR THE RED PEPPER SALSA
3 red peppers
2 tbsp extra virgin olive oil, plus
  extra to drizzle
1 small red onion, finely sliced
juice of ½ lemon
1–2 tbsp baby capers, rinsed
5 fresh mint leaves, finely chopped

1 Preheat the oven to 200°C (180°C fan oven) mark 6. Butter a 4.5 litre (8 pint) roasting tin. Layer the potatoes and onion, seasoning with salt and pepper as you go. Pour the stock over them and cook for 30 minutes.

2 Put the garlic, herbs and butter into a bowl and mix well. Season generously. Put the lamb on a board and trim away any excess fat. Make six or seven deep cuts all over. Use a teaspoon to push the butter mixture into the cuts, then smear the rest all over the leg. Put on a rack over the potatoes. Roast for 1 hour 40 minutes or 20 minutes per 450g (1lb).

3 Meanwhile, make the red pepper salsa. Put the peppers in a roasting tin, drizzle with a little oil and roast in the oven with the lamb for 30–40 minutes until the skins are slightly charred. Put in a bowl, cover with clingfilm and leave to cool.

4 Put the red onion in a bowl, add the lemon juice, season with salt and leave to marinate. Peel the peppers, slice the flesh and put in a bowl with any juice. Add the capers, oil and mint and season well, then stir everything together.

5 Put the lamb on a board, cover with foil and leave to rest for 10 minutes. Leave the potatoes in the oven to keep hot while you carve the lamb. Serve the sliced meat with the potatoes and red pepper salsa.

Meat-free ★

White Nut Roast

Preparation Time 20 minutes • Cooking Time about 1 hour • Serves 8 • Per Serving 371 calories, 28g fat (of which 9g saturates), 20g carbohydrate, 0.8g salt • Vegetarian • Easy

40g (1½oz) butter, plus extra to grease
1 onion, finely chopped
1 garlic clove, crushed
225g (8oz) mixed white nuts, such as brazils, macadamias, pinenuts and whole almonds, ground in a food processor
125g (4oz) fresh white breadcrumbs
grated zest and juice of ½ lemon
75g (3oz) sage Derby cheese or Parmesan, grated (see Cook's Tip)
125g (4oz) cooked, peeled (or vacuum-packed) chestnuts, roughly chopped

½ × 400g can artichoke hearts, drained and roughly chopped
1 medium egg, lightly beaten
2 tsp each freshly chopped parsley, sage and thyme, plus extra sprigs
salt and ground black pepper

1 Preheat the oven to 200°C (180°C fan oven) mark 6. Melt the butter in a pan and cook the onion and garlic for 5 minutes or until soft. Transfer to a large bowl and put to one side to cool.

2 Add the nuts, breadcrumbs, lemon zest and juice, cheese, chestnuts and artichokes to the onion mixture. Season well and bind together with the egg. Stir in the herbs.

3 Put the mixture on to a large piece of buttered foil and shape into a fat sausage, packing tightly. Scatter with the extra herb sprigs and wrap in the foil.

4 Cook on a baking sheet for 35 minutes, then unwrap the foil slightly and cook for a further 15 minutes or until turning golden. Slice and serve.

★ FREEZING TIP

To freeze Complete the recipe to the end of step 3, cool, cover and freeze for up to one month.
To use Cook from frozen for 45 minutes, then unwrap the foil slightly and cook for a further 15 minutes or until turning golden.

★ COOK'S TIP

Vegetarian cheeses: some vegetarians prefer to avoid cheeses that have been produced by the traditional method, because this uses animal-derived rennet. Most supermarkets and cheese shops now stock an excellent range of vegetarian cheeses, produced using vegetarian rennet, which comes from plants, such as thistle and mallow, that contain enzymes capable of curdling milk.

Spiced Bean and Vegetable Stew

Preparation Time 5 minutes • **Cooking Time** about 30 minutes • **Serves 6** • **Per Serving** 262 calories, 7g fat (of which 1g saturates), 44g carbohydrate, 1.3g salt • **Vegetarian** • **Gluten Free** • **Dairy Free** • **Easy**

3 tbsp olive oil
2 small onions, sliced
2 garlic cloves, crushed
1 tbsp sweet paprika
1 small dried red chilli, seeded and finely chopped
700g (1½lb) sweet potatoes, peeled and cubed
700g (1½lb) pumpkin, peeled and cut into chunks
125g (4oz) okra, trimmed
500g (1lb 2oz) passata
400g can haricot or cannellini beans, drained and rinsed
salt and ground black pepper

1 Heat the oil in a large heavy pan over a very gentle heat. Add the onion and garlic and cook for 5 minutes. Stir in the paprika and chilli and cook for a further 2 minutes.

2 Add the sweet potatoes, pumpkin, okra, passata and 900ml (1½ pints) water and season generously with salt and pepper. Cover the pan and bring to the boil, then reduce the heat and simmer for 20 minutes or until the vegetables are tender.

3 Add the beans and cook for 3 minutes to warm through. Serve immediately.

Mushroom and Bean Hotpot

Preparation Time 15 minutes • **Cooking Time** 30 minutes • **Serves 6** • **Per Serving** 280 calories, 10g fat (of which 1g saturates), 34g carbohydrate, 1.3g salt • **Vegetarian** • **Dairy Free** • **Easy**

3 tbsp olive oil
700g (1½lb) chestnut mushrooms, roughly chopped
1 large onion, finely chopped
2 tbsp plain flour
2 tbsp mild curry paste (see Cook's Tip)
150ml (¼ pint) dry white wine
400g can chopped tomatoes
2 tbsp sun-dried tomato paste
2 × 400g cans mixed beans, drained and rinsed
3 tbsp mango chutney
3 tbsp roughly chopped fresh coriander and mint

1 Heat the oil in a large pan over a low heat, then fry the mushrooms and onion until the onion is soft and dark golden. Stir in the flour and curry paste and cook for 1–2 minutes.

2 Add the wine, tomatoes, sun-dried tomato paste and beans and bring to the boil, then reduce the heat and simmer gently for 30 minutes or until most of the liquid has reduced. Stir in the chutney and herbs before serving.

★ COOK'S TIP
Check the ingredients in the curry paste: some may not be suitable for vegetarians.

Black-eye Bean Chilli

Preparation Time 10 minutes • **Cooking Time** 20 minutes • **Serves 4** • **Per Serving** 245 calories, 5g fat (of which 1g saturates), 39g carbohydrate, 1.8g salt • **Vegetarian** • **Easy**

1 tbsp olive oil
1 onion, chopped
3 celery sticks, finely chopped
2 × 400g cans black-eye beans,
 drained and rinsed
2 × 400g cans chopped tomatoes
2 or 3 splashes of Tabasco sauce
3 tbsp freshly chopped coriander
4 warmed tortillas and soured
 cream to serve

1 Heat the oil in a frying pan. Add the onion and celery and cook for 10 minutes or until softened.

2 Add the beans, tomatoes and Tabasco to the pan. Bring to the boil, then reduce the heat and simmer for 10 minutes.

3 Just before serving, stir in the coriander. Spoon the chilli on to the warm tortillas, roll up and serve with soured cream.

★ TRY SOMETHING DIFFERENT
Replace half the black-eye beans with red kidney beans.

Veggie Curry

★

Preparation Time 5 minutes • **Cooking Time** 12 minutes • **Serves 1** • **Per Serving** 468 calories, 20g fat of which 3g saturates), 58g carbohydrate, 1.4g salt • **Vegetarian** • **Gluten Free** • **Dairy Free** • **Easy**

1 tbsp medium curry paste (see
   Cook's Tip, page 228)
227g can chopped tomatoes
150ml (¼ pint) hot vegetable stock
200g (7oz) vegetables, such as
   broccoli, courgettes and
   sugarsnap peas, roughly chopped
½ × 400g can chickpeas, drained
   and rinsed
griddled wholemeal pitta and
   yogurt to serve

1 Heat the curry paste in a large heavy-based pan for 1 minute, stirring the paste to warm the spices. Add the tomatoes and hot stock. Bring to the boil, then reduce the heat to a simmer and add the vegetables. Simmer for 5–6 minutes until the vegetables are tender.

2 Stir in the chickpeas and heat for 1–2 minutes until hot. Serve the vegetable curry with a griddled wholemeal pitta and yogurt.

Spicy Beans with Jazzed-up Potatoes

Preparation Time 12 minutes • **Cooking Time** about 1½ hours • **Serves 4** • **Per Serving** 298 calories, 4g fat (of which 1g saturates), 56g carbohydrate, 0.8g salt • **Vegetarian** • **Gluten Free** • **Easy**

4 baking potatoes
1 tbsp olive oil, plus extra to rub
1 tsp smoked paprika, plus a pinch
2 shallots, finely chopped
1 tbsp freshly chopped rosemary
400g can cannellini beans, drained
   and rinsed
400g can chopped tomatoes
1 tbsp light muscovado sugar
1 tsp Worcestershire sauce
75ml (2½fl oz) red wine
75ml (2½fl oz) hot vegetable stock
a small handful of freshly chopped
   flat-leafed parsley
grated mature vegetarian Cheddar
   to sprinkle
sea salt and ground black pepper

1 Preheat the oven to 200°C (180°C fan oven) mark 6. Rub the potatoes with a little oil and put them on a baking tray. Scatter with sea salt and a pinch of smoked paprika. Bake for 1–1½ hours.

2 Meanwhile, heat 1 tbsp oil in a large pan, then fry the shallots over a low heat for 1–2 minutes until they start to soften.

3 Add the rosemary and 1 tsp paprika and fry for 1–2 minutes, then add the beans, tomatoes, sugar, Worcestershire sauce, wine and hot stock. Season, then bring to the boil and simmer, uncovered, for 10–15 minutes. Serve with the baked potatoes, scattered with parsley and grated Cheddar.

★ TRY SOMETHING DIFFERENT
For a quick meal that takes less than 25 minutes, the spicy beans are just as good served with toast .

Chickpeas with Spinach

Preparation Time 10 minutes • Cooking Time 12–15 minutes • Serves 6 • Per Serving 204 calories, 10g fat (of which 1g saturates), 21g carbohydrate, 0.8g salt • **Vegetarian** • **Gluten Free** • **Dairy Free** • **Easy**

3 tbsp olive oil
2.5cm (1in) piece fresh root ginger, peeled and finely chopped
3 garlic cloves, chopped
2 tsp each ground coriander and paprika
1 tsp ground cumin
2 × 400g cans chickpeas, drained and rinsed
4 tomatoes, roughly chopped
handful of coriander leaves
450g (1lb) fresh spinach
salt and ground black pepper
rice, and grated carrots with lemon juice to serve

1 Heat the oil in a large heavy-based pan, add the ginger, garlic and spices and cook for 2 minutes, stirring. Stir in the chickpeas.

2 Add the tomatoes to the pan with the coriander leaves and spinach and cook gently for 10 minutes. Season to taste with salt and pepper and serve immediately, with rice and a salad of grated carrots tossed in a little lemon juice.

Lentil Casserole

Preparation Time 20 minutes • **Cooking Time** 1 hour • **Serves 6** • **Per Serving** 239 calories, 6g fat (of which 1g saturates), 36g carbohydrate, 0.4g salt • **Vegetarian** • **Gluten Free** • **Dairy Free** • **Easy**

2 tbsp olive oil

2 onions, sliced

4 carrots, sliced

3 leeks, trimmed and sliced

450g (1lb) button mushrooms

2 garlic cloves, crushed

2.5cm (1in) piece fresh root ginger, peeled and grated

1 tbsp ground coriander

225g (8oz) split red lentils, rinsed and drained

750ml (1¼ pints) hot vegetable stock

4 tbsp freshly chopped coriander

salt and ground black pepper

1 Preheat the oven to 180°C (160°C fan oven) mark 4. Heat the oil in a flameproof ovenproof casserole, add the onions, carrots and leeks and fry, stirring, for 5 minutes. Add the mushrooms, garlic, ginger and ground coriander and fry for 2–3 minutes.

2 Stir the lentils into the casserole with the hot stock. Season with salt and pepper and return to the boil. Cover and cook in the oven for 45–50 minutes until the vegetables and lentils are tender. Stir in the chopped coriander before serving.

Beef Tomatoes with Bulgur

Preparation Time 10 minutes • **Cooking Time** 30–35 minutes • **Serves 4** • **Per Serving** 245 calories, 14g fat of which 4g saturates), 21g carbohydrate, 0.7g salt • **Vegetarian** • **Easy**

125g (4oz) bulgur wheat
20g (³⁄₄oz) flat-leafed parsley, finely chopped
75g (3oz) vegetarian feta cheese, chopped
1 courgette, chopped
50g (2oz) flaked almonds, toasted
4 large beef tomatoes
1 tbsp olive oil

1 Preheat the oven to 180°C (160°C fan oven) mark 4. Cook the bulgur according to the pack instructions. Chop the parsley, feta and courgette and stir into the bulgur with the almonds.

2 Chop the top off each tomato and scoop out the seeds. Put on to a baking sheet and spoon in the bulgur mixture. Drizzle with the oil and cook in the oven for 15–20 minutes until the cheese is starting to soften. Serve.

★ TRY SOMETHING DIFFERENT
Try quinoa instead of the bulgur wheat. Put the quinoa in a bowl of cold water and mix well, then soak for 2 minutes. Drain. Put into a pan with twice its volume of water and bring to the boil. Simmer for 20 minutes. Remove from the heat, cover and leave to stand for 10 minutes.

Couscous-stuffed Mushrooms

Preparation Time 3 minutes • Cooking Time about 12 minutes • Serves 4 • Per Serving 373 calories, 25g fat (of which 10g saturates), 25g carbohydrate, 0.6g salt • **Vegetarian** • **Easy**

125g (4oz) couscous

20g pack fresh flat-leafed parsley, roughly chopped

280g jar mixed antipasti in oil, drained and oil put to one side

8 large flat portabellini mushrooms

25g (1oz) butter

25g (1oz) plain flour

300ml (½ pint) skimmed milk

75g (3oz) mature vegetarian Cheddar, grated, plus extra to sprinkle

green salad to serve

1 Preheat the oven to 220°C (200°C fan oven) mark 7. Put the couscous into a bowl with 200ml (7fl oz) boiling water, the parsley, antipasti and 1 tbsp of the reserved oil. Stir well.

2 Put the mushrooms on a non-stick baking tray and spoon a little of the couscous mixture into the centre of each. Cook in the oven while you make the sauce.

3 Whisk together the butter, flour and milk in a small pan over a high heat until the mixture comes to the boil. Reduce the heat as soon as it starts to thicken, then whisk constantly until smooth. Take the pan off the heat and stir in the cheese.

4 Spoon the sauce over the mushrooms and sprinkle with the remaining cheese. Put back into the oven for a further 7–10 minutes until golden. Serve with a green salad.

Spicy Bean and Tomato Fajitas

Preparation Time 15 minutes • **Cooking Time** 25 minutes • **Serves 6** • **Per Serving** 512 calories, 20g fat (of which 6g saturates), 71g carbohydrate, 1.5g salt • **Vegetarian** • **Easy**

2 tbsp sunflower oil
1 onion, sliced
2 garlic cloves, crushed
½ tsp hot chilli powder, plus extra
    to garnish
1 tsp each ground coriander and
    ground cumin
1 tbsp tomato purée
400g can chopped tomatoes
200g can red kidney beans, drained
    and rinsed
400g can borlotti beans, drained
    and rinsed
400g can flageolet beans, drained
    and rinsed
150ml (¼ pint) hot vegetable stock
2 ripe avocados
juice of ½ lime
1 tbsp freshly chopped coriander,
    plus sprigs to garnish
6 ready-made flour tortillas
150ml (¼ pint) soured cream
salt and ground black pepper
lime wedges to serve

1 Heat the oil in a large pan, add the onion and cook gently for 5 minutes. Add the garlic and spices and cook for a further 2 minutes.

2 Add the tomato purée and cook for 1 minute, then add the tomatoes, beans and hot stock. Season well with salt and pepper and bring to the boil, then reduce the heat and simmer for 15 minutes, stirring occasionally.

3 Halve, stone and peel the avocados, then chop. Put the avocado into a bowl, add the lime juice and chopped coriander and mash. Season to taste.

4 Warm the tortillas: either wrap them in foil and heat in the oven at 180°C (160°C fan oven) mark 4 for 10 minutes, or put on to a plate and microwave on full power for 45 seconds (based on a 900W oven).

5 Spoon some beans down the centre of each tortilla. Fold up the bottom to keep the filling inside, then wrap the sides in so they overlap. Spoon on the avocado and soured cream. Sprinkle with chilli powder and coriander sprigs and serve with lime wedges.

Vegetable Tempura

Preparation Time 20 minutes • **Cooking Time** 15 minutes • **Serves 4** • **Per Serving** 450 calories, 21g fat (of which 3g saturates), 55g carbohydrate, 2.1g salt • **Vegetarian** • **Dairy Free** • **A Little Effort**

125g (4oz) plain flour, plus 2 tbsp
    extra to sprinkle
2 tbsp cornflour
2 tbsp arrowroot
125g (4oz) cauliflower, cut into
    small florets
2 large carrots, cut into matchsticks
16 button mushrooms
2 courgettes, sliced
2 red peppers, seeded and sliced
vegetable oil for deep-frying
salt and ground black pepper
fresh coriander sprigs to garnish

FOR THE DIPPING SAUCE
25g (1oz) piece fresh root ginger,
    peeled and grated
4 tbsp dry sherry
3 tbsp soy sauce

1 Sift 125g (4oz) flour, the cornflour and arrowroot into a large bowl with a pinch each of salt and pepper. Gradually whisk in 300ml (½ pint) ice-cold water to form a thin batter. Cover and chill.

2 To make the dipping sauce, put the ginger, sherry and soy sauce in a heatproof bowl and pour in 200ml (7fl oz) boiling water. Stir well to mix, then put to one side.

3 Put the vegetables in a large bowl and sprinkle with 2 tbsp flour. Toss well to coat. Heat the oil in a wok or deep-fryer to 170°C (test by frying a small cube of bread: it should brown in 40 seconds).

4 Dip a handful of the vegetables in the batter, then remove with a slotted spoon, taking up a lot of the batter with the vegetables. Add to the hot oil and deep-fry for 3–5 minutes until crisp and golden. Remove with a slotted spoon and drain on kitchen paper; keep them hot while you cook the remaining batches. Serve immediately, garnished with coriander sprigs and accompanied by the dipping sauce.

Leek and Broccoli Bake

Preparation Time 20 minutes • **Cooking Time** 45–55 minutes • **Serves 4** • **Per Serving** 245 calories, 13g fat (of which 4g saturates), 18g carbohydrate, 0.4g salt • **Vegetarian** • **Gluten Free** • **Easy**

2 tbsp olive oil
1 large red onion, cut into wedges
1 aubergine, chopped
2 leeks, trimmed and cut into
    chunks
1 broccoli head, cut into florets and
    stalks chopped
3 large flat mushrooms, chopped
2 × 400g cans cherry tomatoes
3 rosemary sprigs, chopped
50g (2oz) Parmesan, freshly grated
    (see Cook's Tip, page 226)
salt and ground black pepper

1 Preheat the oven to 200°C (180°C fan oven) mark 6. Heat the oil in a large flameproof dish, add the onion, aubergine and leeks and cook for 10–12 minutes until golden and softened.

2 Add the broccoli, mushrooms, cherry tomatoes, half the rosemary and 300ml (½ pint) boiling water. Season with salt and pepper. Stir well, then cover and cook in the oven for 30 minutes.

3 Meanwhile, put the Parmesan into a bowl. Add the remaining rosemary and season with pepper. When the vegetables are cooked, remove the lid and sprinkle the Parmesan mixture on top. Cook, uncovered, in the oven for a further 5–10 minutes until the topping is golden.

★ TRY SOMETHING DIFFERENT
Use sliced courgettes instead of aubergine.

Bubble and Squeak Cakes

★

Preparation Time 15 minutes • **Cooking Time** 45 minutes, plus cooling • **Makes 12** • **Per Cake** 130 calories, 10g fat (of which 6g saturates), 10g carbohydrate, 0.2g salt • **Vegetarian** • **Easy**

550g (1¼lb) old potatoes
125g (4oz) butter
175g (6oz) leeks, trimmed and finely shredded
175g (6oz) green cabbage, finely shredded
plain flour to dust
1 tbsp oil
salt and ground black pepper

1 Cook the potatoes in a large pan of lightly salted boiling water until tender, then drain and mash.

2 Heat 50g (2oz) butter in a large non-stick frying pan. Add the leeks and cabbage and fry for 5 minutes, stirring, or until soft and beginning to colour. Combine the leeks and cabbage with the potatoes and season well with salt and pepper. Leave to cool. When cool enough to handle, mould into 12 cakes and dust with flour.

3 Heat the oil and remaining butter in a non-stick frying pan and cook the cakes for 4 minutes on each side or until they are golden, crisp and hot right through. Serve.

Mushroom and Roasted Potato Bake

Preparation Time 15 minutes • **Cooking Time** 1¼ hours • **Serves 6** • **Per Serving** 809 calories, 63g fat (of which 31g saturates), 33g carbohydrate, 1.7g salt • **Vegeterian** • **Gluten Free** • **Easy**

900g (2lb) small potatoes, quartered
6 tbsp olive oil
225g (8oz) onions, roughly chopped
450g (1lb) mixed fresh mushrooms, such as shiitake and brown-cap, roughly chopped
2 garlic cloves, crushed
2 tbsp tomato purée
4 tbsp sun-dried tomato paste
25g (1oz) dried porcini mushrooms, rinsed (optional)
2 tsp freshly chopped thyme
300ml (½ pint) each of dry white wine and vegetable stock
300ml (½ pint) double cream
400g (14oz) large fresh spinach leaves, roughly chopped
175g (6oz) Gruyère cheese
125g (4oz) freshly grated Parmesan (see Cook's Tip, page 226)
300g (11oz) Greek yogurt
2 medium eggs, beaten
salt and ground black pepper

1 Preheat the oven to 200°C (180°C fan oven) mark 6. Toss the potatoes with 4 tbsp oil in a roasting tin and cook for 40 minutes or until tender.

2 Heat the remaining oil in a large heavy-based pan. Add the onions and cook for 10 minutes or until soft, then add the fresh mushrooms and garlic and cook over a high heat for 5 minutes. Stir in the tomato purée and tomato paste, the porcini mushrooms, if using, and the thyme and wine. Bring to the boil and simmer for 2 minutes. Add the stock and cream and bring to the boil, then bubble for 20 minutes or until well reduced and syrupy.

3 Pour into a 2.4 litre (4¼ pint) ovenproof dish. Stir in the potatoes, spinach, Gruyère and half the Parmesan. Season well with salt and pepper.

4 Combine the yogurt with the eggs and season. Spoon over the vegetable mixture and sprinkle with the remaining Parmesan.

5 Cook in the oven for 30–35 minutes until golden and bubbling. Serve hot.

⭐ FREEZING TIP
To freeze *Complete the recipe to the end of step 4, then cool and freeze for up to one month.*
To use *Thaw overnight at cool room temperature. Preheat the oven to 200°C (180°C fan oven) mark 6. Bake for 40–45 minutes until golden and bubbling.*

Sesame and Cabbage Rolls

Preparation Time 30 minutes, plus soaking and cooling • Cooking Time about 15 minutes • Makes 12 •
Per Roll 224 calories, 13g fat (of which 2g saturates), 23g carbohydrate, 0.7g salt • Vegetarian • Dairy Free • A Little Effort

50g (2oz) dried shiitake mushrooms
3 tbsp sesame oil
4 garlic cloves, crushed
4 tbsp sesame seeds
450g (1lb) cabbage, finely shredded
1 bunch of spring onions, chopped
225g can bamboo shoots, drained
3 tbsp soy sauce
½ tsp caster sugar
2 × 270g packs filo pastry
1 large egg, beaten
vegetable oil for deep-frying
Spiced Plum Sauce or Thai Chilli
   Dipping Sauce to serve (see
   Cook's Tip)

1 Put the mushrooms into a heatproof bowl and cover with boiling water. Soak for 20 minutes.

2 Heat the sesame oil in a wok or large frying pan. Add the garlic and sesame seeds and fry gently until golden brown. Add the cabbage and spring onions and fry, stirring, for 3 minutes.

3 Drain and slice the mushrooms. Add them to the pan with the bamboo shoots, soy sauce and sugar and stir until well mixed. Remove the pan from the heat and leave to cool.

4 Cut the filo pastry into 24 x 18cm (7in) squares. Keep the filo squares covered with a damp teatowel as you work. Place one square of filo pastry on the worksurface and cover with a second square. Place a heaped tablespoon of the cabbage mixture across the centre of the top square to within 2.5cm (1in) of the ends. Fold the 2.5cm (1in) ends of pastry over the filling. Brush one unfolded edge of the pastry with a little beaten egg, then roll up to make a thick parcel shape. Shape the remaining pastry and filling in the same way to make 12 parcels.

5 Heat a 5cm (2in) depth of vegetable oil in a deep-fryer or large heavy-based saucepan to 180°C (test by frying a small cube of bread: it should brown in 30 seconds). Fry the rolls in batches for about 3 minutes or until crisp and golden. Remove with a slotted spoon and drain on kitchen paper; keep them warm while you fry the remainder. Serve hot with a sauce for dipping.

★ COOK'S TIP
Spiced Plum Sauce
Slice 2 spring onions as thinly as possible. Put them in a small pan with 6 tbsp plum sauce, the juice of 1 lime, ½ tsp Chinese five-spice powder and 2 tbsp water. Heat gently for 2 minutes.
Thai Chilli Dipping Sauce
Put 200ml (7fl oz) white wine vinegar and 6 tbsp caster sugar in a small pan, bring to the boil and simmer for 2 minutes. Add 1 finely chopped red chilli and 50g (2oz) each finely chopped cucumber, onion and pineapple.

Baked Stuffed Pumpkin

Preparation Time about 40 minutes • **Cooking Time** 1½ hours–1 hour 50 minutes, plus standing • **Serves 4** •
Per Serving 438 calories, 24g fat (of which 9g saturates), 38g carbohydrate, 0.7g salt • **Vegetarian** • **Easy**

1 pumpkin, about 1.4–1.8kg (3–4lb)
2 tbsp olive oil
2 leeks, trimmed and chopped
2 garlic cloves, crushed
2 tbsp freshly chopped thyme
    leaves
2 tsp paprika
1 tsp turmeric
125g (4oz) long-grain rice, cooked
2 tomatoes, peeled, seeded and
    diced
50g (2oz) cashew nuts, toasted and
    roughly chopped
125g (4oz) vegetarian Cheddar,
    grated
salt and ground black pepper

1 Cut a 5cm (2in) slice from the top of the pumpkin and put to one side for the lid. Scoop out and discard the seeds. Using a knife and a spoon, cut out most of the pumpkin flesh, leaving a thin shell. Cut the pumpkin flesh into small pieces and put to one side.

2 Heat the oil in a large pan, add the leeks, garlic, thyme, paprika and turmeric and fry for 10 minutes. Add the chopped pumpkin flesh and fry for a further 10 minutes or until golden, stirring frequently to prevent sticking. Transfer the

mixture to a bowl. Preheat the oven to 180°C (160°C fan oven) mark 4.

3 Add the pumpkin mixture to the cooked rice along with the tomatoes, cashews and cheese. Fork through to mix and season with salt and pepper.

4 Spoon the stuffing mixture into the pumpkin shell, top with the lid and bake for 1¼–1½ hours until the pumpkin is softened and the skin is browned. Remove from the oven and leave to stand for 10 minutes. Cut into wedges to serve.

Roasted Stuffed Peppers

Preparation Time 20 minutes • Cooking Time 45 minutes • Serves 8 • Per Serving 189 calories, 14g fat (of which 6g saturates), 11g carbohydrate, 0.9g salt • **Vegetarian** • **Easy**

40g (1½oz) butter
4 Romano peppers, halved, with
   stalks on and seeded
3 tbsp olive oil
350g (12oz) chestnut mushrooms,
   roughly chopped
4 tbsp finely chopped fresh chives
100g (3½oz) vegetarian feta cheese
50g (2oz) fresh white breadcrumbs
25g (1oz) freshly grated Parmesan
   (see Cook's Tip, page 226)
salt and ground black pepper

1 Preheat the oven to 180°C (160°C fan oven) mark 4. Use a little of the butter to grease a shallow ovenproof dish and put the peppers in it side by side, ready to be filled.

2 Heat the remaining butter and 1 tbsp oil in a pan. Add the mushrooms and fry until they're golden and there's no excess liquid left in the pan. Stir in the chives, then spoon the mixture into the pepper halves.

3 Crumble the feta over the mushrooms. Mix the breadcrumbs and Parmesan in a bowl, then sprinkle over the peppers.

4 Season with salt and pepper and drizzle with the remaining oil. Roast in the oven for 45 minutes or until golden and tender. Serve warm.

★ GET AHEAD
To prepare ahead *Complete the recipe to the end of step 4, up to one day ahead. Cover and chill.*
To use *Reheat under the grill for 5 minutes.*

Roast Mushrooms with Pesto

★

Preparation Time 5 minutes • **Cooking Time** 15 minutes • **Serves 4** • **Per Serving** 258 calories, 23g fat (of which 6g saturates), 1g carbohydrate, 0.5g salt • **Easy**

8 portabella mushrooms
8 tbsp fresh pesto (see page 17)
toasted ciabatta, salad and basil
   leaves to serve

1 Preheat the oven to 200°C (180°C fan oven) mark 6. Put the mushrooms into an ovenproof dish, then spoon 1 tbsp fresh pesto on top of each one.

2 Pour 150ml (¼ pint) boiling water into the dish, then cook for 15 minutes or until the mushrooms are soft and the topping is hot. Serve with toasted ciabatta and salad, and scatter a few small basil leaves over the mushrooms.

Cheesy Polenta with Tomato Sauce

Preparation Time 15 minutes, plus cooling • **Cooking Time** 45 minutes • **Serves 6** • **Per Serving** 249 calories, 9g fat (of which 4g saturates), 31g carbohydrate, 0.9g salt • **Vegetarian** • **Gluten Free** • **Easy**

oil to grease
225g (8oz) polenta
4 tbsp freshly chopped herbs, such
as oregano, chives and flat-leafed
parsley
100g (3½oz) freshly grated
Parmesan (see Cook's Tip, page
226), plus fresh Parmesan
shavings to serve
salt and ground black pepper

FOR THE TOMATO AND
BASIL SAUCE
1 tbsp vegetable oil
3 garlic cloves, crushed
500g carton creamed tomatoes or
passata
1 bay leaf
1 fresh thyme sprig
caster sugar
3 tbsp freshly chopped basil, plus
extra to garnish

1 Lightly oil a 25.5 x 18cm (10 x 7in) dish. Bring 1.1 litres (2 pints) water and ¼ tsp salt to the boil in a large pan. Sprinkle in the polenta, whisking constantly. Reduce the heat and simmer, stirring frequently, for 10–15 minutes until the mixture leaves the sides of the pan.

2 Stir in the herbs and Parmesan and season to taste with salt and pepper. Turn into the prepared dish and leave to cool.

3 Next, make the tomato and basil sauce. Heat the oil in a pan and fry the garlic for 30 seconds (do not brown). Add the creamed tomatoes or passata, the bay leaf, thyme and a large pinch of sugar. Season with salt and pepper and bring to the boil, then reduce the heat and simmer, uncovered, for 5–10 minutes. Remove the bay leaf and thyme sprig and add the chopped basil.

4 To serve, cut the polenta into pieces and lightly brush with oil. Preheat a griddle and fry for 3–4 minutes on each side, or grill under a preheated grill for 7–8 minutes on each side. Serve with the tomato and basil sauce, fresh Parmesan shavings and chopped basil.

⭐ GET AHEAD
To prepare ahead *Complete the recipe to the end of step 3. Cover and chill separately for up to two days.*
To use *Complete the recipe.*

Spinach and Goat's Cheese Frittata

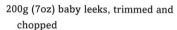

Preparation Time 20 minutes • **Cooking Time** 12 minutes • **Serves 4** • **Per Serving** 280 calories, 21g fat (of which 9g saturates), 3g carbohydrate, 0.9g salt • **Vegetarian** • **Gluten Free** • **Easy**

200g (7oz) baby leeks, trimmed and chopped
4 spring onions, chopped
125g (4oz) baby leaf spinach
6 large eggs
4 tbsp milk
freshly grated nutmeg
125g (4oz) soft goat's cheese, chopped
1 tbsp olive oil
salt and ground black pepper
mixed salad leaves to serve

1 Preheat the grill to high. Blanch the leeks in a pan of lightly salted boiling water for 2 minutes. Add the spring onions and spinach just before the end of the cooking time. Drain, rinse in cold water and dry on kitchen paper.

2 Whisk together the eggs, milk and nutmeg. Season with salt and pepper. Stir the goat's cheese into the egg mixture with the leeks, spinach and spring onions.

3 Heat the oil in a non-stick frying pan. Pour in the frittata mixture and fry gently for 4–5 minutes, then finish under the hot grill for 4–5 minutes until the top is golden and just firm. Serve with mixed salad.

★ TRY SOMETHING DIFFERENT
Use a different cheese, such as Stilton.

Warm New Potato Salad

Preparation Time 15 minutes • Cooking Time 15–20 minutes • Serves 6 • Per Serving 148 calories, 8g fat (of which 1g saturates), 18g carbohydrate, 0.2g salt • **Vegetarian** • **Gluten Free** • **Dairy Free** • **Easy**

650g (1lb 6oz) new potatoes, halved
1 heaped tbsp freshly chopped
  tarragon
1 tbsp caperberries (see Cook's Tip)

FOR THE CAPER DRESSING
1 heaped tbsp capers in sherry
  vinegar, rinsed
1 heaped tbsp Dijon mustard
4 tbsp extra virgin olive oil
salt and ground black pepper

1 Put the potatoes in a large pan of lightly salted boiling water and cook for 15–20 minutes until tender. Drain, cool slightly, then cut each potato into quarters lengthways and keep warm.

2 Meanwhile, make the dressing. Put the capers, mustard and oil in a mini processor and whiz until thick. Season well with salt and pepper.

3 Put the warm potatoes in a large salad bowl, add the dressing and tarragon and toss everything together.

4 Put the caperberries in the bowl with the potatoes and toss together.

 TRY SOMETHING DIFFERENT
Warm Pesto and Rocket Salad
Omit the capers and mustard and make a dressing by mixing 4 tbsp pesto (see page 17) with 1 tbsp olive oil. Toss with the warm potatoes, along with a good handful of wild rocket instead of the tarragon and caperberries.

 COOK'S TIP
Caperberries are the fruit from the caper bush. They are larger than capers, which are the buds.

Puddings and Desserts

Rustic Blackberry and Apple Pie

Preparation Time 25 minutes, plus chilling • Cooking Time 40 minutes • Serves 6 • Per Serving 372 calories, 19g fat (of which 11g saturates), 49g carbohydrate, 0.4g salt • Vegetarian • Easy

200g (7oz) plain flour, plus extra
  to dust
125g (4oz) chilled unsalted butter,
  diced
1 medium egg, beaten
75g (3oz) golden caster sugar, plus
  3 tbsp
a pinch of salt
500g (1lb 2oz) eating apples,
  quartered, cored and cut into
  chunky wedges
300g (11oz) blackberries
¼ tsp ground cinnamon
juice of 1 small lemon

1 Pulse the flour and butter in a food processor until it resembles coarse crumbs. Alternatively, rub the butter into the flour by hand or using a pastry cutter. Add the egg, 2 tbsp sugar and the salt, and pulse again to combine, or stir in. Wrap in clingfilm and chill for at least 15 minutes. Meanwhile, preheat the oven to 200°C (180°C fan oven) mark 6.

2 Put the apples, blackberries, 75g (3oz) sugar, the cinnamon and lemon juice in a bowl and toss together, making sure the sugar dissolves in the juice.

3 Grease a 25.5cm (10in) enamel or metal pie dish. Using a lightly floured rolling pin, roll out the pastry on a large sheet of baking parchment to a 30.5cm (12in) circle. Lift up the paper, upturn the pastry on to the pie dish and peel away the paper.

4 Put the prepared fruit in the centre of the pie dish and fold the pastry edges up and over the fruit. Sprinkle with the remaining sugar and bake for 40 minutes or until the fruit is tender and the pastry golden.

Rhubarb and Pear Crumble

Preparation Time 25 minutes • **Cooking Time** 40–45 minutes • **Serves 6** • **Per Serving** 255 calories, 14g fat (of which 6g saturates), 32g carbohydrate, 0.2g salt • **Vegetarian** • **Easy**

450g (1lb) rhubarb, cut into 2.5cm (1in) pieces
2 ripe pears, peeled, cored and roughly chopped
75g (3oz) demerara sugar
1 tsp ground cinnamon
50g (2oz) unsalted butter, chilled
75g (3oz) self-raising flour
2 shortbread fingers
50g (2oz) hazelnuts
Greek yogurt to serve

1 Preheat the oven to 180°C (160°C fan oven) mark 4. Put the fruit into a small shallow baking dish and sprinkle with 25g (1oz) sugar and the cinnamon. Mix together well.

2 Next, make the crumble mixture. Put the butter in a food processor, add the flour and the remaining sugar and whiz until it looks like rough breadcrumbs. Alternatively, rub the fat into the flour by hand or using a pastry cutter, then stir in the sugar.

3 Break the shortbread fingers into pieces and add to the processor with the hazelnuts, or crush the shortbread with a rolling pin and chop the hazelnuts. Whiz again for 4–5 seconds until the crumble is blended but still looks rough. Sprinkle the crumble over the fruit, spreading it up to the edges and pressing down with the back of a wooden spoon.

4 Bake for 40–45 minutes until the topping is golden brown and crisp. Serve with Greek yogurt.

Apple and Blueberry Strudel

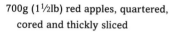

Preparation Time 15 minutes • **Cooking Time** 40 minutes • **Serves 6** • **Per Serving** 178 calories, 2g fat (of which trace saturates), 40g carbohydrate, 0g salt • **Vegetarian** • **Dairy Free** • **Easy**

700g (1½lb) red apples, quartered, cored and thickly sliced
1 tbsp lemon juice
2 tbsp golden caster sugar
100g (3½oz) dried blueberries
1 tbsp olive oil
6 sheets of filo pastry, thawed if frozen
crème fraîche to serve

1 Preheat the oven to 190°C (170°C fan oven) mark 5. Put the apples into a bowl and mix with the lemon juice, 1 tbsp sugar and the blueberries.

2 Warm the oil. Lay three sheets of filo pastry side by side, overlapping the long edges. Brush with the oil. Cover with three more sheets of filo and brush again.

3 Tip the apple mixture on to the pastry and roll up from a long edge. Put on to a non-stick baking sheet. Brush with the remaining oil and sprinkle with the remaining caster sugar. Bake for 40 minutes or until the pastry is golden and the apples soft. Serve with crème fraîche.

Classic Apple Pie

Preparation Time 20 minutes • Cooking Time 35–40 minutes • Serves 6 • Per Serving 268 calories, 11g fat (of which 4g saturates), 43g carbohydrate, 0.4g salt • **Vegetarian** • **Easy**

900g (2lb) cooking apples, peeled, cored and sliced
50g (2oz) caster sugar, plus extra to dust
flour to dust
Shortcrust Pastry (see Cook's Tip), made with 225g (8oz) plain flour, a pinch of salt, 100g (3½oz) chilled butter and 1 large egg

1 Preheat the oven to 190°C (170°C fan oven) mark 7.

2 Layer the apples and sugar in a 1.1 litre (2 pint) pie dish. Sprinkle with 1 tbsp water.

3 Roll out the pastry on a lightly floured surface to a circle 2.5cm (1in) larger than the pie dish. Cut off a strip the width of the rim of the dish, dampen the rim of the dish and press on the strip. Dampen the pastry strip and cover with the pastry circle, pressing the edges together well. Decorate the edge of the pastry and make a slit in the centre to allow steam to escape.

4 Bake for 35–40 minutes until the pastry is lightly browned. Sprinkle with caster sugar before serving.

 COOK'S TIP
Shortcrust Pastry
This is a basic recipe for shortcrust pastry. Adjust the quantities of ingredients as specified in individual recipes.
Sift 125g (4oz) plain flour and a pinch of salt into a bowl and add 50g (2oz) chilled unsalted butter, cut into small pieces. Using your fingertips or a pastry cutter, rub or cut the butter into the flour until the mixture resembles fine breadcrumbs. Using a fork, mix in 1 medium egg yolk and 1½ tsp water until the mixture holds together; add a little more water if necessary. Knead lightly to form a firm dough. Gather the dough in your hands and lightly knead. Form the pastry into a ball, wrap tightly in clingfilm and chill for at least 1 hour before using. (This allows the pastry to 'relax' and prevents shrinkage when it is baked.) Makes 125g (4oz) pastry.

Express Apple Tart

··· ★

Preparation Time 10 minutes • **Cooking Time** 20 minutes • **Serves 8** • **Per Serving** 197 calories, 12g fat (of which 0g saturates), 23g carbohydrate, 0.4g salt • **Vegetarian** • **Easy**

375g pack ready-rolled puff pastry
500g (1lb 2oz) dessert apples, such as Cox's Orange Pippins, cored and thinly sliced, then tossed in the juice of 1 lemon
golden icing sugar to dust

1 Preheat the oven to 200°C (180°C fan oven) mark 6. Put the pastry on to a 28 x 38cm (11 x 15in) baking sheet and lightly roll over it with a rolling pin to smooth down the pastry. Score lightly around the edge, leaving a 3cm (1¼in) border.

2 Put the apple slices on top of the pastry within the border. Turn the edge of the pastry inwards to reach the edge of the apples, pressing it down and using your fingers to crimp the edge.

3 Dust heavily with icing sugar. Bake for 20 minutes or until the pastry is cooked and the sugar has caramelised. Serve warm, dusted with more icing sugar.

Lemon Meringue Pie

★

Preparation Time 30 minutes • **Cooking Time** about 1 hour, plus standing • **Serves 8** • **Per Serving** 692 calories, 36g fat (of which 21g saturates), 83g carbohydrate, 0.6g salt • **Vegetarian** • **Easy**

23cm (9in) ready-made sweet
  pastry case

FOR THE FILLING
7 medium eggs, 4 separated, at
  room temperature
finely grated zest of 3 lemons
175ml (6fl oz) freshly squeezed
  lemon juice (about 4 lemons),
  strained
400g can condensed milk
150ml (¼ pint) double cream
225g (8oz) golden icing sugar

1 Preheat the oven to 180°C (160°C fan oven) mark 4. To make the filling, put 4 egg yolks into a bowl with the 3 whole eggs. Add the lemon zest and juice and whisk lightly. Mix in the condensed milk and cream.

2 Pour the filling into the pastry case and bake for 30 minutes or until just set in the centre. Put to one side to cool while you prepare the meringue. Increase the oven temperature to 200°C (180°C fan oven) mark 6.

3 For the meringue, whisk the egg whites and sugar together in a heatproof bowl set over a pan of gently simmering water, using a hand-held electric whisk, for 10 minutes or until very shiny and thick. Remove from the heat and whisk at a low speed for a further 5–10 minutes until the bowl is cool.

4 Pile the meringue on top of the lemon filling and swirl with a palette knife to form peaks. Bake for 5–10 minutes until the meringue is tinged brown. Leave to stand for about 1 hour, then serve.

Treacle Tart

Preparation Time 25 minutes, plus chilling • Cooking Time 45–50 minutes, plus cooling • Serves 6 •
Per Serving 486 calories, 15g fat (of which 8g saturates), 88g carbohydrate, 1.1g salt • Vegetarian • Easy

Sweet Shortcrust Pastry (see
  Cook's Tip), made with 225g
  (8oz) plain flour, 150g (5oz)
  unsalted butter, 15g (½oz) golden
  caster sugar and
  1 medium egg yolk
flour to dust

FOR THE FILLING
700g (1½lb) golden syrup
175g (6oz) fresh white breadcrumbs
grated zest of 3 lemons
2 medium eggs, lightly beaten

1 Preheat the oven to 180°C (160°C
fan oven) mark 4. Roll out the pastry
on a lightly floured surface and use
to line a 25.5cm (10in), 4cm (1½in)
deep, loose-based fluted tart tin.
Prick the base all over with a fork
and chill for 30 minutes.

2 To make the filling, heat the
golden syrup in a pan over a low
heat until thinner in consistency.
Remove from the heat and mix in
the breadcrumbs and lemon zest.
Stir in the beaten eggs.

3 Pour the filling into the pastry case
and bake for 45–50 minutes until
the filling is lightly set and golden.
Allow to cool slightly. Serve warm.

★ COOK'S TIP
Sweet Shortcrust Pastry
Make as for shortcrust pastry on
page 255, adding 50g (2oz) caster sugar
and 2 medium egg yolks at step 2.
Makes 125g (4oz) pastry.

Orange Syrup Cake

Preparation Time 20 minutes, plus soaking • **Cooking Time** 30–40 minutes • **Cuts into 10 slices** • **Per Slice** 291 calories, 20g fat (of which 10g saturates), 27g carbohydrate, 0.4g salt • **Vegetarian** • **Easy**

175g (6oz) unsalted butter, plus extra to grease
225g (8oz) caster sugar
2 medium eggs, beaten
200g (7oz) rice flour
2 tsp baking powder
75g (3oz) ground almonds
grated zest and juice of 1 large orange
250ml carton orange juice
2 large oranges, peeled and thickly sliced
2 tbsp lemon juice
blueberries to serve

1 Preheat the oven to 190°C (170°C fan oven) mark 5. Grease a shallow 20.5cm (8in) round tin and baseline with greaseproof paper.

2 Cream the butter and 75g (3oz) sugar, then beat in the eggs gradually. Fold in the rice flour, baking powder and ground almonds. Stir in the zest and juice of the orange and 8 tbsp orange juice. The mixture should be of a soft, dropping consistency. Spoon the mixture into the prepared tin and level the surface.

3 Bake in the oven for 40 minutes or until firm. Leave to cool in the tin for 10 minutes, then turn out on to a wire rack to cool completely.

4 Just before serving, combine the remaining sugar and orange juice plus the lemon juice in a small pan. Add the orange slices, bring to the boil and cook for 1–2 minutes. Take the pan off the heat and leave to cool for 5 minutes. Remove the orange slices from the syrup and put to one side. Put the cake on a serving plate and, with a cocktail stick, prick the cake in a number of places. Drizzle with the syrup and leave to soak in for 30 minutes. Serve with the orange slices and blueberries.

★ FREEZING TIP
To freeze *Complete the recipe to the end of step 3, wrap and freeze.*
To use *Thaw at a cool room temperature for 2–3 hours. Complete the recipe.*

Pear and Ginger Steamed Pudding

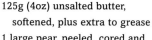

Preparation Time 20 minutes • Cooking Time 1 hour 35 minutes • Serves 8 • Per Serving 314 calories, 14g fat (of which 9g saturates), 45g carbohydrate, 0.6g salt • **Vegetarian** • **Easy**

125g (4oz) unsalted butter,
    softened, plus extra to grease
1 large pear, peeled, cored and
    diced
2 tbsp golden caster sugar
2 balls stem ginger, finely chopped,
    plus 2 tbsp ginger syrup
4 tbsp golden syrup
125g (4oz) light muscovado sugar
finely grated zest of 1 lemon
2 medium eggs, beaten
175g (6oz) self-raising flour
2 tsp ground ginger
3 tbsp perry or pear juice

1 Grease a 900ml (1½ pint) pudding basin. Put the pear into a pan with 2 tbsp water and the caster sugar and simmer for 5 minutes. Stir in the stem ginger and the ginger and golden syrups and leave to cool. Tip into the basin.

2 Beat the butter, muscovado sugar and lemon zest in a bowl with a hand-held electric whisk until light and fluffy. Beat in the eggs a little at a time.

3 Fold in the flour and ground ginger, then fold in the perry or pear juice. Pour the mixture into the basin on top of the pear compote. Cut out a piece each of greaseproof paper and kitchen foil, each measuring 30.5 x 30.5cm (12 x 12in). Place the greaseproof on the foil and fold a pleat in the middle. Put on top of the pudding basin – it should overhang the sides. Tie the paper under the rim of the basin with string, using extra to make a knotted handle over the top. Trim off excess paper and foil.

4 Sit the basin on an upturned saucer in a large pan. Pour in enough boiling water to come halfway up the basin. Cover and steam for 1¼–1½ hours, topping up with boiling water as necessary. Turn out on to a plate and serve.

Steamed Syrup Sponge Puddings

Preparation Time 20 minutes • **Cooking Time** 35 minutes or 1½ hours • **Serves 4** • **Per Serving** 580 calories, 29g fat (of which 17g saturates), 76g carbohydrate, 0.7g salt • **Vegetarian** • **Easy**

125g (4oz) unsalted butter,
   softened, plus extra to grease
3 tbsp golden syrup
125g (4oz) golden caster sugar
few drops of vanilla extract
2 medium eggs, beaten
175g (6oz) self-raising flour, sifted
about 3 tbsp milk
custard or cream to serve

1 Half-fill a steamer or large pan with water and put it on to boil. Grease four 300ml (½ pint) basins or a 900ml (1½ pint) pudding basin and spoon the syrup into the bottom.

2 Cream the butter and sugar together until pale and fluffy. Stir in the vanilla extract. Add the eggs, a little at a time, beating well after each addition.

3 Using a metal spoon, fold in half the flour, then fold in the remaining flour with enough milk to give a dropping consistency. Spoon the mixture into the prepared pudding basin(s).

4 Cover with greased and pleated greaseproof paper and foil (see opposite), and secure with string. Steam for 35 minutes for individual puddings or 1½ hours for one large pudding, checking the water level from time to time and topping up with boiling water as necessary. Turn out on to warmed plates and serve with custard or cream.

⭐ TRY SOMETHING DIFFERENT
Instead of syrup, try the following.
Steamed Jam Sponge Puddings
Put 4 tbsp raspberry or blackberry jam into the bottom of the basins instead of the syrup.
Steamed Chocolate Sponge Puddings
Omit the golden syrup. Blend 4 tbsp cocoa powder with 2 tbsp hot water, then gradually beat into the creamed mixture before adding the eggs.

Cherry and Tangerine Sticky Puddings

Preparation Time 20 minutes, plus soaking • Cooking Time 25 minutes • Serves 8 • Per Serving 664 calories, 39g fat (of which 22g saturates), 79g carbohydrate, 0.7g salt • Vegetarian • Easy

about 25g (1oz) white vegetable fat, melted
200g (7oz) dried cherries
2 tbsp orange-flavoured liqueur
¾ tsp bicarbonate of soda
75g (3oz) unsalted butter, softened
150g (5oz) golden caster sugar
2 medium eggs, beaten
175g (6oz) self-raising flour

FOR THE SAUCE
175g (6oz) light muscovado sugar
125g (4oz) unsalted butter
6 tbsp double cream
25g (1oz) pecan nuts, chopped
juice of 1 tangerine

1 Preheat the oven to 180°C (160°C fan oven) mark 4. Using the melted fat, lightly oil eight 175ml (6fl oz) metal pudding basins or ramekins, then put a circle of non-stick baking parchment into the base of each.

2 Put 175g (6oz) dried cherries into a bowl and pour 150ml (¼ pint) boiling water over them. Stir in the liqueur and bicarbonate of soda, then leave to soak for 1 hour.

3 Whisk the butter and sugar in a large bowl until pale and fluffy, then beat in the eggs a little at a time. Fold in the cherry mixture.

4 Add the flour and fold in with a large metal spoon. Divide the mixture equally among the basins, then place on a baking sheet and bake for about 25 minutes or until well risen and firm.

5 Meanwhile, make the sauce. Put the sugar, butter, cream, pecans and remaining cherries in a pan. Heat gently until the sugar has dissolved, then stir in the tangerine juice.

6 Leave the puddings to cool for 5 minutes, then turn out. Serve topped with the sauce.

 FREEZING TIP
To freeze *Cool the puddings completely. Wrap in clingfilm. Pour the sauce into a freezerproof container and leave to cool. Freeze both for up to one month.*
To use *Thaw the puddings and sauce overnight in the fridge. Warm the sauce. Meanwhile, put the puddings on a microwaveable plate. Spoon 1 tbsp sauce over each. Warm in the microwave on High for 2 minutes. Serve with the remaining sauce.*

Bread and Butter Pudding

Preparation Time 10 minutes, plus soaking • Cooking Time 30–40 minutes • Serves 4 • Per Serving 450 calories, 13g fat (of which 5g saturates), 70g carbohydrate, 1.1g salt • **Vegetarian** • **Easy**

50g (2oz) unsalted butter, softened, plus extra to grease

275g (10oz) white farmhouse bread, cut into 1cm (½in) slices, crusts removed

50g (2oz) raisins or sultanas

3 medium eggs

450ml (¾ pint) milk

3 tbsp golden icing sugar, plus extra to dust

1 Lightly butter four 300ml (½ pint) gratin dishes or one 1.1 litre (2 pint) ovenproof dish. Butter the bread, then cut into quarters to make triangles. Arrange the bread in the dish(es) and sprinkle with the raisins or sultanas.

2 Beat the eggs, milk and sugar in a bowl. Pour the mixture over the bread and leave to soak in for 10 minutes. Preheat the oven to 180°C (160°C fan oven) mark 4.

3 Put the pudding(s) in the oven and bake for 30–40 minutes. Dust with icing sugar to serve.

Chocolate Cherry Roll

Preparation Time 30 minutes • **Cooking Time** 30 minutes, plus cooling • **Serves 8** • **Per Serving** 185 calories, 5g fat (of which 2g saturates), 30g carbohydrate, 0.3g salt • **Vegetarian** • **Gluten Free** • **A Little Effort**

4 tbsp cocoa powder, plus extra
   to dust
100ml (3½fl oz) milk, plus 3 tbsp
   extra
5 medium eggs, separated
125g (4oz) golden caster sugar
1–2 tbsp cherry jam
400g can cherries without stones,
   drained and chopped
icing sugar to dust

1 Preheat the oven to 180°C (160°C fan oven) mark 4. Line a 30.5 x 20.5cm (12 x 8in) Swiss roll tin with baking parchment. In a bowl, mix together the cocoa and 3 tbsp milk. Heat 100ml (3½ fl oz) milk in a pan until almost boiling, then add to the bowl, stirring. Leave to cool for 10 minutes.

2 Whisk the egg whites in a clean grease-free bowl until soft peaks form. In a separate bowl, whisk together the egg yolks and caster sugar until pale and thick. Gradually whisk in the cooled milk, then fold in the egg whites. Spoon the mixture into the prepared tin and smooth the surface. Bake in the oven for 25 minutes or until just firm.

3 Turn out on to a board lined with baking parchment and peel off the lining parchment. Cover with a damp teatowel.

4 Spread the jam over the sponge and top with the cherries. Roll up from the shortest end, dust with cocoa and icing sugar, then cut into slices and serve.

★ TRY SOMETHING DIFFERENT
You can add whipped cream to the roll, but you will need to cool it first. To do this, turn out the sponge on to baking parchment. Do not remove the lining paper but roll the sponge around it while still warm. Leave to cool, unroll and peel off the paper. Spread with the jam and fruit, then the cream, and re-roll.

Warm Chocolate Fondants

★

Preparation Time 25 minutes • Cooking Time 10–12 minutes • Serves 6 • Per Serving 502 calories, 37g fat (of which 21g saturates), 39g carbohydrate, 0.5g salt • Vegetarian • Easy

150g (5oz) unsalted butter, plus extra to grease
3 medium eggs, plus 3 egg yolks
50g (2oz) golden caster sugar
175g (6oz) plain chocolate (at least 70% cocoa solids), broken into pieces
50g (2oz) plain flour, sifted
6 chocolate truffles

1 Preheat the oven to 200°C (180°C fan oven) mark 6. Lightly grease six 200ml (7fl oz) ramekins. Put the eggs, egg yolks and sugar into a large bowl and beat with a hand-held electric whisk for 8–10 minutes until pale and fluffy.

2 Meanwhile, melt the chocolate and butter in a heatproof bowl set over a pan of gently simmering water, making sure the base of the bowl doesn't touch the water, stirring occasionally.

3 Stir a spoonful of the melted chocolate into the egg mixture, then gently fold the remaining chocolate mixture into the egg mixture.

4 Put a large spoonful of mixture into each ramekin. Put a chocolate truffle in the centre of each, taking care not to push it down. Divide the remainder of the mixture among the ramekins to cover the truffle; they should be about three-quarters full. Bake for 10–12 minutes until the top is firm and starting to rise and crack. Serve warm.

Sticky Toffee Puddings

Preparation Time 20 minutes • Cooking Time 25–30 minutes, plus resting • Serves 4 • Per Serving 565 calories, 38g fat (of which 21g saturates), 53g carbohydrate, 0.9g salt • Vegetarian • Easy

1 tbsp golden syrup
1 tbsp black treacle
150g (5oz) unsalted butter, softened
25g (1oz) pecan nuts or walnuts, finely ground
75g (3oz) self-raising flour
125g (4oz) caster sugar
2 large eggs, beaten
cream or custard to serve

1 Preheat the oven to 180°C (160°C fan oven) mark 4. Put the syrup, treacle and 25g (1oz) butter into a bowl and beat until smooth. Divide the mixture among four 150ml (¼ pint) timbales or ramekins and put to one side.

2 Put the nuts into a bowl, sift in the flour and mix together well.

3 Put the remaining butter and the sugar in a food processor and whiz briefly. (Alternatively, use an electric hand mixer.) Add the eggs and the

flour mixture and whiz or mix again for 30 seconds. Spoon the mixture on top of the syrup mixture in the timbales or ramekins. Bake for 25–30 minutes until risen and golden.

4 Remove the puddings from the oven and leave to rest for 5 minutes, then unmould on to warmed serving plates. Serve immediately with cream or custard.

Baked Apples

Preparation Time 5 minutes, plus soaking • Cooking Time 15–20 minutes • Serves 6 • Per Serving 280 calories, 13g fat (of which 1g saturates), 36g carbohydrate, 0g salt • Vegetarian • Gluten Free • Dairy Free • Easy

125g (4oz) hazelnuts
125g (4oz) sultanas
2 tbsp brandy
6 large Bramley apples, cored
4 tbsp soft brown sugar
100ml (3½fl oz) apple juice
thick cream to serve

1 Preheat the oven to 190°C (170°C fan oven) mark 5. Spread the hazelnuts over a baking sheet and toast under a hot grill until golden brown, turning them frequently. Put the hazelnuts in a clean teatowel and rub off the skins, then chop the nuts. Put to one side.

2 Soak the sultanas in the brandy and put to one side for 10 minutes. Using a small sharp knife, score around the middle of the apples to stop them from bursting, then stuff each apple with equal amounts of brandy-soaked sultanas. Put the apples in a roasting tin and sprinkle with the brown sugar and apple juice. Bake in the oven for 15–20 minutes until soft.

3 Serve the apples with the toasted hazelnuts and a dollop of cream.

Spiced Winter Fruit

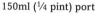

Preparation Time 20 minutes • **Cooking Time** about 20 minutes • **Serves 6** • **Per Serving** 222 calories, 0g fat, 48g carbohydrate, 0g salt • **Vegetarian** • **Gluten Free** • **Dairy Free** • **Easy**

150ml (¼ pint) port
150ml (¼ pint) freshly squeezed orange juice
75g (3oz) light muscovado sugar
1 cinnamon stick
6 whole cardamom pods, lightly crushed
5cm (2in) piece fresh root ginger, peeled and thinly sliced
50g (2oz) large muscatel raisins or dried blueberries
1 small pineapple, peeled, cored and thinly sliced
1 mango, peeled, stoned and thickly sliced

3 tangerines, peeled and halved horizontally
3 fresh figs, halved

1 First, make the syrup. Pour the port and orange juice into a small pan, then add the sugar and 300ml (½ pint) water. Bring to the boil, stirring all the time. Add the cinnamon stick, cardamom pods and ginger, then bubble gently for 15 minutes.

2 Put all the fruit into a serving bowl. Remove the cinnamon stick and cardamom pods from the syrup, then pour the syrup over the fruit. Serve warm or cold.

 FREEZING TIP
To freeze *Tip the fruit and syrup into a freezerproof container, leave to cool, then cover with a tight-fitting lid. Freeze for up to three months.*
To use *Thaw overnight in the fridge and serve cold.*

 COOK'S TIPS
● *It might sound odd freezing a fruit salad, but it saves all the last-minute chopping and slicing.*
● *Not suitable for children due to the alcohol content.*

Toffee Apples

★

Preparation Time 10 minutes • Cooking Time 15 minutes • Serves 6 • Per Serving 413 calories, 0g fat, 109g carbohydrate, 0g salt • Vegetarian • Gluten Free • Dairy Free • Easy

550g (1¼lb) sugar
300ml (½ pint) water
6 eating apples

1 Put the sugar into a heavy-based pan with 300ml (½ pint) water and heat gently until the sugar dissolves.

2 Meanwhile, spear the apples with a stick or fork. Once the sugar has dissolved completely (otherwise it will crystallize), increase the heat and let the mixture boil until it turns a caramel colour. Take the pan off the heat and immediately dip the pan in cold water to stop the caramel cooking further.

3 Quickly dip each apple into the caramel to coat, then put on non-stick baking parchment to cool. They should last for 2–3 hours before the caramel starts softening.

White Chocolate and Berry Crêpes

Preparation Time 2 minutes • Cooking Time 10 minutes • Serves 4 • Per Serving 476 calories, 37g fat (of which 15g saturates), 37g carbohydrate, 0.2g salt • Vegetarian • Easy

500g bag frozen mixed berries, thawed
100g (3½oz) good-quality white chocolate, broken into pieces
142ml carton double cream
4 thin ready-made crêpes

1 Put the thawed berries into a large pan and cook over a medium heat for 5 minutes or until heated through.

2 Meanwhile, put the chocolate and cream into a heatproof bowl set over a pan of simmering water, making sure the bottom of the bowl doesn't touch the hot water. Heat gently, stirring, for 5 minutes or until the chocolate has just melted. Remove the bowl from the pan and mix the chocolate and cream to a smooth sauce. Alternatively, microwave the chocolate and the cream together on full power for 2–2½ minutes (based on a 900W oven), then stir until smooth.

3 Meanwhile, heat the crêpes according to the pack instructions.

4 To serve, put each crêpe on a warmed plate and fold in half. Spoon a quarter of the berries into the middle of each, then fold the crêpe over the filling and pour the hot chocolate sauce over the top.

★ COOK'S TIP
Instead of mixed berries, try using just one type of berry.

Instant Banana Ice Cream

★

Preparation Time 5 minutes, plus freezing • Serves 4 • Per Serving 173 calories, 1g fat (of which 0g saturates),
42g carbohydrate, 0g salt • **Vegetarian** • **Gluten Free** • **Easy**

6 ripe bananas, about 700g (1½lb),
    peeled, cut into thin slices and
    frozen (see Cook's Tip)
1–2 tbsp virtually fat-free fromage
    frais
1–2 tbsp orange juice
1 tsp vanilla extract
splash of rum or Cointreau
    (optional)
a few drops of lime juice to taste

1 Leave the frozen banana slices to
stand at room temperature for 2–3
minutes. Put the still frozen pieces in
a food processor or blender with
1 tbsp fromage frais, 1 tbsp orange
juice, the vanilla extract and the
liqueur, if using.

2 Whiz until smooth, scraping down
the sides of the bowl and adding
more fromage frais and orange juice
as necessary to give a creamy
consistency. Add lime juice to taste
and serve at once or turn into a
freezerproof container and freeze
for up to one month.

★ COOK'S TIP
*To freeze bananas, peel them and slice
thinly, then put the banana slices on a
large non-stick baking tray and put into
the freezer for 30 minutes or until frozen.
Transfer to a plastic bag and store in the
freezer until needed.*

Lemon Sorbet

Preparation Time 10 minutes, plus chilling and freezing • **Serves 4** • **Per Serving** 130 calories, 0g fat, 33g carbohydrate, 0g salt • **Vegetarian** • **Gluten Free** • **Dairy Free** • **Easy**

3 juicy lemons
125g (4oz) golden caster sugar
1 large egg white

1 Finely pare the lemon zest, using a zester, then squeeze the juice. Put the zest into a pan with the sugar and 350ml (12fl oz) water and heat gently until the sugar has dissolved. Increase the heat and boil for 10 minutes. Leave to cool.

2 Stir the lemon juice into the cooled sugar syrup. Cover and chill in the fridge for 30 minutes.

3 Strain the syrup through a fine sieve into a bowl. In another bowl, beat the egg white until just frothy, then whisk into the lemon mixture.

4 For best results, freeze in an ice-cream maker. Otherwise, pour into a shallow freezerproof container and freeze until almost frozen; mash well with a fork and freeze until solid. Transfer the sorbet to the fridge 30 minutes before serving to soften slightly.

★ TRY SOMETHING DIFFERENT
Orange Sorbet
Replace two of the lemons with oranges.
Lime Sorbet
Replace two of the lemons with four limes.

Summer Pudding

Preparation Time 10 minutes, plus overnight chilling • **Cooking Time** 10 minutes • **Serves 8** • **Per Serving** 173 calories, 1g fat (of which trace saturates), 38g carbohydrate, 0.4g salt • **Vegetarian** • **Dairy Free** • **Easy**

800g (1lb 12oz) mixed summer berries, such as 250g (9oz) each redcurrants and blackcurrants and 300g (11oz) raspberries
125g (4oz) golden caster sugar
3 tbsp crème de cassis
9 thick slices slightly stale white bread, crusts removed
crème fraîche or clotted cream to serve

1 Put the redcurrants and blackcurrants into a medium pan. Add the sugar and cassis. Bring to a simmer and cook for 3–5 minutes until the sugar has dissolved. Add the raspberries and cook for 2 minutes. Once the fruit is cooked, taste it – there should be a good balance between tart and sweet.

2 Meanwhile, line a 1 litre (1¾ pint) bowl with clingfilm. Put the base of the bowl on one piece of bread and cut around it. Put the circle of bread in the base of the bowl.

3 Line the inside of the bowl with more slices of bread, slightly overlapping them to prevent any gaps. Spoon in the fruit, making sure the juice soaks into the bread. Keep back a few spoonfuls of juice in case the bread is unevenly soaked when you turn out the pudding.

4 Cut the remaining bread to fit the top of the pudding neatly, using a sharp knife to trim any excess bread from around the edges. Wrap in clingfilm, weigh down with a saucer and a can and chill overnight.

5 To serve, unwrap the outer clingfilm, upturn the pudding on to a plate and remove the inner clingfilm. Drizzle with the reserved juice and serve with crème fraîche or clotted cream.

Classic Tiramisù

★

Preparation Time 20 minutes, plus chilling • **Serves 8** • **Per Serving** 420 calories, 33g fat (of which 18g saturates), 24g carbohydrate, 0.3g salt • **Vegetarian** • **Easy**

4 medium egg yolks
75g (3oz) golden caster sugar
200g tub mascarpone cheese
1 tbsp vanilla extract
300ml (½ pint) double cream,
   whipped until softly peaking
100ml (3½fl oz) grappa
200g packet sponge fingers or
   Savoiardi biscuits
450ml (¾ pint) warm strong black
   coffee
1 tbsp cocoa powder

1 Using an electric hand-held beater, whisk the egg yolks and sugar in a large bowl until pale and thick – about 5 minutes. Add the mascarpone and vanilla extract and beat until smooth. Fold in the cream and grappa.

2 Spread half the mascarpone mixture over the bottom of eight small serving dishes. Dip the sponge fingers, in turn, into the coffee and arrange on the mascarpone layer. Top with the remaining mascarpone mixture.

3 Cover and chill for at least 2 hours. Dust with cocoa powder, through a sieve, just before serving.

Rich Chocolate Pots

★

Preparation Time 10 minutes, plus chilling • **Cooking Time** 10 minutes • **Serves 6** • **Per Serving** 895 calories, 66g fat (of which 41g saturates), 66g carbohydrate, 0g salt • **Vegetarian** • **Gluten Free** • **Easy**

300g (11oz) plain chocolate (at least 70% cocoa solids), broken into chunks
300ml (½ pint) double cream
250g (9oz) mascarpone cheese
3 tbsp cognac
1 tbsp vanilla extract
6 tbsp crème fraîche
chocolate curls to decorate (see Cook's Tip)

1 Melt the plain chocolate in a heatproof bowl over a pan of gently simmering water, making sure the base of the bowl doesn't touch the water. Remove from the heat and add the cream, mascarpone, cognac and vanilla. Mix well – the hot chocolate will melt into the cream and mascarpone.

2 Divide the mixture among six 150ml (¼ pint) glasses and chill for 20 minutes.

3 To serve, spoon some crème fraîche on top of each chocolate pot and decorate with the chocolate curls.

★ GET AHEAD
To prepare ahead *Make the chocolate curls and keep in a sealed container in the refrigerator for up to one day.*

Profiteroles

Preparation Time 25 minutes • Cooking Time 30 minutes, plus cooling • Serves 6 • Per Serving 652 calories, 59g fat (of which 33g saturates), 35g carbohydrate, 0.3g salt • Vegetarian • A Little Effort

65g (2½oz) plain flour
a pinch of salt
50g (2oz) butter, diced
2 large eggs, lightly beaten
300ml (½ pint) double cream
a few drops of vanilla extract
1 tsp caster sugar

FOR THE CHOCOLATE SAUCE
225g (8oz) plain chocolate (at least 70% cocoa solids), broken into pieces
140ml (4½ fl oz) double cream
1–2 tbsp Grand Marnier to taste (optional)
1–2 tsp golden caster sugar to taste (optional)

1 Preheat the oven to 220°C (200°C fan oven) mark 7. Sift the flour with the salt on to a sheet of greaseproof paper. Put the butter into a medium heavy-based pan with 150ml (¼ pint) water. Heat gently until the butter melts, then bring to a rapid boil. Take off the heat and immediately tip in all the flour and beat thoroughly with a wooden spoon until the mixture is smooth and forms a ball. Turn into a bowl and leave to cool for about 10 minutes.

2 Gradually add the eggs to the mixture, beating well after each addition. Ensure that the mixture becomes thick and shiny before adding any more egg – if it's added too quickly, the choux paste will become runny and the cooked buns will be flat.

3 Sprinkle a large baking sheet with a little water. Using two damp teaspoons, spoon about 18 small mounds of the choux paste on to the baking sheet, spacing well apart to allow room for them to expand. (Alternatively, spoon the choux paste into a piping bag fitted with a 1cm (½in) plain nozzle and pipe mounds on to the baking sheet.)

4 Bake for about 25 minutes or until well risen, crisp and golden brown. Make a small hole in the side of each bun to allow the steam to escape and then put back in the

oven for a further 5 minutes or until thoroughly dried out. Slide on to a large wire rack and put to one side to cool.

5 To make the sauce, put the chocolate and cream in a medium pan with 4 tbsp water. Heat gently, stirring occasionally, until the chocolate melts to a smooth sauce; do not boil. Remove from the heat.

6 To assemble, lightly whip the cream with the vanilla extract and sugar until it just holds its shape. Pipe into the hole in each choux bun, or split the buns open and spoon in the cream. Chill for up to 2 hours.

7 Just before serving, gently reheat the chocolate sauce. Add Grand Marnier and sugar to taste, if you like. Divide the choux buns among serving bowls and pour the warm chocolate sauce over them. Serve immediately.

★ FREEZING TIP
To freeze Complete the recipe to the end of step 4, then cool, wrap, seal, label and freeze.
To use Put the frozen buns on a baking sheet in the oven at 220°C (200°C fan oven) mark 7 for 5 minutes. Cool, then complete the recipe.

Fruity Rice Pudding

★

Preparation Time 10 minutes, plus cooling and chilling • **Cooking Time** 1 hour • **Serves 6** • **Per Serving** 323 calories, 17g fat (of which 10g saturates), 36g carbohydrate, 0.2g salt • **Vegetarian** • **Gluten Free** • **Easy**

125g (4oz) pudding rice
1.1 litres (2 pints) full-fat milk
1 tsp vanilla extract
3–4 tbsp caster sugar
200ml (7fl oz) whipping cream
6 tbsp wild lingonberry sauce

1 Put the rice into a pan with 600ml (1 pint) cold water and bring to the boil, then reduce the heat and simmer until the liquid has evaporated. Add the milk and bring to the boil, then reduce the heat and simmer for 45 minutes or until the rice is very soft and creamy. Leave to cool.

2 Add the vanilla extract and sugar to the rice. Lightly whip the cream and fold through the pudding. Chill for 1 hour.

3 Divide the rice mixture among six glass dishes and top with 1 tbsp lingonberry sauce.

★ TRY SOMETHING DIFFERENT
● *Although wild lingonberry sauce is used here, a spoonful of any fruit sauce or compote such as strawberry or blueberry will taste delicious.*
● *For an alternative presentation, serve in tumblers, layering the rice pudding with the fruit sauce; you will need to use double the amount of fruit sauce.*

Sticky Banoffee Pies

★

Preparation Time 15 minutes, plus chilling • **Serves 6** • **Per Serving** 827 calories, 55g fat (of which 32g saturates), 84g carbohydrate, 1.2g salt • **Vegetarian** • **Easy**

150g (5oz) digestive biscuits
75g (3oz) unsalted butter, melted, plus extra to grease
1 tsp ground ginger (optional)
450g (1lb) dulce de leche toffee sauce
4 bananas, peeled, sliced and tossed in the juice of 1 lemon
300ml (½ pint) double cream, lightly whipped
plain chocolate shavings

1 Put the biscuits into a food processor and whiz until they resemble fine crumbs. Alternatively, put them in a plastic bag and crush with a rolling pin. Transfer to a bowl. Add the melted butter and ginger, if using, then process, or stir well, for 1 minute to combine.

2 Butter six 10cm (4in) rings or tartlet tins and line with greaseproof paper. Press the biscuit mixture evenly into the bottom of each ring. Divide the toffee sauce equally among the rings and top with the bananas. Pipe or spoon on the cream, sprinkle with chocolate shavings and chill. Remove from the rings or tins to serve.

★ COOK'S TIP
Slightly overripe bananas are ideal for this recipe.

Custard Tart

Preparation Time 25 minutes, plus chilling • Cooking Time 1¼ hours • Serves 10 • Per Serving 399 calories, 28g fat (of which 16g saturates), 32g carbohydrate, 0.4g salt • Vegetarian • Easy

225g (8oz) plain flour, sifted, plus
  extra to dust
175g (6oz) cold butter, diced
50g (2oz) golden caster sugar
finely grated zest of 1 lemon
1 medium egg yolk

FOR THE FILLING
8 large egg yolks
75g (3oz) golden caster sugar
450ml (¾ pint) single cream
nutmeg for grating

1 Put the flour into a bowl and, Using your fingertips or a pastry cutter, rub in the butter until it resembles breadcrumbs. Stir in the sugar and lemon zest. Lightly beat the egg yolk with 2–3 tbsp ice-cold water and, using a knife, stir small amounts into the flour until it starts to clump together but isn't too sticky or dry. Bring together with your hands and knead lightly until smooth. Shape into a disc, wrap in clingfilm and chill for 30 minutes.

2 Roll out the pastry on a lightly floured surface to a 3mm (⅛in) thickness. Use to line a 23cm (9in) round, 4cm (1½in) deep flan tin. Prick the base all over with a fork and chill for 30 minutes.

3 Preheat the oven to 200°C (180°C fan oven) mark 6. Put the flan tin on a baking sheet. Line the tin with greaseproof paper, cover with baking beans and bake blind for 12–15 minutes. Remove the beans and paper and continue baking for 5–10 minutes until cooked through. Reduce the oven temperature to 130°C (110°C fan oven) mark ½.

4 Mix the egg yolks and sugar together with a wooden spoon. Gradually stir in the cream, then strain into a jug to remove any eggy strands. Pour the mixture into the pastry case and bake for 40–50 minutes until just set with a little wobble. Grate plenty of nutmeg over it and cool in the tin on a wire rack. Serve at room temperature.

 COOK'S TIP
Freeze the leftover egg whites in a clean container for up to three months and use to make meringues.

Toffee Cheesecake

Preparation Time 15 minutes, plus chilling • **Cooking Time** 45 minutes–1 hour • **Serves** 10 • **Per Serving** 379 calories, 24g fat (of which 13g saturates), 34g carbohydrate, 1.1g salt • **Vegetarian** • **Easy**

300g pack digestive biscuits
125g (4oz) unsalted butter, melted

FOR THE FILLING
450g (1lb) curd cheese
140ml (4½fl oz) double cream
juice of ½ lemon
3 medium eggs, beaten
50g (2oz) golden caster sugar
6 tbsp dulce de leche toffee sauce,
   plus extra to drizzle

1 Put the biscuits into a food processor and whiz until they resemble fine crumbs. Alternatively, put them in a plastic bag and crush with a rolling pin. Transfer to a bowl. Add the butter and blend briefly, or stir in, to combine. Tip the crumb mixture into a 20.5cm (8in) springform cake tin and press evenly into the base and up the sides, then chill for about 1 hour or until firm.

2 Preheat the oven to 200°C (180°C fan oven) gas mark 6. To make the filling, put the curd cheese and cream into a food processor or blender and whiz until smooth. Add the lemon juice, eggs, sugar and toffee sauce, then blend again until smooth. Pour into the chilled biscuit case and bake for 10 minutes. Reduce the oven temperature to 180°C (160°C fan oven) mark 4, then bake for 45 minutes or until set and golden brown.

3 Turn off the oven and leave the cheesecake inside, with the door ajar, until it is cool. When completely cool, chill for at least 2 hours to firm up the crust.

4 To remove the cheesecake from the tin, run a knife around the edge of the cake. Open the tin carefully, then use a palette knife to ease the cheesecake out. Cut into wedges, put on a serving plate and drizzle with toffee sauce.

★ COOK'S TIP
To slice the cheesecake easily, use a sharp knife dipped into a jug of boiling water and then wiped dry.

Toffee Crunch Ice Cream

Preparation Time 20 minutes, plus overnight freezing • Cooking Time 5 minutes • Serves 8 • Per Serving 535 calories, 33g fat (of which 19g saturates), 60g carbohydrate, 0.4g salt • Vegetarian • Easy

3 chocolate-covered fudge finger bars, about 100g (3½oz) total weight

284ml carton double cream

2 medium eggs, separated

50g (2oz) icing sugar

5 chocolate bars with a butter almond centre, 175g (6oz) total weight, broken into pieces

500g carton chilled ready-made custard

1 Break the fudge bars into a heatproof bowl. Add 2 tbsp double cream and heat slowly over a pan of simmering water. Leave to cool until tepid but still liquid.

2 Whisk together the egg yolks and sugar until pale, fairly thick and mousse-like.

3 Whip the remaining cream and egg whites in separate bowls until they both form soft peaks.

4 Fold together the whipped cream, custard, egg yolk mixture, fudge bar mixture and most of the chocolate bar pieces. Finally, fold in the egg whites.

5 Pour the mixture into a shallow freezerproof container to a depth of about 5cm (2in) and freeze overnight. Before serving, leave to soften for about 40 minutes in the fridge, then stamp out into shapes, if you like. Decorate with the remaining chocolate bar pieces to serve.

Rhubarb Fool

Preparation Time 5 minutes, plus chilling • Cooking Time 10 minutes • Serves 6 • Per Serving 107 calories, 3g fat (of which 1g saturates), 20g carbohydrate, 0.1g salt • **Vegetarian** • **Gluten Free** • **Easy**

450g (1lb) rhubarb, thickly chopped
50ml (2fl oz) orange juice
1 cinnamon stick
25g (1oz) golden caster sugar
1 tbsp redcurrant jelly
150g (5oz) fat-free Greek-style yogurt
2 tbsp soft brown sugar

1 Put the rhubarb, orange juice, cinnamon stick and caster sugar into a pan. Cover and cook gently for 10 minutes or until tender.

2 Remove the lid and cook for 5 minutes or until the liquid has evaporated. Discard the cinnamon stick. Stir in the redcurrant jelly, then leave to cool.

3 Roughly fold in the yogurt, then spoon the mixture into six glasses and sprinkle with the soft brown sugar. Chill for 2 hours.

⭐ TRY SOMETHING DIFFERENT
Use blackberries instead of rhubarb – you will need 400g (14oz) – and a squeeze of lemon juice instead of the orange juice. Blend in a food processor after stirring in the redcurrant jelly.

Exotic Fruit Salad

Preparation Time 10 minutes • **Serves 4** • **Per Serving** 187 calories, 1g fat, 47g carbohydrate, 0.1g salt • **Vegetarian** • **Gluten Free** • **Dairy Free** • **Easy**

2 oranges

1 mango, peeled, stoned and chopped

450g (1lb) peeled and diced fresh pineapple

200g (7oz) blueberries

½ Charentais melon, cut into cubes

grated zest and juice of 1 lime

1 Using a sharp knife, peel the oranges, remove the pith and cut into segments. Put into a bowl.

2 Add the mango to the bowl with the pineapple, blueberries and melon.

3 Add the lime zest and juice and gently mix together. Serve immediately.

⭐ TRY SOMETHING DIFFERENT

● *Use 2 papayas, peeled, seeded and chopped, instead of the pineapple.*

● *Mix the seeds of 2 passion fruit with the lime juice before adding to the salad.*

Fruity Teacake

Preparation Time 20 minutes, plus soaking • **Cooking Time** 1 hour • **Cuts into 12 slices** • **Per Slice** 185 calories, 1g fat (of which trace saturates), 42g carbohydrate, 0.1g salt • **Vegetarian** • **Gluten Free** • **Dairy Free** • **Easy**

150ml (¼ pint) hot black tea, made
with 2 Earl Grey teabags
200g (7oz) sultanas
75g (3oz) ready-to-eat dried figs,
roughly chopped
75g (3oz) ready-to-eat dried prunes,
roughly chopped
a little vegetable oil
125g (4oz) dark muscovado sugar
2 medium eggs, beaten
225g (8oz) gluten-free flour
2 tsp wheat-free baking powder
2 tsp ground mixed spice

1 Pour the tea into a bowl and add all the dried fruit. Leave to soak for 30 minutes.

2 Preheat the oven to 190°C (170°C fan oven) mark 5. Oil a 900g (2lb) loaf tin and baseline with greaseproof paper.

3 Beat the sugar and eggs together until pale and slightly thickened. Add the flour, baking powder, mixed spice and soaked dried fruit and tea, then mix together well. Spoon the mixture into the prepared tin and level the surface.

4 Bake on the middle shelf of the oven for 45 minutes–1 hour. Leave to cool in the tin.

5 Serve sliced, with a little butter if you like.

★ TO STORE
Wrap in clingfilm and store in an airtight container. It will keep for up to five days.

Index

CONVERSION TABLES

TEMPERATURE

°C	FAN OVEN	GAS MARK	°C	FAN OVEN	GAS MARK
110	90	¼	190	170	5
130	110	½	200	180	6
140	120	1	220	200	7
150	130	2	230	210	8
170	150	3	240	220	9
180	160	4			

LIQUIDS

METRIC	IMPERIAL	METRIC	IMPERIAL
5ml	1 tsp	200ml	7fl oz
15ml	1 tbsp	250ml	9fl oz
25ml	1fl oz	300ml	½ pint
50ml	2fl oz	500ml	18fl oz
100ml	3½ fl oz	600ml	1 pint
125ml	4fl oz	900ml	1½ pints
150ml	5fl oz / ¼ pint	1 litre	1¾ pints
175ml	6fl oz		

MEASURES

Metric	Imperial	Metric	Imperial
5mm	¼ in	10cm	4in
1cm	½ in	15cm	6in
2cm	¾ in	18cm	7in
2.5cm	1in	20.5cm	8in
3cm	1¼ in	23cm	9in
4cm	1½ in	25.5cm	10in
5cm	2in	28cm	11in
7.5cm	3in	30.5cm	12in